MYTHICAL INTENTIONS
IN MODERN LITERATURE

Mythical Intentions in Modern Literature

Eric Gould

PRINCETON UNIVERSITY PRESS

5-13-92

For Diane: "*A book without room for the world would be no book. It would lack the most beautiful pages . . .*"
Edmond Jabès

CONTENTS

ACKNOWLEDGMENTS

Portions of Chapter 3, section II appeared in *English Studies*, Vol. 58, no. 6, December 1977. Part of Chapter 3, section III appeared in *Sub-Stance*, no. 22, 1979.

My thanks are due to the University of Denver, and particularly to Dean Robert Amme of the Graduate School, for faculty research grants which enabled me to complete this book.

Several colleagues and friends offered helpful suggestions and encouragement: Gunnar Boklund, Catherine Gallagher, Stuart James, Robert Richardson, Raymond Tripp, and Douglas Wilson. Burton Feldman read all of the manuscript, and his criticism, always constructive and sometimes chastening, was indispensable.

This was not an easy book to write, for it attempts to show the cross-references between a theory of myth and a theory of literature, which made it necessary to dart between principles drawn from interpretation theory, Structuralism, psychoanalytic writings, and anthropology. I must acknowledge, then, an entire network of influences upon the theoretical content of this book—however imperfect it may be—which includes the work of Lévi-Strauss, Barthes, Lacan, Derrida, Gadamer, Ricoeur, and de Man. What might appear as an unholy alliance between their differing ideas remains my problem, not theirs.

Mrs. Arthur Sherwood of Princeton University Press has been a most patient and encouraging editor. Judith May has with tact saved me a number of embarrassments with the copy. Donn Calkins typed the manuscript speedily and with fastidious care. And most of all, my wife Diane's concern and support during the writing made it all worthwhile.

Denver, 1980

MYTHICAL INTENTIONS
IN MODERN LITERATURE

INTRODUCTION

Any account of the relation between myth and literature has a responsibility first to define "myth." And there, with historical stubbornness, lies not merely a problem, but perhaps the entire subject of myth studies. On the one hand, there is a question as to what myths actually refer to, since they have come to mean many things, from primitive and sacred ritual to propaganda and ideological statements. On the other, there is a good deal of confusion and conflicting argument over how to define the significance of myth. Is it primarily a matter of thematics, or form, or function—or some or all of these categories?

There are only two ways, I think, of making sense of either of these questions of reference and significance. We can argue historically, trying to establish details of what myth did say and do and how it has developed, and then myth may become part of a mythology once we have sifted the evidence and reached a conclusion about historical validity. The other way of making sense of myth is to concentrate on the nature of the mythic (on *mythicity*, for want of a better word) and not simply on certain myths. From this perspective, there has developed since the eighteenth century the increasingly self-conscious discipline of mythography which warns us that we cannot even discuss myth until we have some working propositions for an approach to the subject. We can even become concerned with the ontological status of myth as part of a general theory of human expression.

It is probably fair to say that almost all contemporary studies of myth and literature have tended to argue for the meaning of myth from the former approach and to alight on one or other of the categories of myth's historical function and form.

We find there a daunting range of possibilities. If we consider the importance of *reference* alone, we are confronted with the problem of deciding on the authenticity of standard, received classical or totemistic myths—whose authority literary studies does tend to take for granted—and how they compose mythologies and infiltrate literature. We must decide, too, whether myth is an ancient and not a modern phenomenon: whether, say, the myth of the machine or current ethnic mythologies can acquire quite the same status as ancient myth. And if we turn to the *significance* of myth, then our task is even harder. The meaning of myth has been historically evoked through many versions of its main themes: myth as the source of history (euhemerism), or as religion, morality, or an expression of psychological origins. There is mythic form, in which the structural significance of myth is said to lie in its metaphorical word-play (as Vico, Müller, and Schlegel pointed out) or in its symbolic consciousness (Jung and Cassirer). These arguments are closely linked to theories of the function of myth as ritual, speculation, or wish-fulfillment, and even as primitive science.

All aspects of the thematic, formalist, and functionalist arguments seem to be relevant to literary studies. Mythological references in literature establish our psychological origins, or the structure of the collective unconscious. They can be said to reveal binary structures of thought, or fantasy-dislocation or problem-reflection. They may ironically prefigure literary meaning, or act as the primary language of experience. In addition to these thematic variations, literary myth studies, from the German Romantics to Roland Barthes, have argued for the importance of *mythopoesis*: the mythopoeic imagination as the source of the power of both myth and the best literature. This is close to Frank Kermode's well-known idea that myth "short-circuits the intellect and liberates the imagination," or Northrop Frye's view of literature as displaced mythology, or John Vickery's argument that *The Golden Bough* has propelled the modern imagination along an important mythopoeic course.

In short, in literary myth studies the question of myth's reference and significance as history and moment is still unresolved. Indeed, the temptation is to say that given theories of its thematic form and function and its importance as a theory of the imagination, myth is now so encyclopedic a term that it means everything or nothing. We can find in it whatever we want to say is essential about the way humans try to interpret their place on earth. Myth is a synthesis of values which uniquely manages to mean most things to most men. It is allegory and tautology, reason and unreason, logic and fantasy, waking thought and dream, atavism and the perennial, archetype and metaphor, origin and end. What a burden myth has to carry as a portmanteau term! Thematics and the search for the powerful motif have given rise to unearned optimism, befuddlement, and even, in their notorious political uses, fascism. Formalism has eroded the morality of myth, and functionalism has quickly led to myth as a superior kind of positivism. Literary studies in particular have relentlessly stuffed into myth's large compartments everything they have ever wanted to declare about the liveliness and failure of art and the life of the imagination in the modern: its ancient values and its current excessively fragmented form.

I certainly hope this study will ease some of the dismay, but I doubt whether it will please the historicists or the formalists. It seems to me that the issue for literary studies has long been the synchronic problem, that of trying to explain what the mythic is, and thence of trying to establish our optimism or pessimism over its place in the modern. So at the risk of seeming to oversimplify the subject and to overemphasize certain characteristics of myth in order to right the mythographic balance, I am concerned with mythicity rather than with particular myths, with the origins of myth in language, and with myth as allegorical, logical, conscious, creative, and very much alive in modern literature. This is not a discussion of the conditions of mythology, but it does venture into the conditions by which myth seems to be an autonomous production in a thoroughly interdisciplinary context. I found that I wanted to be as fundamentalist as possible in approaching the subject of myth, and this is primarily a study—at once speculative and pragmatic—of what makes myth mythic in the modern and of its relationship to literature, and not another paean of praise for the atavistic importance of myth. But it is also not another formalist study of mythic structure which forgets that myth has a function in recovering some sense of the numinous.

The starting point is this: whenever we try to define the form, value, or ontological status of a myth (in any of its versions, ancient or modern), we confront the fact that somehow it has proven itself essential, or very close to essential, within the cultural and social scheme of things. What I want to examine is how it has always done so as language, as an act of interpretation, and as a discourse about origins and values which is even conscious of being a problem-solving event. These are the key facts which make myth a value system and an exemplary function of discourse. Myths apparently derive their universal significance from the way in which they try to reconstitute an original event or explain some fact about human nature and its worldly or cosmic context. But in doing so, they necessarily refer to some essential meaning which is absent until it appears as a function of interpretation. If there is one persistent belief in this study, it is that there can be no myth without an *ontological gap between event and meaning*. A myth intends to be an adequate symbolic representation by closing that gap, by aiming to be a tautology. The absent origin, the arbitrary meaning of our place in the world, determines the mythic, at least in the sense that we cannot come up with any definitive origin for our presence here. So what I continually turn to is the fact that myth is both hypothesis and compromise. Its meaning is perpetually open and universal only because once the absence of a final meaning is recognized, the gap itself demands interpretation which, in turn, must go on and on, for language is nothing if it is not a system of open meaning.

From this point of view, superstition is not a prerequisite for myth. A myth may deal with ultimate questions—and it most often does—but its repeated exploitation of the fact that its questions have no answers leads to a linguistic crisis, to the inadequacy of human language, rather that to a need to resort to supernatural powers. The fact that classical and totemistic myths have to refer to some version of translinguistic fact—to the Gods and Nature—proves not that there are Gods, but that our talents for interpreting our place in the world may be distinctly limited by the nature of language.

So in the first part of this study, I examine the essential in myth from the only starting point I think we can have any confidence in: language itself as a system of signs. This initially limits the mythic to a semiological fact, and one can define its interdisciplinary function via linguistics, anthropology, and psychology, following that path to literature itself. In the beginning, the gap which lies at the heart of myth is no more or less than the perpetual tension we find in any sign, between the signifier (in all its arbitrary indifference) and the signified (which depends on our intention to locate meaning in language). To put it another way: event and meaning are never simultaneously present. We have no meaning without interpretative processes, given the perennial failure of verbal expression to be adequate to experience and to be an adequate naming of the world. The nature of the mythic, therefore, must have something to do with semiotics and interpretation theory.

There is, though, a risk of becoming obsessed with this ontological gap as the fatal condition of myth. It can pessimistically force us to acknowledge our incompleteness and drive us to apocalyptic theories. We are well aware of the arguments for the trans-rationality of myth from the traditional Jungian perspective. The problem lies in determining the extent of that unreason. We still find a certain reverence for myth in the modern as a means of preserving an unknowable (and by transference, a sacred) motive for myth. No less than any more primitive age, the modern still more than occasionally holds the view that myth is an item of religious belief, and that we might be able to preserve a sense of the numinous today through a renewed awareness of ancient mythology. The mystery of the origin of myth most often finds its place in some version of that powerful theory of the collective unconscious in Jung. Cassirer and Langer, too, are not far from this position as they suggest that the gap demands the verbalization of some "motor expression" of "feeling states" to replace the "motor expression" of the "holy" (such as, say, Rudolf Otto and Mircea Eliade propose).

On the other hand, there is the related problem of dealing with the possibility of bridging the gap through some positivistic and rationalist approach. There has steadily developed since the turn of the eighteenth century and Vico's *New Science* (1725) an alignment of myth and rationality, which has reached a climax in our time in the work of Lévi-Strauss. It has become increasingly difficult to separate the function of myth from the growth of consciousness, whether it be in Herder's allegoric treatment or Max Müller's theory of myth as a kind of linguistic disease. The view that myth is a superior reason has linked such eminent moderns as Lévi-Strauss, Roland Barthes, and Jean Piaget, while varying degrees of rationality in myth are discoverable in the work of Malinowski, Durkheim, and Mauss. These arguments can lead directly to formalist treatments of the grammar of myth, but I want to make it clear that although my argument owes more to this position than to Jungian essentialism and is even a post-Structuralist study, it is concerned less with poetics in any strictly codified summary than it is with the question of whether modern literature can attain the ontological status of myth as a superior treatment of fact.

I am concerned not only with the more generalized condition of narrative transformation which takes place when myth appropriates literature (and the converse), but also with the process whereby writing makes literal the way to and from a sense of translinguistic fact. The argument is that literature at its best is always something more than entertainment or incidental event. Specifically, I am interested in discovering the reasons a narrative gives for its own necessity, which seem to transcend the descriptive or even generative terms of modern poetics. The highly self-conscious literature I have chosen to discuss is not without ontological motive. It is the need to say it all, to recover the status of mythological narrative for the modern consciousness that offers a great challenge to the reader now.

I do not want to enter the problem of defining terms as part of the history of myth, for the intent of this study is to account for the mythicity of reading and writing as the clue to the status of myth. But it is essential for anyone attempting to explain the function of myth either *in* or even *as* literature to acknowledge, as Burton Feldman and Robert Richardson have shown in their essential critical anthology *The Rise of Modern Mythology* (1972), that the twentieth century is not strikingly original in its attitudes to myth. I would say, for example, that some of my claims for the mythic nature of modern writing (based on an understanding of the mythicity of writing itself) presuppose an awareness of that rich intellectual continuum from German Idealism to modern phenomenology. That is, the line from Herder to Jaspers, Heidegger, and now Gadamer, and the development of phenomenological methods in philosophy (not to mention anthropology, literary criticism, and psychoanalysis), imply the semiotic viewpoint. Semiotics must appear to the historically minded as one aspect of the growth-into-consciousness through language which is part of the romantic revival of myth.

Furthermore, I do realize that it is by no means new to align myth and literature in the attempt to explain a sense of the sacred, the essential, and the reasonable. The modern has thrived on that central paradox of German Idealism that man comes into consciousness of the world as spirit manifested in ideas. If anything, our anxiety can be said to have grown over that very point rather than to have diminished. Kierkegaard, Jaspers, and Heidegger all echo Kant's questions "What can I know? What shall I do? What may I hope?" which also find frequent repetition in modern art and philosophy. We see, for example, Kierkegaard reestablishing the writer in a position of paradox, with all communication qualified in some way by reflection. Jaspers' Encompassing tries to reconcile "Being itself" and "Being for us": we are always enclosed within that at which we are looking. We have also not recovered yet from the shock waves of Heidegger's confrontation with Nothing, with the lack of an answer to his question "Why is there any being at all and not rather Nothing?" It is to Heidegger that we have most often turned recently to find the crisis of consciousness which has its beginning in the hermeneutical issues of German Idealism.

For Heidegger, all metaphysical questions make sense only as "being" concerned with the nature of all Being, while all Being is available only as a phenomenological crisis, a coming-into-consciousness. Furthermore, "What-is" is nothing more than itself, so what is Nothing? The problem lies in defining—as I want to show myth itself always tries to do—why that Nothing-more always seems like something-more. Nothing is not an object, yet we live with the experience of nihilation. It has a presence in our consciousness. Even in the midst of our cultural contexts, we are beings projected into Nothing. We have always been beings projected into Nothing, and for that reason there has always been myth. For it is first myth, and then, I would suggest, modern interpretation theory, that reminds us strongly today that without a sense of Nothing, there is no selfhood or freedom. In Heidegger's annoying paradox, Nothing is the ground of Being. And flirting with that proposition is like flirting with the stuff of myth. For myth, as I shall discuss it further in the first part of this study, is, if nothing else, the history of our inability to authenticate our knowledge of Being, and yet it is at the same time a history of our attempts to understand that inability.

I want to emphasize that the mythic, therefore, does not and cannot disappear in the modern so long as these questions remain. For reasons which should be clear to the reader by the end of this study, I do not believe that we must differentiate sharply between some pristine, original, and sacred myth of origins which has somehow receded from our grasp, and which we can only pessimistically hope to recover and, on the other hand, myth as semiotic fact. True myth, it is very often said, even by such opposites as Eliade and Lévi-Strauss, can no longer be a reality for civilized man. My point is that mythicity is alive insofar as we rely on fictions to make sense of our world, and indeed, on the inadequacies of language to explain the inexplicable. Instead of disappearing, our myths have become more and more obsessed, as literature is too, with the hermeneutics of expression, with the linguistic limits to mythicity itself. The urge to define myth continues unabated in the modern, and even more important, the deep human need for myth persists. In this way, we have turned often to literary myths about myth in order to re-create it.

This is a difficult point to explain, and I have had to resort to the fact that myth, in order to be mythic, has to create itself, has to be a self-contained system deriving its ontology from language. The second and third chapters of this study explore the Structuralist model for myth's reproduction in narrative. I argue that literature and myth must exist on a continuum, by virtue of their function as language: myth tends to a literary sense of narrative form, and fictions aspire to the status of myth. The key question remains not that of the literary use of mythological motifs, but the possibility that fictions can recover the structure of mythic thought and expression—indeed, that there might be some kind of equivalence between mythic and fictional narrative. Only a theory of fictions, it would seem, can cope with the meaning of both mythological and novelistic plots. But again, I stop short of offering a poetics for mythic form, for that has been well documented by Propp, Lévi-Strauss, and perhaps, by implication, by Todorov and Kristeva. Rather, we need to concentrate now on the more speculative issue of how fictional narratives seek to justify their importance both in and out of the history of literary language and genre. For myths and fictions reveal the paradox of language itself as a system, defined in linguistic terms as both sequence (syntagm) and schemata (paradigm). Whatever we have to say about a meaning of a text is necessarily part of this paradox, which describes the ontological limits of both myth and literature.

The work of James Joyce is a clear example of a self-conscious flirtation with this paradox. In *Portrait*, *Ulysses*, and *Finnegans Wake*—and particularly in his increasingly complex emphasis on "epiphany" and "transubstantiation"—we find examples of how mythic thought can be recovered in the novel. This is achieved less by a simple re-use of motifs from *The Odyssey* and other quest mythology than it is by Joyce's clever entry into the logic of mythological plotting, which is carefully reconstituted in his writing. Plot transformations tend to the absurd (while preserving the dialectical reasoning of the original myth), and solutions to social compromise are reached by rearranging patterns of experience into constantly changing sign systems. So myth insists that reality is not static but a changing systematic, and this is recoverable in Joyce's logic of the pun, the epiphany, and the multilayered plot.

Indeed, the whole subject of mythicity in the modern strikes me as showing itself most cogently in the relationship between myth and literature. Again, this is not particularly new, for German Idealism took this task very seriously. But once we have relocated that interest, the question remains fresh for us: Is the created myth of modern narrative different from "primary" myth as we find it in archaic or primitive-historical examples? Because I argue from the start that it is the nature of language that determines myth and not the reverse, the conclusion of this study is that mythicity is no less modern than it is ancient, that it is preserved in the gap which has always occasioned it, through our attempts symbolically to represent and give meaning to our place in the world through discourse. Insofar as literature preserves the fullness of that intent, then it preserves mythicity.

But one cannot leave the argument there, or else we become locked into mere circularity. In the end, it is not enough to argue from linguistic premises alone and expect to have spoken intelligently about the mana of myth, which has supposedly been rather more universal than the mana of literature.

I do want to examine something we all know, that ancient myths survive in the modern with all their problematic intensity as they deal with the numinous and the sacred. The question is how and why. The "why" relates to the argument for the ontological status of myth to be found in the first part of this study. The "how" is discussed in specific examples drawn from the work of Lawrence and Eliot. If myth seeks to achieve understanding, to reach an unconcealed presence, to recover the numinous, to locate the universal in the Beingness of beings, then it must still cope with the Nothing of the modern. That remains our intellectual crisis, which is why I begin by trying to define essentiality and end by encountering the problem of mythical intentions in the contrasting attempts of Lawrence and Eliot to restore literature to the task of defining the absence of the "holy" as an aspect of literature.

A post-Structuralist approach to the problem makes the absence cogent enough. The fascination with that absent element, the semiotic gap, is implicit in our fascination with structure, even with the very hermeneutical intentions of a Lawrence or an Eliot. We find the attempt to recover the numinous in literature in these authors' belief in the logocracy of writing, in the text establishing the dominance of writing as expression, yet struggling with its limitations at the same time. Again, our problems with the sacred—as with any attempt to define essentiality—are with the linguistic. Discourse alone institutionalizes apodictic experience. So, too, all the genuinely ontological issues discussed so widely in the modern—the Underground Man's boredom and spite, Heidegger's Nothing, Kierkegaard's irony, Jaspers' Encompassing, and now Derrida's Deconstruction—are all issues which are only defined in language and about language. So it is appropriate that we turn to the language of literature where the full weight of nihilation, irony, paradox, and transformation can be carried.

From a critical standpoint, then, this study is an introduction to the course myth-and-literature studies might further take along less pessimistic lines than it has followed in the past. We need to go beyond the old obsession with the "failures" of the modern fragmented sensibility to preserve myth in our time. There have certainly been defenders of the lacerated faith, but we need to note too that it is precisely the fragmentation which can be seen to keep myth alive. I attempt to offer fresh readings of Joyce, Lawrence, and Eliot with the motive of showing how they perpetuate mythicity. And since I am insisting that myth is a function of language and interpretation, it must be said that the subject under discussion is also the business of literary criticism. It is currently fashionable to declare that the reach of the Structuralist enterprise has far exceeded its grasp, and that its attempt to seek meaning through networks, vast and small, of symbolic connections and disconnections has neutralized the text. We are confronted by a theory of the autonomy of structures, and at the same time, as René Girard has said, we are forced to find a context in which to study those structures. It is to combat that problem that I argue that Structuralism must be intimately linked to interpretation theory.

I do not think that one can saturate myth by discovering a formalistic grammar for it or a specific rhetoric of functions—here I only scratch the surface and offer some ideas based on principles language itself determines—but it is possible to show, after Lévi-Strauss, that mythic narratives do perform repetitively, negatively, transformationally, and in allegorical forms. The real task, though, is to keep alive in any approach to both myth and literature not only the problems of form, but the ontological issues which drive myth and much modern writing to the structures they embody. That is why it is so important to locate modern myth and literature studies in some theory of reading and writing as well as structure. We have to argue now for the relationship between a structure of the mythic and its reach, which will always, by necessity, exceed its grasp. For it is the nature of language itself to be symbolic, and the nature of myth to be the rhetoric of that intent.

CHAPTER 1

ON THE ESSENTIAL
IN MYTH: INTERPRETING
THE ARCHETYPE

> There are no inborn ideas, but there are inborn possi-
> bilities of ideas that set bounds to even the boldest fan-
> tasy and keep our fantasy activity within certain cate-
> gories: *a priori* ideas, as it were, the existence of which
> cannot be ascertained except from their effects.
> —Jung, "Instinct and the Unconscious"[1]

> The unconscious is not an ambiguity of acts, future
> knowledge that is already known not to be known, but
> lacuna, cut, rupture inscribed in a certain lack.
> —Lacan, *The Four Fundamental Concepts
> of Psychoanalysis*[2]

THE ESSENTIALIST'S ARCHETYPE

The archetypalist position is a very familiar one in literary
studies, where it has sanctioned a long history of interpretation
as the art of translating symbols into universal archetypes.
From this we learn, according to Jung, that the creative process
"consists in the unconscious activation of an archetypal image,
and in elaborating and shaping this image into the finished
work. By giving it shape, the artist translates it into the language of the present, and so makes it possible for us to find
our way back to the deepest springs of life."[3] Jung is clearly
the most influential figure in modern archetypalist argument,
offering what has appeared to many to be a workable nostalgia over the universal and supposedly sacred origins of art.
He suggests a radical departure from Freudian orthodoxy in

his explanation of what the human mind does as it creates fictions, largely through his theory of the archetype. Freud used mythological tales as the expression of repressed instinctual drives in the unconscious. He treated these narratives as sources of dream material which derive from the infantile psychological life of man. Jung, on the other hand, finds in myth a mature psychological life, and isolates there certain primordial images: the shadow, the *anima* and *animus*, the wise old man, and so on. These he believes have not only revelatory powers—they indicate repetitive psychological fixations rather than repressions—but therapeutic ones also: they insist on our sacred origin, on the existence of God, and on a universal human nature.

For Jung, the meaning of "fantasy activity" lies primarily in recovering a religious significance to an event. The world is not merely surface and symbol, but *numinously* so. In fact, the surface and the symbol are not really what is important at all. Jung makes a fundamentalist effort to get us "back," as he would have it, from an empirical reality to the "primitive wonder world" of the unconscious which, he claims, informs the meaning of every event and of every act of interpretation we make. This process is apparently both "mythic" and mysterious, and also "dialectical" and democratic. Here, then, we have at first sight an enticing version of the phenomenology of mythical thinking, especially as it attempts to make a link between theology and what Kenneth Burke has called logology: between *mythos* and *logos*, mythology and literature. Jung's belief that he has joined heaven and earth, the unconscious and the conscious, in the archetype is indeed what literary studies has found most interesting about his approach:

> The primordial image, or archetype, is a figure—be it daemon, a human being, or a process—that constantly recurs in the course of history and appears wherever creative fantasy is freely expressed. Essentially, therefore, it is a mythological figure. When we examine these images more closely, we find that they give form to countless

typical experiences of our ancestors. They are, so to speak, the psychic residua of innumerable experiences of the same type. They present a picture of psychic life in the average, divided up and projected into the manifold figures of the mythological pantheon. But the mythological figures are themselves products of creative fantasy and still have to be translated into conceptual language. Only the beginnings of such a language exist, but once the necessary concepts are created they could give us an abstract, scientific understanding of the unconscious processes that lie at the roots of the primordial images.[4]

Great poetry draws its strength from the life of mankind, and we completely miss its meaning if we try to derive it from personal factors. Whenever the collective unconscious becomes a living experience and is brought to bear upon the conscious outlook of an age, this event is a creative act which is of importance for a whole epoch. A work of art is produced that may truthfully be called a message to generations of men.[5]

A great work of art is like a dream; for all its apparent obviousness it does not explain itself and is always ambiguous. A dream never says "you ought" or "this is the truth." It presents an image in much the same way as nature allows a plant to grow, and it is up to us to draw conclusions. . . . we let a work of art act upon us as it acted upon the artist. To grasp its meaning, we must allow it to shape us as it shaped him. Then we also understand the nature of his primordial experience. He has plunged into the healing and redeeming depths of the collective psyche, where man is not lost in the isolation of consciousness and its errors and sufferings, but where all men are caught in a common rhythm which allows the individual to communicate his feelings and strivings to mankind as a whole.

This re-immersion in the state of *participation mys-*

tique is the secret of artistic creation and of the effect which great art has upon us, for at that level of experience it is no longer the weal or woe of the individual that counts, but the life of the collective. That is why every great work of art is objective and impersonal, and yet profoundly moving.[6]

These quotations give a sense of the familiar appeal Jung makes to the democratic and therapeutic values of art. He has proposed a special significance for art by suggesting that it reveals a close working relationship with the sacred and with the unconscious life. If we accept that analytical psychology does indeed provide some of the rudiments for a "science" of the unconscious, then his explanation of the birth of both myth and art from archetypal images must attract our attention. Psychology has apparently provided the encouragement for many readers to follow Jung and treat the archetype as both temporally adjustable and yet eternally present in all creative activity. So it has long been a commonplace among "myth critics" to assume that the unconscious is universally disposed to distribute archetypal images into consciousness. Exactly why, we do not know, beyond the fact that it probably has something to do with our sharing versions of the same human body.

And it is not only the mystique of the origin which has proven fascinating. Jung has also established something of a hermeneutical spirit in modern myth and literature studies. As the archetypalist argues, the conscious mind, in circular fashion, both creates concepts and fictions out of the "primordial images" and attempts to relocate their sacred origin in symbolic discourse in order to keep their power alive. Art and myth, then, reveal this intent, and can supposedly merge their interests in art's recovery of the numinous, even if a myth's significance as a "universal" fact remains unchallenged.

If we are going to take this theory seriously, then we are immediately confronted with the need to define what an archetype is and to try and locate its function as an antecedent to creative fantasy. It is possible to counter Jung with Jean Piaget's theories, pointing out that archetypal symbols are not genetic or inborn, but are recurrent images derived from the process of child development.[7] But let us first acknowledge the need to approach Jung on his own terms, even though, as I want to argue, we find only paradox. Archetypal motifs do have some identity of their own in his schema before they become symbolic discourse or metaphysical language, but they are available only as "effects" of an unknown cause. They are prior "psychic phenomena" which somehow reveal the nature of both the universal "soul" and creativity at once. By displaying the language of the unconscious at work (or is it the unconscious dimension of language?) they offer a radical intuition into the self, and even demand that one be "lost" (in Jung's words) "in oneself." Since it "defines" this power, the essentialist theory of archetypes has become useful because it aims to objectify psychological processes, even while it satisfies our need to locate somewhere (however mysterious) the universalizing function of symbols. Archetypes are treated as the beginning and end of both the "meaning" of myth and art and of our attempts to understand them. They are above all a solution to our teleological yearnings. We need archetypes, Jung seems to imply, because we crave the "essential." We continually query the conditions for our need to understand the surplus of meaning, the urge for transcendence, inherent in symbolic discourse.

Furthermore, if we accept this archetypalist theory, then it follows quite naturally, but no less problematically, that myths, as the verbal structures in which archetypes appear most frequently, must share the mystique of the archetype as a symbol-making process, reorganizing experience "in images and of images." It is this hermeneutic process which is perhaps even more problematic than the mystique of origins, for even as we concentrate on it, we are no wiser about the nature of the archetype's originality. The symbol-making results in concepts in which the signifier is seen to have a primary relationship only to itself. Myths are clearly thought of by Jung as dealing less with ideas than with more diagrammatically available behavior (the image) originating in the "primitive wonder world." The antecedent remains stubbornly pictorial; Jung insists that the archetype is not in essence a concept. The issue is complicated further by the fact that although mythology and literature both constitute second-order metaphorical systems dependent on the same supposedly talismanic figures, they are somehow not equivalent (a point even Lévi-Strauss is careful to preserve, as we shall see). Thus a clear distinction remains for us between image and concept, myth and art, even as we recede from the primordial image into the necessity for some kind of hermeneutical enterprise. Somehow the "imagistic" quality of myth (including its highly stylized design) more directly reveals the transcendent value of an archetype in the group imagination. Literature, on the other hand, is too obsessed with its affectivity and cannot consistently achieve this. Literature may even be too conceptual, and it rarely taps the archetypal roots of the imagination with such pictorial clarity.

Now literary theory has shown considerable respect for the hermeneutic intentions (based on his symbol-making process theory) which Jung displayed in his application of psychology to the search for the sacred and originary in art-activity. But it also goes without saying that contemporary criticism has become increasingly skeptical of the mystical nature of this process as it "objectifies" the unconscious into something as intangible as "figures" in the group imagination. For by "figure" Jung does not mean a rhetorical trope, but a daemonic or mediatory image. This intermediary can then conveniently be seen to include whatever its interpreter chooses to declare is essential, either by statistical sleight of hand ("this is a universal symbol"), or because the aura of the archetype once alighted on is somehow irresistible. The primordial image, in short, is not interpretable; it simply dominates consciousness and gives birth to an art which lives in its shadows.

But that conclusion should be balanced. It is true, on the

other hand, that Jungianism has been a powerful corrective to various trends in critical interpretation. It has polarized the remains of Cartesian solipsism and positivist methodology in modern literary criticism, reasserting that we cannot expect to know all of what is going on in reading and writing. The word does not simply contain the world, and therefore there will always be room for surmising on the theme of transcendence. Jung imaginatively revives the whole question, after German Idealism and Coleridge, of the status of "creative fantasy," of translinguistic fact, and of the "sacred" relationship between myth and art. It is comforting to be told, even by an archetypalist, that the symbol-making process constitutes a kind of socially essential behavior, the seeking of further knowledge of the human condition in art. Yet, in spite of all this, it is disturbing in several ways to live with the explanation which Jungianism offers for these activities. Once we become interested in interpreting the symbol-making process, we find evidence for the repetition of *a priori* images in our own imaginations. We can, if we follow Jung, discover that our conscious life is always condemned to be subservient to some kind of unattainable, superior fact. We are, that is, always on the defensive. Most troublesome is the fact that archetypalist interpretation is entirely dependent on the *arbitrary* emergence of those primordial image-symbols, in spite of Jung's continual insistence that the recovery of these figures is a "dialectical process." We are in their grip, whether we like it or not,. and yet we never really know what we are in the grip of. The peculiar combination of "instincts and archetypes," as he defined it in "Instinct and the Unconscious" in 1919, "together form the 'collective unconscious,' "[8] and this quite emphatically determines our conscious lives, constantly presenting us with the possibility that what we understand is never real enough, and that the "truth" might always be "other" than what we think it is. "In contrast to the personal unconscious, the collective unconscious shows no tendency to become conscious under normal conditions, nor can it be brought back to recollection by any analytical technique, since it was never repressed or forgotten."⁹ Fantasy, then, must dominate, and its archetypalizing becomes very difficult (if not deliberately impossible) to explain. Yet the theory of myth-as-sacred-history has turned on this point, and on its rather dubious definition of the "dialectical process" of converting images into ideas even while the images remain somehow pristine and intractible in their mysterious essence.

Jung describes consciousness as a "rhythm of negative and positive, loss and gain, dark and light," a rhythm of the psyche as *anima* and *animus* which, in turn, is all that can allow the integration of archetypes into consciousness. Reason, apparently, cannot. Another real problem with the theory, then, is that it does not provide us with a transition in language from the supernatural to the natural, regardless of whether we believe the supernatural exists or not. The problem of the self-subsistence and reference of the archetype as language is not taken up in terms that will do language justice. What Jung calls a "dialectic" is more like an eternal dualism, for he believes that archetypes are "autonomous" and cannot be integrated *ab origine* with ideas, and that they never fully partake of language later. As they are assimilated into consciousness and discourse, they remain somehow apart, and finally resist an objective and conceptualized status. Yet all the while, "the collective consciousness is not to be thought of as a self-subsistent entity; it is no more than a potentiality handed down to us from primordial times in the specific form of mnemonic images or inherited in the anatomical structures of the brain."¹⁰ Yet no matter what we think we know, consciousness always depends on some arbitrarily present "other," beyond nature, language, the socio-political context, or sensory evidence. Archetypes move hesitantly from the dimly lit world of unconscious figures, under mysterious conditions, to a tentative union with consciousness, constantly struggling, it would seem, to return from whence they came. Indeed, a large part of our fascination with Jungian theories would seem to derive from this attempt to have one's metaphysical cake and eat it too, an effort reminiscent of, if less impressive than,

Idealist attempts to link spirit and reason. But as far as literary theory is concerned, we must say that this is achieved by devious means, for no reliable theory of *language* as both the interpretative medium and the very process of coming-into-consciousness accompanies the argument.

The main barrier, then, to accepting Jung's account of the universal unconscious and the emergence of its archetypes remains (for literary criticism, at least) the nature of his "interpretation theory." He seeks meaning not so much "in images and of images"—that is, in a discourse concretely evoking such figures and merging them with concepts—but in a transformational process beyond language, and therefore beyond anything we can consciously know. This, in turn, is revealed helplessly in dream and the self-reflecting life of creative fantasy. Understanding, as he puts it, is reached "alchemically," as in the "definition of the *meditatio*: 'an inner colloquy with one's good angel.' Usually the process runs a dramatic course, with many ups and downs. It expresses itself in, or is accompanied by, dream symbols that are related to the '*representations collectives*,' which, in the form of mythological motifs, have portrayed psychic processes of transformation since the earliest times."[11]

The "dialectic" and the "transformation" are made dependent on the *a priori* status of the primordial images which then have no tangible form as collective psychological motifs and which are not to be thought of as deriving their essence from their modification in either the human imagination or in language. The archetype, then, leads a life rather like the boulder of Sisyphus, deliberately strained time after time to the top of the cliff, only to quiver for a moment, disappear out of control, and demand that the process be begun all over again. So the unconscious life in Jung's analysis is, not surprisingly, awe-inspiring; it is the mysterious origin of the instincts and intuition, personified into a force which not only nurtures archetypes, but which is more powerful in its intent to reveal them than man can possibly tolerate. The unconscious always contains a potential danger to our equilibrium:

Primitives are afraid of uncontrolled emotions because consciousness breaks down under them and gives way to possession. All man's strivings have therefore been directed towards the consolidation of consciousness. This was the purpose of rite and dogma. . . .

Whether primitive or not, mankind always stands on the brink of actions it performs itself but does not control. The whole world wants peace and the whole world prepares for war, to take but one example. Mankind is powerless against mankind, and the gods, as ever, show it the ways of fate.[12]

To many modern readers this defensive need for a "consolidation of consciousness" has not been a distortion of the symbol-making process, which it has long been fashionable to see as developing from a psyche quite as uncontrollable, but nonetheless, it is hoped, as "androgynous," as Jung's *anima / animus*. It is a theory which has lent itself to the now traditional modernist fascination with apocalypse, and it contains its own conditions for the inevitable human failure to hold on to the "barriers" of consciousness. These, we are told, collapse in the face of "waves" from the unconscious "when the symbols become weak with age." The theory of the entropic nature of language ironically takes on, then, a highly pessimistic form in the hands of Jung when applied to the relationship between myth and literature, even though it is true that Jungianism is most often considered rather optimistic in its implications. Archetypalism has been deeply influential in discussions of the "magical" relation between literature and dream in the attempt to develop a phenomenology of the imagination.

Yet, of course, the *intent* of the Jungian critic is indeed hermeneutical, for Jung does say that "psychic existence can be recognised only by the presence of contents that are capable of consciousness" and therefore of interpretation and understanding. But such "hermeneutics" insists that the creative process allows at best that the writer be *possessed* by an archetype, and hence the business of "becoming lost in oneself" is an irrational and even a deterministic one. (This countering argument has, of course, been used before by Freudians, in their turn reacting to Jungian causative psychology.) The unconscious defined in terms of the "wonder-world" theory offers us little more than a grab bag of anthropomorphic meaning, and little scope for interpretation beyond an insistence that the function of language is to aim (hopelessly) to create paradigmatic events: events in which meaning is somehow entirely *full*, as if the historic function of language were always subservient to (and not in a genuine dialectic with) its synchronic axis. The repetition of the archetype can be as neurotic as it is comforting.

We will examine this point further, but it is worth reminding ourselves here (should it be necessary) that when Jungianism has come into contact with literary studies, certain subtleties have emerged from this paradox which have played an important role in the development of modern interpretation theory. I do not want to appear to believe that one can dismiss Jungianism summarily, for Jung's paradox reveals the problem of talking sensibly about myth at all. Furthermore, within the very broad and popular scope of Jung's influence, the question of how to assign meaning to the relationship between literature and recurring motifs in human experience has been answered with perhaps a little more accuracy for *writing* (though with no less historicism about mythology) by Northrop Frye. He declares that literature is displaced mythology and that archetypes are structural units offering a possible synthesis and a genuine science of interpretation in their formal interrelationship in literature. The significance of this logical progression of applied Jungianism he explains as follows:

> Our first step . . . is to recognize and get rid of meaningless criticism: that is, talking about literature in a way that cannot help to build up a systematic structure of knowledge. . . . Criticism, as a science, is totally intelligible; literature as the subject of a science, is, so far as

we know, an inexhaustible source of new critical discoveries. . . . there is a quality in literature which enables it to be so, an order of words corresponding to the order of nature in the natural science. An archetype should be not only a unifying category of criticism, but itself a part of a total form, and it leads us at once to the question of what sort of total form criticism can see in literature.[13]

This is, indeed, an enduring question, but I am not sure that Frye has answered it for us with the assertion that criticism as a "science" either is or can be "totally intelligible." That seems of doubtful validity when psychology, sociology, and other related disciplines have been telling us quite persistently, and surely by now with adequate argument, that intelligence is a *process*, self-contained even if incomplete, at best a kind of cybernetic system (as even Jung himself seemed to idealize it) and not an objective totality. Literary criticism bears this out in two ways. The first, albeit an anecdotal one, is its traditional broad-minded accommodation of many approaches to engagement with a text. The second, more serious and theoretical, is the development over the last few years of phenomenological interests in order to justify criticism's own existence as one of the "sciences of man" amid the highly problematic discourse (let alone the "final meaning") of literature. Criticism, that is, deliberately attempts to be as suggestive of interpretative processes as it is of the writing to which it refers. Mere allegorical criticism, in the sense of a one-to-one interpretation, is in severe disrepute. We should be currently concerned, in these post-Saussurean days, with the dynamics of signification as endlessly suggestive, yet not so open-ended as to be meaningless. That is, we expect suggestiveness to be endless, while the suggestions themselves have a certain finite and systematic nature, which in turn have something to do with the problems of perception and the limitations of language. When Frye implies that the appeal of myth is to a sense of "total form," we can be skeptical for, like Jung, he wants to say that the real totality has in the end nothing much to do with the text at all.

Frye has very few suggestions as to how mythic thought actually operates in its attempt to recover that lost unity, how it tangibly evolves archetypes into narrative form. On the one hand, there is his theory of displacement whereby myths become fictions, mainly because we can find mythological motifs *in* fictions. On the other, there is his idea of the conveniently large and very tempting rubric of social revelation created by all serious narratives, mythological and literary. This gives myths and fictions a common intent: to be moral allegories of man's fate. After reading *Anatomy of Criticism*, one might say—I hope not unfairly—that the presence of archetypes is located with a certain authoritarian, even if, at times, a highly subtle flair for allegorical commentary.[14] Archetypes themselves again provide the reason for writing, as well as the instigation to translate a text with the certainty that one has a definitive reading.

But Frye does not confuse myths and fictions, even though he writes of the latter as determined by primordial symbols. If anything, there is a lingering interest in showing that the importance of literature in our time is a revelation of myth. He is careful to point out in "Literature and Myth" that "a mythical story or theme is not a Platonic idea of which all later treatments are approximations, but an informing structural principle of literature." Nevertheless, "the more we study the literary development of a myth the more we learn about the myth."[15] Thus he writes in the same essay that *The Golden Bough* is above all "a work of literary criticism"; that all myths are already a literature and depend on the literary characteristic of *mythos* or plot; that the language of myth is metaphorical; and that the real meaning of a myth is revealed not by its origin but by its later career.

Now these are all points I want to return to later in this study, but here I should say how suggestive Frye's writing on myth is. The argument I want to develop concerning the structure of myth can only restate these points even while they are given a theoretical backing rather different from Frye's. For one thing, he seems unaware of some of the more pressing problems of interpretation. One reads—a process without explanation—and in so doing, finds archetypes that will inspire us to euphoric acts of recognition, and a singular confidence that we can justify a universal meaning for a text: "The myth is the central informing power that gives archetypal significance to the natural and archetypal narrative to the oracle. Hence the myth is the archetype, though it may be convenient to say myth only when referring to the narrative, and archetype when speaking of significance."[16] But it is not so convenient to speak of myth as narrative unless we treat it as such, that is, unless we offer more information than Frye does anywhere in his writings on the structure of narratives *as* myth, and the way they demand our attention through a particular kind of signification. Like Jung, he is more concerned to show, as he does in the *Anatomy of Criticism*, how myths essentialize themselves and eventually become one myth, the quest. So however subtle and comprehensive his reading of a wide body of important literature, it is finally a narrow "science" of myth and criticism that lies behind the syncretism: a cloistering of literature which seeks an order determined by the very representational fallacy he claims criticism must avoid. In this case, his science is still dependent on proving the value of literature through the presence of archetypes, about which nothing further can be said, for as we all know, their presence speaks of our need for them.

This has been but a short consideration of a very prolific school of criticism, but I want to suggest that however complex the readings which may derive from archetypalist principles, they offer the possibility only of translating vague, mythic antecedents. Theirs is a kind of impressionism of the unconscious (if such is possible) which takes too much for granted about the interpretative process. What I want to argue instead is that it is precisely in whatever common conditions we can determine for language and the act of interpretation that one can locate a more accurate sense of myth and archetype in literature. It seems inevitable that we try to do this, for our received, standard version of modern myth-and-literature studies (after the essentialists) shows little concern for the compromising function of reading and writing, without which even the most sacred of archetypal images makes no sense. But both symbols and myths are metaphorical language and therefore demand interpretation, and myth criticism has not yet come up with a theory of reading and writing consistent with the nature of archetypal activity. The universality of the archetype has rather more to do with what we do know about it than what we do not; that is, with its act of symbolic representation, however paradoxical, rather than with its hypothetically sacred origins. If mythicity has any primary significance, it must relate to the mythicity of language, to the fact that all signs are transformational events and not simply the single, dominant "image" of archetypalism. The strange irony of Jung's position, anyhow, is that the mana and suggestiveness of the sign become the demythologization of the imperial archetype. For the result of any attempt to create an identity between archetype and experience, without accounting for the changing nature of the symbolic, must be to insist on an ever-shrinking range of content as the symbol becomes more essential. Hence interpretation is limited. Again, for Jung not only must all symbols eventually become one symbol, but experience becomes merely incidental to unconscious meaning itself. While perhaps that statement does simplify Jung's theories down to some bare essentials, it does not oversimplify his persistent supposition concerning the mystery and arbitrariness of the interpretative process, which is our concern here, and which we can argue against as leading to reductionism and pessimism in myth studies.

Instead, it is important to reexamine—and any theory of myth now depends on this—the conditions under which universal meaning can be articulated at all. This intent, I hasten to add, will be only tentatively explored here, for it demands a synthesis of linguistics, philosophy, anthropology, psychology, and literary criticism which only a community of texts can adequately develop. But I want to argue in this study that the potentiality of myth must lie in the potentiality of language. Then the question is: What are the limits which are imposed on our discovery of evidence of unconscious archetypal knowledge by the nature of language itself? Are we implicated mythically in the business of writing and interpretation? And if so, how? We cannot deny the unconscious, yet in literature we only know archetypes and myths as language events. Of course, it is still very much open to speculation as to what that genetic mechanism is in language and story-telling which accounts for myth and the recovery of the sacred. Above all, we need to find a model for the relationship of the unconscious to language which would be useful for exploring this large question in the area of myth-and-literature studies.

I start with the problem of interpretation itself in order to speak of the nature of myth as language. Given that we have no escape from language, that we can never move outside it, that language precedes truth and that myth as narrative is no exception to this rule, then what needs to be discussed first is the relationship between "linguisticality" and "mythicity." But I hasten to add that my aim is not to insist in a positivist manner that if myths and fictions are both narrative systems, then myth is nothing more than fiction. Instead, I want to argue that while myths are fictions, there is something about the symbolic nature of mythic performance as ritual, narrative, or archetype which really determines mythicity, and which can make us more hopeful about the mythic dimensions of literature. (My subject, again, is *mythicity* rather than myth.) Related to this intent, to repeat another point, is the assumption that the genetic mechanism accounting for myth must have something to do with language and its interpretation, especially since language is in full complicity with human desires, ranging from ontological yearnings to our very existential need to solve the compromises of the self among other selves. We have learned much from Jung and essentialist argument concerning the determination of language by the unconscious, but we are learning more now from interpretation theory, psychoanalysis, anthropology, and literary studies (as will be discussed in the next few sections) about the determination of the unconscious by language, to the extent that whatever we know of the unconscious mind, of its supposed archetypes, and of the occasionally epiphanic nature of experience, must be called, in a very important sense, linguistic.

In considering the problematic nature of archetypal significance, we have been directed to a tautology: if symbols—archetypal or not—have any human value at all, then they have the potentiality to be understood. And if this is the case, then since understanding is always a matter of interpretation, it follows that the archetype must be interpretable for it to exist at all; that is, it must have a discernible presence, a context, and a history. An archetype must create some kind of code and enter some kind of a dialectic with a perceiving mind, and not merely be a vague memory from "the mists of time." Let us begin by assuming the possibility of the archetype as open to understanding. How then do we define its singularity? For if it is to carry meaning, surely it must be part of discourse itself? Is it then wise to follow Frye's lead and "say myth only when referring to the narrative, and archetype when speaking of significance"?[17] Frye's statement does to some extent circumvent the problem, though not, as I have said, by following Frye's reasoning. Is the archetype a word or a sentence? Is it a word-centered or a statement-centered metaphor? These are questions to which we must continually return, as we have traditionally wanted the archetype to be both essence and distribution, to be the source and inspiration. For even if we turn to the *leitmotif* theory of the archetype as a stubbornly resonating symbol, we are still driven to its *act* of self-revelation in extended discourse. (And even if we turn, say, to Lévi-Strauss's lengthy accounts of the transformations of a single myth, we must still ask what is the significance of the repetition.) Insofar as it is unavoidable that the archetype infuses narrative, and that it is open to interpretation in the process, then it is persistently linguistic, and its effect, at least superficially, is not to be differentiated from myth. Archetypal significance would seem to be the equivalent of the mythicity of discourse. But is it really an archetype as sign which is the effective carrier of mythic meaning, the focus of our attention and the essential event, either through repetition or elaboration? (So we find the quest is a dominating theme or motif in, say, the story of Ulysses, and the incest taboo in the story of Oedipus.) The question also follows as to whether the myth is a narrative event which modifies and develops the archetype, perhaps more accurately interpreting the iconic value of such a symbol and returning us always to that origin which is the word which cannot be substituted for anything but itself.

It is surely the case that for interpretation to take place at all, and for us to make sense of any of these closely related questions which one can legitimately raise about mythicity, we have to turn to the nature of interpretation and the metaphoric nature of language. For behind myth lies the ancient desire to make comprehensible that which is not in a shared language. In order to tackle the problem of interpreting narrative mythicity we must approach this state as one which involves (a) the play of signs, representational events incorporating the tension between something signifying and something signified (some of which we want to call archetypes); and (b) the possibility of meaning, through our involvement in attempting to understand such a play. These two positions are related. The revelation of significance in the word needs a semiotic theory to explain its status, but also a semantic theory to account for its metaphorical extension: its history, and its function as an interpretive act. If myth or archetype have meaning, then they implicate a subject via predication. Mythicity, that is, is not a simple aura surrounding some essential thing, not something instinctively known, but something discovered through a whole network of interpretation, in which the archetype and its discursive extension are impossible to differentiate.

The argument must pass through several stages in this study.

First, if the archetype is such a powerful sign, then whatever mythicity is, it is tied up with a theory of interpreting the sign ("The Archetype as Concealing Nothing"). Second, once the question of the scope of the interpretative act is raised, the possibility of the importance and survival of myth as metaphorical language also arises; so myth and metaphor must be discussed ("Mythicity and Metaphor"). Third, some answer must be attempted to the difficult question of how the archetype, as both moment and metaphor, symbol and predication, relies on promptings from the unconscious ("The Unconscious as Lack").

THE ARCHETYPE AS CONCEALING NOTHING

We begin with the fact that archetype / myth must be interpretable for it to exist and to exert any power at all. Of course, we cannot be sure whether the archetype has any objective and *a priori* life, but we have been so involved with the concept of the unconscious that is has been difficult to avoid begging the question and inventing the term "preconscious." But we must always ask what the need is for this dimension to myth in the first place. Surely myth is at its most efficient as a sign system. If I have opened this chapter with a certain skepticism over the nature of essentialist myth and archetype, it is not because I must be uncertain of having established a *cogito*, or that I want to deny the unconscious, but because I assume that the archetype is *a priori* no absolute in the terms that Jung insists on, for we have no way of proving its independence from consciousness, nor of denying open-endedness as part of a system of signs.

If this is the case, then the archetype is but a representation of experience resulting itself from the quite distinct intent to make an interpretation of the world. This is very much the assertion of modern structural anthropology, as we now well know from Lévi-Strauss. But no amount of detail about the structuring of myth as intentional narrative, such as Lévi-Strauss does offer, will have any power of persuasion unless

it seems to follow from the very conditions of human interpretation which, in turn, underpin the *necessity* for myth. In
other words, behind all definitions of mythicity—including
implicitly that of Lévi-Strauss, as we shall see—must lie a clear
allegory of intent, which I want to examine in the next few
pages. What we consider essential about myth seems to me
to be no more or less than its exemplary function of intending-
to-interpret, whether its object is social compromise, the
supernatural, questions covering the self and its place in the
world, or those issues we think of as ultimate, unanswerable,
and metaphysical. The need to interpret the nature of experience which we call myth results in commentary which, in
reproducing that intent, can inevitably reach no conclusion
other than its own necessity.

The key to understanding that circularity lies very much in
post-Saussurean linguistics and its place in modern philosophical hermeneutics. Neither subject will bear full repetition
here, for each has been discussed frequently in contemporary
criticism,[18] but short summaries are in order. The linguistic
model for interpretation developed by Structuralism and semiotics declares there is no escape (in Fredric Jameson's terms)
from "the prison-house of language." The word always reveals
an unbridgeable gap between a signifier and a signified, a text
and a reader, a sign and its meaning. Language itself is always
prior to meaning and relies for its shared quality not on a
fusion of word and thing, text and authority, but on its figural
capacity to exploit this gap between signifier and signified.
Thus semiotics has insisted that language has a life of its own.
It thinks man as much as man claims to think language. However clearly words refer out to some thing, they also draw
specific attention to their tropes of reference, the inside and
the outside of their metaphors, the science of their signifiers,
because the word is never fused with the thing itself. As Paul
de Man has put it, "the demystifying power of semiology
. . . has been considerable. It demonstrated that the perception
of the literary dimensions of language is largely obscured if
one submits uncritically to the authority of reference."[19] But

even as semiotics *de*mystifies the old historicist impulses in criticism, it must *re*mystify the text by raising the whole issue of how words mean not only through references that we can share, but through the text's metaphorical ability to suggest absent meanings. Texts have hidden complexes of meaning, unstated intentions implied by the very play of the tropes themselves.

As reading and writing become objects of study, acts of intervention attempting to reduce the nonmeaning of the word as signifier, so they involve the discovery of specific historical conditions to meaning. Any act of interpretation implies a mediation between a subject intent on understanding an event and an object to be interpreted. But rather than insist that the mediation is simply a matter of turning an inherent dualism of self and other into some kind of conveniently endless "dialectical interchange" (or into the assumption that the two can never actually merge even in symbolic discourse, and so knowledge is doomed to pessimistic incompletion), we can treat the *phenomenology* and *history* of the subject and object as facts that work against such a dualism. They establish both the gap between the two and the attempt to close it. By the phenomenology of the subject or object, I mean again their presence in the activity of consciousness discoverable in language, an activity that defines both the sciences of man and the science of phenomena once the full complicity of a perceiving self and of an other for it to perceive have been constituted in the play.

The question has been posed often enough: which is central to interpretation theory, the phenomenology of perception or the historical conditions of the participants? The answer, one can argue (after much recent interpretation theory), lies in defining the historicity of consciousness and language which makes of interpretation a network of possibilities. The act of interpretation, that is, is one of psychologically reconstituting the object in the subject which establishes (a) an empathic, pleasure-and-knowledge-seeking *cogito* (Freud's *desidero*) as well as (b) the activity of an other, in (c) an historical context embracing each. The reconstruction is of the subject, the object, and historical meaning all at once. The act of interpretation is a discovery of the way the historical contingency of self and other actually allows each to be in some way related and even transformed in the effort of understanding.

We can postulate a hypothetical origin to consciousness and history in the mystery of the unconscious, as in Jung's primordial image or, say, in René Girard's sacred but surrogate act of violence.[20] But any exclusivity of mythic origin used to explain history is bound to be an oversimplification and to congeal the play of interpretation. As Jacques Derrida has argued in "Structure, Sign and Play in the Discourse of the Human Sciences"—an essay which is surely one of the key texts for modern interpretation theory—the central signifier never exists outside a system of differences:

> There is no unity or absolute source of the myth. The focus or the source of the myth are always shadows and virtualities which are elusive, unactualizable, and nonexistent in the first place. Everything begins with structure, configuration, or relationship. The discourse on the acentric structure that myth itself is, cannot itself have an absolute subject or an absolute center. It must avoid the violence that consists in centering a language which describes an acentric structure if it is not to shortchange the form and movement of myth. Therefore it is necessary to forego scientific or philosophical discourse, to renounce the *episteme* which absolutely requires, which is the absolute requirement that we go back to the source, to the center, to the founding basis, to the principle, and so on.[21]

A belief in the primacy of the subject's reconstruction of intention, or the primacy of the sociological conditioning of the subject's or object's history, is also an oversimplification attempting to center meaning. Some bias in both the psychological and the social directions has achieved useful results, especially in reader-centered criticism and Marxist geneticist theories, both of which are suspicious of Cartesian logic. But even sophisticated psycho-sociological theorizing often seeks an impossibly firm center. The problem with René Girard's assumption, for example, in his recent major discussion of the sacred, ironically lies in his most useful claim: that it is the Structuralist method of interpretation that forms some kind of genetic mechanism which can lead us back to a metaphysical or sacred origin. It is true that this theory is rather more enticing than, say, Jung's fundamentalism. (I do intend to argue in the last chapters that Structuralism can help define the implied transcendence in language-activity because interpretation always depends on an absent meaning: it is always incomplete because language is always incomplete.) But the Structuralist approach to transcendence need not be idealized, and is oversimplified in Girard's work. It is turned into an allegorical presence (in the perjorative sense of defining a direct one-to-one relationship between image and belief) when it demands a *specific* origin to the consciousness in the "sacred" act of violence. Girard's sense of the self does not endorse the play of the signifier among the signified. As he says: "There is a unity that underlies not only all mythologies and rituals but the whole of human culture, and this unity of unities depends on a single mechanism, continually functioning because perpetually misunderstood—the mechanism that assures the community's spontaneous and unanimous outburst of opposition to the surrogate victim."[22] Girard's sense of the sacred is finally no less archetypalist than Jung's, no matter how much more thoroughgoing his appreciation of existential fact seems to be and how subtle an adjustment of Jung's premises he seems to make. Therefore it is no more helpful in the end to our attempt to account for mythicity.

To return to the question of the historicity of language and consciousness, one of the major problems in interpretation theory since Friedrich Schleiermacher[23] has been the need to explain the mediation between subject and object (on which our whole concept of the history of language and understanding hangs) without mystifying the process in some origin and thus arbitrarily widening the temporal gap between the two or even naively foreshortening it. Again, this intent has consistently resulted in lively opposition between interpretation as the act of reconstituting an event psychologically (that is, in the consciousness of the subject) and interpretation as the discovery of the specific historical conditions of the meeting of subject and object. This opposition drove Schleiermacher to separate linguistic and historical knowledge. He differentiated, that is, between language as the phenomenon of being conscious and language as the account of what has been understood and has apparently constituted historical knowledge. With Schleiermacher we find that the only way the hermeneutical principle can be constructed at all is through the imperialism of the individual consciousness. That is, only through the uniqueness of individual discourse, feelings, and empathy is a particular representation of universal conditions achieved. One's psychological fate is to discover that this understanding is separated from historical knowledge, and that an analytic psychology must be developed to provide the conditions for any understanding at all.

Wilhelm Dilthey[24] developed this theory, again emphasizing that it is the interpreter's own individuality which is the presupposition for understanding. Through an awareness of singularity, as the romantic principle had long claimed, the universal and historical can be reached. Bultmann and the Christian Existentialists,[25] too, have pursued this same argument. Scientific understanding is a question of embracing an entelechial principle inherent not in language but in one's own possibilities. From Schleiermacher to Dilthey to Bultmann runs the faith in a typical human psychology on which rests the burden of creating historical meaning. Again, this Romantic link to the existentialist ethic has been a powerful mythologizing force in the modern, but it is Heidegger and more clearly Gadamer[26] who have shown us that to be preoccupied with the hermeneutical principle of *self*-construction as the way out into the ground of Being is only part of the answer, until self-consciousness actually embraces history and objectivity in language itself.

The urge to generalize, to establish the historical conditions of language as the ground of Being, remains implicit in the urge to interpret. The singular cannot be postulated universally as if it were simply an emotional state; the temporal distance between subject and object cannot be shortened by insisting that it has been absorbed into the individual consciousness once and for all without being conceptualized. The center of consciousness cannot be impressionistically established, and will not hold steady. These are familiar enough realizations in modern literature. Experience of the *cogito*'s unreliability now demands less the reference to a preconsciousness than it does to the decentering of the self in language, allowing it to be, at best, what Jacques Lacan has called a "locus of signifiers." In other words, we are tied to giving full purchase to the apparently unmotivated and incomplete system of signs which we call reality, and to their expression in the arbitrariness of the signifier (which needs no wonder world to make it arbitrary, for that is established solidly enough by its relationship to significance). In short, interpretation theory, via Heidegger and more importantly, Gadamer, has translated the *cogito* into all the tensions of the linguistic order: language has appropriated the self as its humanizing context and as the reflection of history. The process of humanization cannot ignore that words are not things, and that as we use words we are psychologically decentered (a process I shall discuss later in relationship to Jacques Lacan) in order to allow concealing as well as revealing meaning to emerge. This theory, in different forms, is common to Nietzsche, Freud, Heidegger, and, more recently, Derrida and Lacan. What I want to treat as this stubborn fact about interpretation theory—more stubborn, that is, than the romantic psychologizing of a Schleiermacher, or even a Girard—is the clue to our defining the mythicity of myth and literature in the modern. *Since myth is language, it is a response to the conditions of language itself.*

But let us not assume that we can set up the Schleiermacher "school" of interpretation theory as the straw man. For one thing, it is the tradition of interpreting from one's own possibilities, associated with the psychoanalytic persuasion, that brings an important perspective to our understanding of myth. The therapeutic value which Jung emphasized is one way of putting it, but Paul Ricoeur's interest in unifying a theory of the imagination and feelings with language philosophy (which I shall discuss in the section on metaphor and mythicity) is a more powerful romantic interest. Indeed psychological *re*construction (after Schleiermacher and Dilthey) as well as the more recent *de*construction (after Gadamer and Derrida) can both be seen as related in the evolution of the modern insistence on keeping open the gap between signifier and signified, even as the possible transcendence of the sign remains an important issue. It is the deconstructionists, however (critics like Paul de Man and Derrida) who seem most uncompromising about their persuasion of the way language works as we know it from post-Saussurean linguistics. They insist that a theory of understanding literary discourse must take into account the arbitrariness of symbols comprising both the text and the language of the self.

The moment of radical decentering in interpretation, as has often been pointed out, occurs with Heidegger as he attempted to reconstitute metaphysics as an existentialist philosophy. The history of "what-is" becomes a summary of the scope of our inability (as much as our ability) fully to authenticate Being in language. And in the modern, I think, mythicity has little chance of adhering to anything more important than this lack: a knowledge of language's deconstructive talents, which is not merely nihilistic, but an attempt to account realistically for the limits of our understanding. More fruitful than Heidegger's theory is Gadamer's development of the negative underpinnings of interpretation. Insofar as authenticity has a phenomenological status, dependent on descriptive and psychological terms, and a history generated by the contingent object and subject, dependent on a context, then the authentic and its lack are defined, as Gadamer has insisted, by the nature of the language we all use. The historicity of consciousness is located in the play of language which carries in its every use the possibility of its own denial. The incompleteness of the sign (after Saussure's well-known theory) insists that no complete meaning is possible, only *a system of differences*: form and meaning are never present at once; the meaning of a word is a tension between its paradigmatic and historical roles.

It is scarcely unusual to remark now that this congenital "lack" in language creates the *necessity* for coming into further consciousness as part of our need for unifying the self, if for no other reason than that it is impossible to comprehend the totality of "what-is," which always has surplus meaning. So we become as concerned over the play of differences and absences of meaning as we are over what Derrida has called the "metaphysics of presence." We are tantalized in interpretation by language that suggests both meanings and the ability to undercut them. Mythical thinking might even be said to stem from the fact that we have no way of avoiding Heidegger's Nothing (and the history of ideas about Nothing). And thanks to Gadamer, Heidegger's intuition of selfhood and consciousness as highly nihilating events leads to the hermeneutical experience of grasping the limitations and situatedness of *being human*. Metaphor, as Ricoeur puts it, is not a stylistic choice but is forced on us by a real deficiency. Selfhood includes acceptance of the insufficiency of language, the projection into Nothing, beyond what-is, because we are finite. This embrace of negation in the play of language has become one of the more cogent and surprisingly rational ways adopted by the modern for describing the nature of possible transcendence, a transcendence explained in terms of continual openness to more experience (Gadamer's *Erfahrung*). Our confidence in asserting this optimism in the face of negation can exist only because a unity is recognized between the act of interpretation and our self-consciousness of the act, *which exists entirely because of and in spite of language*. For us, language is both the sickness and the cure. Consequently, Gadamer, by following Heidegger, can make this large claim which David Hoy has paraphrased in his recent, fine study of literature and hermeneutic theories:

> It is not that language reflects thought or is "prior" to the world in some way, but rather that both language and the world appear together—as one changes, so does the other. Thus Gadamer claims that language is "the behavior of the world itself in which we live." The problem of reflection, of the antithetical relation of mind and world, subject and object, is transcended. The world is not an independent object *for* language; rather, "the world presents itself *in* language."[27]

What has this to do with defining myth and archetype? Language embodies the semiotic gap which determines all interpretation, and myth is that function of language which intentionally tries to close that gap. For, as Gadamer insists, language is not merely our behavior, but the history and behavior of the world. His hermeneutical consciousness (*wirkungsgeschichtlichen Bewusstseins*) can be concretely located not simply in self-construction, but in self-construction in language, in what he calls the "linguisticality of understanding." The lack which is exemplified in Saussure's gap between sign and thing, and so on, is no less contained in and cordoned off in the sentence, for we know that we are at least trying to "fill the gap with signs," as Norman Holland has put it. A language event has meaning primarily because of its semiological appropriations, and not just because the speaker or writer exerts a subjectivity. Indeed the question of the *absence* not only of meaning but of an author—which is important here, as one might guess, for myths are anonymous—is central to the meaning of any literary text. Jacques Derrida has explained this as the condition in which all writing symbolizes the death of the "I," which need not be present to validate the text.[28] The consciousness (of reader and writer) must *nihilate* (to use Heidegger's term) in the act of interpreting what-is. And it does so not out of sheer pessimism or dread, which one finds in more essentialist prescriptions, but in continuing to affirm one's being-in-the-world through language as a part of selfhood. "Nothing," that is, is not mere negation but—as Lévi-Strauss has shown of the kinds of negative transformation in myth—involves the necessity for metaphor and the closing of the gap.

There is, then, a determinant of "essential thinking" beyond the syllogistic because thinking is conditioned as much by what is other, *by what is concealed,* as it is by what-is or might be. But the concealed is not necessarily an archetype or something at all. The unconcealedness of Being, the sheer directedness of experience, in Heidegger's terms, hides the possibility of Nothing. The mythic, I believe, emerges from that very existential awareness and not from some primitive wonder-world. I want to emphasize that as we come to define the nature of the link between literature and mythicity in the modern—in the work of Joyce, Lawrence, and Eliot, for example—we must begin with this fact that the act of interpretation on which the archetype, myth, and mythicity depend for their existence does not allow in the modern anything more compromising than this insight into absence as central to understanding. If metaphor is built on that lack—and is the result of it—then no metaphorical language confronts non-being quite so squarely and definitively as myth. Mythicity, I would suggest, is the condition of filling the gap with signs in such a way that Being continues to conceal Nothing as a predication for further knowledge. We may think it is possible to avoid the problem by assuming that Nothing should not play any role at all in modern writing except as some decadent proposal, some failure of emotional realism, an idea which many contemporary writers can still quite happily pursue. But since the modernist questions the linguisticality of his world, treats language, that is, as the ground of discovery (which is now surely established as a commonplace since the Symbolist aesthetic), then we are drawn, more acutely perhaps than we have cared to admit, to questions concerning the mythicity of *writing* itself as it evokes the simultaneously open and closed nature of experience.

There is in writing no lost origin to be sought after, no inherent monomyth to celebrate, but only the enigmatic myth of interpretation as play, dependent on concealed lack. Quite literally, all myth reveals that man cannot get out of this paradox of language or history; even his yearning for the supernatural has this existential basis. Once we accept that the semiological gap conditions all human attempts to reach the essential, then we realize that mythicity depends on being part of the ongoing process of making acts of interpretation in order to shorten the gap.

In terms of this very compressed "ontological hermeneutics," the archetype can attain universality not by conditioning a singular perspective (for Jung has not given full play to the subversiveness of language), nor by returning us to an origin (for the essential center, once articulated, is always absent), but by cogently suggesting that it is always open to interpretation. Myth, as the narrative of archetypal significance, is not an objective fact, nor a mere focus on an informing primordial image, nor a matter of received knowledge, but a working proposition, an unfolding of understanding which persuades us of its logic. What this logic amounts to and can do in the face of absence, I will attempt to outline in "The Structuralist Model" and the chapters following, but first the sense of the mythic as involved in the act of interpretation needs to be examined for its function of endowing symbols with archetypal qualities. The implication is that it is language itself which is the most powerful symbolic order of either consciousness or the unconscious. How then do words successfully mediate between our historic conditions and our need to solve the very human *negative* compromises of language? What is the respite from the shared negative condition of the subject and object in language?

MYTHICITY AND METAPHOR

If archetypal significance in myth lies in its universal meaning—say that of the quest, the incest taboo, or the sacredness of the fire—then, as I have been arguing, its universality depends not on the statistical recurrence of some motif we call a "quest," or an "incest taboo," or "fire," but on our interpretation of such events. In semiological vocabulary, it is not the constant recurrence of the signifier which creates the universality of myth, but the repetition of the signified. If I locate something I call archetypal significance in a given set of events, then I should be able to show that those "outside" conditions create over and over again a similar "inside" meaning.

But that in turn does not simply imply that the link between the inside and the outside is static. For the outside is as much my inherited convention of language as it is sensory evidence, and the conscious inside is never free of language at all. Again, the common factor is language itself. We know that mythicity cannot reside in the exact coincidence of the inside with the outside for that is linguistically impossible: the sign is not a thing, and the signifier and signified cannot be one. It resides, then, in the shared capacity for language. Mythicity, insofar as it is a condition of the interpretative act, lies in the interchangeability of the outside and the inside, which is dependent on the play of language. Then, as this dialectic is made apparent, it becomes itself an outside fact for others to interpret, And so the mythic signified becomes the signifier of the next myth, endlessly repeating the so-called archetype.

This slippery but roughly coincidental meeting of the inside and the outside (in these now widely used terms of psychoanalytic interpretation theory such as we find, say, in the work of Norman Holland or Jean Starobinski)[29] can only develop from a recognition of metaphor as the primary function of language. For as the current terms would have it, amid all the constructing and deconstructing of the sensory world which occupies my centering and decentered consciousness, I recognize that a relationship exists between my perception of an event and the significance I give to it. The problem, however, is to define the logic of that necessity in metaphor, which remains a controversial issue but one which should lead us closer to an explanation of mythicity.

For a mythological narrative to have any useful meaning there must be some human release from the fantastic reference of its terms. I sense, that is, that Oedipus's plight is not literally a result of Cadmus's killing the dragon, planting its teeth, and founding the fated Theban race. There is instead some logic to the metaphor, some interchangeability between the outside fact (mythology itself) and the inside (my knowledge of human nature) which allows me to interpret the tale. Even the arbitrary choice of terms in a mythological plot—which Jung too hastily translated into the arbitrariness of the unconscious archetype—implies a contingency between interpretation and a narrative's symbol. What that contingency is lies somewhere in the very nature of metaphor: that is, language which is at once figurative and suggestive of an unlikely conjunction between two events. But it is not enough merely to say that language is shared between subject and object. Interpretation theory must also concern itself with the definition of metaphor. How is language shared so that it can accommodate the lack?

The theory of metaphor is enormously complex, ranging historically from Aristotle's version of metaphor as *epiphora* or displacement of the name by another name to a current theory that the explanation of metaphor is grounded in the substitution of one sign for another in a paradigmatic exchange. (With the latter theory, metaphor is said to exist in a polar relation to metonymy, in which substitution is an accident or coincidence in time and space.) This is not the place to elaborate on the history of the ideas about metaphor, and besides, Paul Ricoeur's recent work, *The Rule of Metaphor*, does just that and is perhaps the most thoroughgoing commentary we have on the subject.[30] But if the reader will continue to assume that this is to be largely a study of mythicity in literature and not of interpretation theory itself—and that I must rely on necessarily short explanations of such key terms as "metaphor" and "metonymy"—then I should risk an outline of my premises concerning myth and archetype as metaphorical / metonymical language in the light of Ricoeur's comprehensive scholarship.

The arguments for the nature of metaphor reduce themselves to a categorical opposition between theories involving the substitution of a work for another word (either resembling it or paraphrasing it) and theories which shift the focus away from word change to their performance in the whole sentence as the carrier of meaning. (Our major source for this insight into the historical dichotomizing of metaphor—and it is Ricoeur's—is Emil Benveniste's *Problems in General Linguistics*.)[31] The emphasis on the word-metaphor is a semiotic theory (developing from Aristotle's *epiphora* through the work of Fontanier, Saussure, and Jakobson to writers like Barthes and Genette). On the other hand, metaphor as sentence is a semantic concern related to the predicative function of discourse. (This is also an emphasis found in Aristotle's poetics, but this time passing through the link between *mythos*, *mimesis*, and *poesis*, down to modern British ordinary language philosophy after Ryle, Austin, and Strawson, and thence to Ricoeur's own attempt to link the semantics of metaphor to modern interpretation theory.) I want to deal first briefly with Ricoeur's theory of metaphor, which is the most interesting of contemporary theories for the way it tries to accommodate the strengths of both sides of the argument, a synthesis he takes pains to make.

Ricoeur's theory of metaphor is primarily tensional. In a recent article,[32] he refers to metaphor (after Max Black) as a "deviant predication" and, following Jean Cohen, as "a semantic impertinence." He had summed this up in *The Rule of Metaphor*:

> The theory of the statement-metaphor puts the accent on the predicative operation. It seems now that it is not incompatible with the theory of the word-metaphor. The

metaphorical statement achieves its statement of meaning by means of an *epiphora* of the word. . . . the "analytical" definition and the "contextual" definition of the word are compatible with each other to the extent that the perspectives of language and of speech call for and complete each other. Now it must be said that the theory of the word-metaphor and the theory of the statement-metaphor relate to each other in just the same way.[33]

Ricoeur is of course attacking a dualism inherent in early Structuralism: Roman Jakobson's insistence that all language is either a matter of *combination* (metonymy, the syntagmatic axis of language) or *substitution* (metaphor, the paradigmatic axis). Ricoeur, developing a hermeneutics under the influence first of Heidegger, and now more clearly influenced by British ordinary language philosophy, sees the dichotomy in a different way:

> Like Jakobson, indeed, but in a different sense from his, we form a concept of "metaphorical process" for which the rhetorical trope plays the role of agent of revelation. But we part ways with Jakobson in that what can be generalized in metaphor is not its substitutive essence but its predicative essence. Jakobson generalized a semiotic phenomenon, the substitution of one term for another. We are generalizing a semantic phenomenon, assimilation to each other of two networks of the signification by means of an unusual attribution. At the same time, being properly predicative or attributive in essence, the "metaphorical pole" of language does not have a metonymic pole as its counterpart. The symmetry of the two poles is broken. Metonymy—one name for another name—remains a semiotic process, perhaps even the substitutive phenomenon *par excellence* in the realm of signs. Metaphor—unusual attribution—is a semantic process, in the sense of Benveniste, perhaps even the *genetic* phenomenon *par excellence* in the realm of the instance of discourse.[34]

This intent to unify the semiotic and semantic will strike many readers as necessary, and Ricoeur is not exactly alone in wanting to achieve this. Jean Cohen, too, has developed a syncretistic approach[35] as has Jacques Lacan.[36] The problem with Ricoeur's analysis, however, is that he is not really breaking out of the dualisms of language at all. Whereas Jakobson emphasizes substitution for metaphor in opposition to metonymy's combination, Ricoeur wants to point up attribution for metaphor, a semantic process, in opposition to metonymy's semiosis, which he calls substitutive. In other words, he has replaced Jakobson's dualism with a new one: that between semantics and semiotics. The matter becomes further complicated in "The Metaphorical Process" where he returns to his old preoccupation with defining "imagination" and "feeling," this time in relation to metaphor.

There is "a *structural analogy* between the cognitive, the imaginative, and the emotional components of the complete metaphorical act. . . . the metaphorical process draws its concreteness and its completeness from the structural analogy and this complementary functioning."[37] Ricoeur makes it clear that he is not interested in "a new kind of intuitionism" or a "new emotional realism," nor is he merely semanticist: "metaphorical meaning does not merely consist of a semantic clash but of the *new* predicative meaning which emerges from the collapse of the literal meaning, that is, from the collapse of the meaning which obtains if we rely only on the common or usual lexical values of our words. The metaphor is not the enigma but the solution of the enigma."[38] So the semantics of metaphor are now broadened by a psychology of the imagination and feelings which aims to align itself with cognition. By "feeling," Ricoeur does not mean "our usual interpretation of emotion as both inner and bodily states. . . . To *feel*, in the emotional sense of the word, is to make *ours* what has been put at a distance by thought in its objectifying phase. Feelings, therefore, have a very complex kind of intentionality. They are not merely inner states but interiorized thoughts."[39] Ricoeur argues that the synthesis of thought, imagination, and feeling in the yoking of two incongruous events in metaphor is as follows. In the making of metaphor, we assert not so much an association by resemblance as a "predicative assimilation." In spite of differences between two events, new kinds of assimilations are made involving "a specific kind of tension which is not so much between semantic incongruence and congruence. The insight into likeness is the perception of the conflict between the previous incompatibility and the new compatibility."[40] And we too are assimilated into the predication: "we feel like what we see like." This process is brought to concretion as poetic language merges "sense and senses. . . . In reading, Bachelard says, the verbal meaning generates images which, so to speak, rejuvenate and reenact the traces of sensorial experience."[41] (By images, Ricoeur is referring not to mental pictures but to Bachelard's "being pertaining to language . . . and emerging meaning.") That is, coextensive with the play of thought and imagination together, the meaning of a metaphor is a "mood" (after Frye's use of the term): "nothing other than the way in which the poem affects us as an icon."

The last aspect of Ricoeur's version of the metaphoric is the *epoché*, the moment of suspension of meaning, the negativity of the image, which he derives from Jakobson's theory of the "split-reference" of the sign:

> . . . poetic language is no less *about* reality than any other use of language but refers to it by means of a complex strategy which implies, as an essential component, a suspension and seemingly an abolition of the ordinary reference attached to descriptive language. . . . The poet is this genius who generates split references *by* creating fictions. It is in fiction that the "absence" proper to the power of suspending what we call "reality" in ordinary language concretely coalesces and fuses with the *positive insight* into the potentialities of our being in the world which our everyday transactions with manipulatable objects tend to conceal."[42]

And poetic feelings, too, reveal this negativity and split-reference: "an *epoché* of our bodily emotions."

Now Ricoeur's theory of metaphor may very well be the most comprehensive we have (if *The Rule of Metaphor* is also taken into account). It would seem valuable to apply his broadly syncretistic approach to the question of mythicity, combining imagination, thought, and feeling, as classical rhetoric has always wanted to do. Ricoeur preserves the unbridgeable gap within the sign, even as he allows the imagination to have power to construct meaning. There is clearly more optimism to his *epoché* and his sense of the negative than there is, say, in deconstruction theory and practice as we find it in either Derrida or de Man. But although Ricoeur will be the first to admit that the theory of cognition and affectivity combined in the metaphor is "in its infancy," the fact remains that it needs adjusting further to be comprehensive enough to cope with mythicity.

We might restate Ricoeur's attempt to break down the Jakobsonian dualism of metaphor and metonymy as follows. In purely semiotic terms (that is, in terms of what the sign arbitrarily signifies), metaphor is a matter of word substitution. But substitution is revealed in the act of discourse. And in discourse, to use one of Kenneth Burke's favorite terms, language operates on the entelechial principle, which is nothing less than metaphor as process: language is the instrument developing a potentiality of the sign into an actuality by creating reference and meaning. In every metaphor there is both substitution and statement. All discourse reveals the synchronous and paradigmatic relationship between words. Meaning is only possible because the two functions of language exist simultaneously in the act of predication. In spite of Ricoeur's privileging of the semantic function, there is a distinctly semiological element even in his notion of the *epoché* or surplus of meaning. Through the predicative assimilation, we are drawn in by metaphor's distinct attempt to *imply* an absent element, another signifier, a metonymical relationship where there is no hope of one. It is as if two signifiers might originally be metonymically related. One of the signifiers in metaphor takes the place of the other in the signifying chain, even while the hidden signifier remains present. It is not simply a *split* reference which is at stake—and certainly not just a split signifier—but the possible substitutive relationship between two signifiers, which informs any predication at all. Metonymy itself is somehow natural, independent of predication, defined simply by proximity in time and space: a name for a name.

It seems a simple-minded but nevertheless unavoidable point that the semanticist position is so closely related to the semiotic that any sharp differentiation must be an oversimplification. Metonymy as a substitutive process must become a type of metaphorical performance. Metaphor must always strive toward the clarity of exact substitution. The dialectic between the two, then, belies any essence at all, substitutive or predicative. In other words, the opposition between semiotics and semantics—at least in the area of metaphor and myth theory—in spite of the partisanship each has shown, has never really been ideologically thoroughgoing. While these relative emphases may allow for functional differences (e.g., one may argue, as I will, for T. S. Eliot's largely metonymic emphasis in his early poetry and *The Waste Land*, compared with the metaphorical expansiveness of *Four Quartets*), one finally makes no sense without the possibility of the other. Metaphor predicates, fashions resemblance, shows a generic relatedness, mediates between opposites, and constructs new meanings for our instruction, but always because it is at some point focused on the possibility of achieving the kind of accuracy only metonymy can offer: the exact word substitution which we ideally want to make; as it were, the rhetorical degree zero of metaphor.

The focus of metaphor, then, even as it is both the word itself which is substituted and the sentence carrying the substitution, is on the *absent metonymy which lies behind the metaphor.* The sentence *frame* does remain in the ground of metaphor in Ricoeur's theory (and in the vocabulary of Max Black).[43] But when metaphor slides over the absent metonymy, it borders on the non-sense which tantalizes us in our interest in accurate meaning. It raises the paradox that we can search via metaphor for a verifiable meaning, for a tautology, which can only be metonymy. We might prefer "floating fortress" to replace "sail" for "ship," for metaphor with its logic of "plenitude" and "congruence," as Ricoeur puts it, draws out the sense of representationality of an object. But it must always return us to that object and its uncertain name to have any meaning at all. Metaphor is nostalgic for the act of substitution begun in metonymy, and could, in theory, go on forever if it were not for the metonym which becomes the absent element holding it back to some relatively empirical and stable terms. In effect, metaphor relies on emulating metonymy so that it need *not* go on endlessly, but can tentatively close the circle of its own meaning and escape non-sense.

The theoretical paradox of metaphor is evident in that metaphor not only expands and increases meaning in the face of the metonym, but it does so by *internalizing* the evidence of metonymy as words play. The metaphor hides and abolishes even as it has to draw attention to this absent element in order to create any meaning at all. By literally appearing to go on forever, metaphor ironically denies that it can ever be fully unveiled. If there is a predicative ideal, then, it is not endless play, but play-for-substitution, a process in which metaphor aspires to the status of metonymy. Interpretation must acknowledge the free play of language, but it is always interpretation-for: reading and writing in the pursuit of accurate significance.

What can this tell us about archetypes and myth? It would seem that we may yearn to be absorbed by the archetype as primordial symbol, but all that language will ever let us find is the absent metonymy in the metaphor. We cannot substitute a literal meaning for the figurative (as in classical rhetoric), for if all language is metonymy / metaphor, then it is never literal: only metaphor, or at best metonym, can interpret a metaphor. As Ricoeur puts it: "We would be substituting (with Black and Beardsley) the systems of connotations and commonplaces. I would rather say that metaphorical attribution is essentially the construction of the network of interactions that causes a certain context to be one that is real and unique. Accordingly, metaphor is a semantic event that takes place at the point where several semantic fields intersect. It is because of this construction that all of the words, taken together, make sense."[44] But, again, to accommodate this to the point I have been pursuing, metaphor (after Beardsley) may stabilize and construct at once, but the stability lies in rooting the system of connotations and commonplaces in an absent *metonymy-demanding-interpretation*. It is this metonymy which seems to inform the development of meaning in the sense that the most definitive connotations are closer to metonymy than metaphor.

Ricoeur's emphasis (after Stephen Ullman) on the *polysemy* of language—the fact that there is always more than one sense for a word and that language is vague and cumulative—emphasizes the innovativeness of language, but it is only one side of the creative battle. The polysemy is always undercut by the need for the aphoristic, the limited, and the tautologous. At the heart of the crisis remains, that is, the Structuralist problem (first made clear by Saussure) of the impossibility of totally unifying event and meaning. So the gap is further describable not as created by an absolute opposition, but by the interrelationship of this dialectic of language performance, metaphor and metonymy, which leads us out to the way the world means.

What we call mythic narratives can now be said to be exemplary versions of how that gap *might* be filled. Such discourse—and I want to show that literature is capable of it, too—reveals a heightened sense of reliance on metaphor to explore serious ontological questions and social compromises and can only serve to screen us temporarily from the gap between word and thing. This screening, reaching its full effectiveness in poetry and myth as metaphor, is so intense and becomes so instrumental to our maintaining a cumulative knowledge of experience, that we can argue, as Genette has done, that metaphorical language is "real" language while the nonfigurative is a "virtual" language. This is an important point concerning myth, for myth does acquire a status not as ornament or mere poeticizing about the world (in some pejorative sense) but, like poetry itself, as metaphor actively trying to give itself the status of metonymy—that is, the status of being most accurate. Like the questing hero Ulysses, we must fight the protean world to find elusive fact. We can understand polysemy, on which Ricoeur relies so heavily for metaphorical innovation, as real language *in the face of* the lack which lies at the heart of all discourse: the gap between words and things which forces language to offer transforming versions of an original signifier.

Structuralist theory, then, is by no means as purely "formalistic" or as "agnostic" as is often thought. It is fascinated by the ontological status of language which enters modern poetics in practical terms in semiotics: for example, Jakobson's theory of poetry as the message concerned with itself, Genette's differentiation in *Figures I* between real and unreal language, Todorov's opaque figure and concern with the "absent element" in discourse and, as we find it in the more psychoanalytic of the Structuralists, the *distancing* and *configuration* of the "inner space of language." We learn that real language lives with its own insecurity, but hides the lack even while metaphor ironically increases the intensity of that problem. Yet the transparency of language can never be without the rhetorical degree zero of metonymy. Since language can never be fully denotative—even in this figure—it insists on leaving the play of spatial figures in the lacuna. In this way it connotes a surplus of meaning in order to say anything at all.

I have been edging toward a description of the mythicity of literature (a) by showing that the archetype is not essentialist, but a function of the open-endedness of discourse; (b) by establishing the need for mythicity to be dependent on the openness of interpretation and its Structuralist basis; and (c) by arguing that the interrelationship of semantics and semiotics is the necessary clue to our understanding of how metaphor and hence interpretation works. The question now is: How does one move from the metaphoric to the mythic?

There are at least three routes open to us implied by the previous discussion. In the first, we develop the semiotic dimension of language to include the possibility of an essentializing, hierarchical function of language. In the second, we further describe the process of metaphor to consider the possibility of a closure to interpretation. In the third, we complement both these functions of language with a theory not simply of how the self occupies language (in reading and writing), but of how the unconscious dimension of the self determines the mythicity of language. I will consider the first two possibilities here—to be taken up again later—and continue with the third in the next section.

The value of the semiotic approach to the nature of the mythic is that it can ground us in unavoidable, and not simply hypothetical, first principles based on the nature of language. My overstatement of the gap between signifier and signified, word and meaning, in every sign has been deliberate, for it is that fact which allows us to consider from various perspectives the grounding of interpretation and metaphor in the conditions of language. It also suggests—as Roland Barthes, for one, has made very clear—that all mythological systems are based on the function of the sign. One can speak of the virtual meaning of a poem, for example, on several levels: at the level of the play of its metaphorical language in the self-referential system of the poem; at the level of the poem functioning as a signified of the signifier "poetry"; and then at the level of the poem as a signified of the signifier "literature." There is a fourth level , implied by this study, which emerges when we consider the poem as a signified of "language," when we move out of genre into potential discourse, and thence into a range of criteria relevant to the entelechial principle of language itself. This level, currently occupied by deconstruction theory and the insistence that meaning must reside in the signifier's evasiveness, defines what we might understand as the ontological status of literature. At no point, as we move through a synchronic reading of a poem, does the gap diminish in its presence, nor the perpetual change of a signified into the signifier of another sign system ever cease. Interpretation itself becomes a *necessary* metaphor for the literary event, and the paradigmatic play of language the source of its attempt to essentialize itself.

This genetic model is in turn related to our second alternative for expanding the metaphoric to include the mythic: the possibility, or impossibility, of closure in language. I have been faithful to the semiotic assumption of endless play in language, but I have also been suggesting that behind the play lies the yearning for completeness inherent in the absent metonymy of every metaphor. This does not imply actual closure but offers the possibility of reaching some position of confidence in language. I think the most useful explanation of this position, at least from the psychological perspective, is that of Jacques Lacan, who has shown that at the heart of creating or interpreting metaphorical statement lies the opposition of an infinite subject occupying any number of places in a finite "series of signifiers" in any particular instance. We can say that Lacan is deconstructing Ricoeur's "split reference." That implies, again, our union of semiotics and semantics: "interpretation is directed not so much at the meaning as towards reducing the *non-meaning of the signifiers* [emphasis mine], so that we may rediscover the determinants of the subject's entire behavior":[45]

> . . . there can be no relations between the signifier and itself, the peculiarity of the signifier being the fact that it is unable to signify itself, without producing some error in logic.
>
> .   .   .   .
>
> It is so much easier to realize that what is happening is that a substitutive signifier has been put in place of

another signifier to constitute the effect of metaphor. It refers the signifier that it has usurped elsewhere. . . .

Consequently, it is false to say, as has been said, that interpretation is open to all meaning under the pretext that it is a question only of the connection of a signifier to a signifier, and consequently, of an uncontrollable connection. Interpretation is not open to any meaning. This would be to concede to those who rise up against the character of uncertainty in analytic interpretation that, in effect, all interpretations are possible, which is patently absurd. The fact that I have said that the effect of interpretation is to isolate in the subject a kernel, a kern, to use Freud's own term, of *non-sense*, does not mean that interpretation is in itself nonsense.

. . . .

Interpretation is not open to all meanings. It is not just any interpretation. It is a significant interpretation, one that must not be missed. This does not mean that it is not this signification that is essential to the advent of the subject. What is essential is that he should see, beyond this signification, to what signifier—to what irreducible, traumatic, non-meaning—he is, as a subject, subjected.

In so far as the primary signifier is pure non-sense, it becomes the bearer of the infinitization of the value of all, which is different. . . . What, in effect, grounds, in the meaning and radical non-meaning of the subject, the function of freedom, is strictly speaking this signifier that kills all meanings.[46]

This primary signifier is the absent metonymy in the metaphor and it seems readily available, for example, in modern and postmodern writing. Its play emerges from the uncertainty that many modernist writers have experienced over risking metaphor at all, in order to preserve the hidden (and, ironically, pristine and numinous) status of things (*quidditas*) in the world. Joyce in *Ulysses* and *Finnegans Wake*, Lawrence, and Eliot in the poetry before *Four Quartets*—as I want to show—develop a discipline for the imagination which restates the place of the author amid the real *as an art of metonymy.* Postmodern writing maintains the primacy of the signifier, and not surprisingly this leads, in the art of, say, Pynchon, Marquez, or Barthelme, to the freedom of the author to indulge pure non-sense. The infinitely elastic metaphors of modern fiction are ironically dependent on metonymy to lay down the conditions for the irreducible signifier, which is, in Pynchon's and Lacan's terms, none other than the paranoia of the imagination. Indeed, since all language must be either metonymy or metaphor (as Jakobson has pointed out), then, as Lacan seems to have decided for psychoanalysis, and literary theory might decide for interpretation, all that interpretation can ever do is tangle with the paradox of seeking the metonym in the metaphor, even while we know that no signifier is a static entity. And so we are thrust into the troublesome but exciting prospect, which always needs exploring, that the mythicity of any statement cannot be more than a "complicity mixed with antagonism" (in Starobinski's terms), not just between signifier and signified but between metonymy and metaphor, reader and reading. Metaphor must create a *constantly shifting interior distance*: the "infinity of the subject," as Lacan puts it, is mediated only in metaphor (which for him is specifically the "experience of analysis"), and therefore by the troublesome metonymy of desire.

The same conclusion can be reached in terms of the recent, widespread descriptions of the *act of reading* as the act of interpretation. This reader-centered critical theory has become the common property of psychoanalysis and linguistic and literary studies in recent years, and I think it is useful at this point to expand on Ricoeur's relationship of imagination and feeling to metaphor and outline some of the implications of that important relationship for the study of metaphor and mythicity. In the first place, the therapeutics which clinical psychoanalysis aims for is implicitly the recovery of a lost unity both within ourselves and between ourselves and what lies beyond. That is, it is both the identification of genuine desire and the fulfillment of that desire. (The metapsychology of Freud explores desire's mythical origin.) This is the transformation process of inner and outer which Jean Starobinski, Norman Holland, and Jacques Lacan have located in the metaphorical nature of language. The therapeutic moment, then, is in this sense linguistic: a matter of experiencing the lack in language and somehow superseding it. Experience is, literally, interchangeable in language and only in language, or else it can never be shared, and the therapeutic change cannot be achieved. All this is no less implied in literature's compensatory satisfactions for a reader or writer.

The interesting point, though, is that in each case the "subject" (be it reader or patient), encouraged to put the wheels of interpretation in motion by the perplexing nature of the signs confronting him, must at some point substitute illusion for reality in the intricate process of understanding. As the reader fantasizes, the metaphorical or "unrealistic" version of the inside world ironically becomes a specific test of his desire to enter the real world and accept that it is open to interpretation. So metaphors must be risked again and again— as they are in psychoanalysis.

As readers, Norman Holland points out, we expend a certain amount of energy to reach an end or meaning by adapting to the promptings (and gaps) of the text and its context. We do this in order to try to come into consciousness of some process of understanding discourse as well as to protect our pleasure. Both the prompting to do this and the medium of our activity are words themselves. And, ironically, we must introject our fantasies of expectation and our foreknowledge of genre into the text in order to read it at all and, especially, in order to locate and further yield some kind of socially acceptable mode, some moral / intellectual / conceptual space which is the point that enables us to find in the work unity, significance, and consolidated pleasure. This is the primary act of defining both good and bad reading, and surely it defines, too, our interpretation of any system, such as nature and the reality around us. The transformation process—the making of metaphor—does not deny judgments, but sets the ground on which judgments are made. As Holland describes it:

> . . . one becomes "locked in" to a positive experience and "locked out" of a negative one. Having created his characteristic defensive structures from the work, the reader has warded off anxiety. He can therefore project into it the fantasies that give him pleasure, and he can use his defenses to transform the fantasies into themes that give the work intellectual cohesion and sense. Having achieved this transformation, his style has indeed created itself: as he goes through the work line by line, he finds in it characteristic expectancies for them. At this point, he can perceive no difference between the process "in" him and what he sees "in" the work, and he finds that special sense of absorption or merger that literary experiences can give us.[47]

Does this mean, then, that a reader can only get from a text what he already is? Or that he is happy only when the text fulfills his metaphorical expectations? Is criticism a vicious circle? And is myth by implication only in the eye of the beholder?

The answer is "no" to all these related questions for, as I have been arguing, the active introjection of fantasy must be open to determination by language itself. Holland makes this point clearly. Introjection is, in fact, a subtle form of *mutual assimilation* by the inside and the outside, text and reader. Ricoeur refers to this process as "appropriation," and Gadamer speaks of understanding as always a conscious application to a present situation, an "implicit moment" which exists only in constant alteration. So this hermeneutical principle of introjection into the lack is, after Heidegger, more Being than consciousness alone. It is lived through rather than conceptualized: a process made possible only *in* language rather than simply as a use of language. Hence Gadamer's *wirkungsgeschichtlichen Bewusstseins*—the linguisticality of understanding—most importantly refers to what is lived in and understood, and this, I have implied, is metonymy itself. Understanding can be complete enough that the reader's personal "horizons" (to use Gadamer's term) are fused (*Verschmeltzung*) with the "horizons" of the text.

An important addition to the linguistic basis for metaphor is that the reader and work create a metaphorical transformation *together*, and only then has the reader, in Holland's terms, made the work his own:

> The reader reconstructs, as we have seen, part of his characteristic pattern of adaptive or defensive strategies from the work, and this re-creation must be rather delicately and exactly made. Once he has done so, however, he can admit through the filter of his particular style some or all of the work, which then becomes the material from which he very freely creates a kind of fantasy that is important to him. He then (again, with great freedom) transforms that fantasy by means of the defensive strategies he has created toward the coherence and significance he consciously demands. Altogether, then, he has duplicated his own style of mind. Neither he nor we can see any difference between his characteristic mental processes and those that seemingly belong to the work. The question "Where is the fantasy and defense, in the work or in the reader?" ceases to have any meaning.[48]

Reader, writer, and language itself are each an appropriate system. Mythicity, and indeed any other condition for narrative experience, is born of the competition between the participants in the interpretative event, each caught in a metaphorical world seeking stability. Myths, we might assume, form perhaps the most demanding system among narratives that we have, a point which can be defined in several ways: traditionally in ritual performance, which can be found in wide-ranging civilizations, or else in its psychological function as either an imperial Jungian archetype or as some version of what Bruno Bettelheim has described as myth's "typical" involvement with "superego demands in conflict with id-motivated action, and with the self-preserving desires of the ego." But, again, those approaches do not seem to me to get to the heart of the matter: the *mythicity of discourse* as metaphor relies on metonymy. Myth is, after all, an historical consciousness only available in discourse, which does reveal a growing awareness of some literal meaning in our finitude through metaphorical expansion. But the importance of myth in our culture, it would seem, is the result of the fact that we have no option but to use metaphor in order to find truth.

That is, any theory of the appropriativeness of myth as a language event refers to the appropriativeness of language itself, which in turn has something to do with the ongoing process of transacting meaning in the business of metaphor-making and interpretation. We experience a union and a cutting from discourse at the same time. At best, all we can declare about the experience of interpretation is that we occupy a potential (and not an ideal) space in the world of language. As opposed to the hypothetical objectivity of archetypes which Jung and Frye proclaim, we find instead that metaphor drives us to what Starobinski calls "the contact surface," the place where inner and outer actually meet.

So we continue to need the "archetype" as a description of this site, as a hypothetical space created by the subject's search for himself as well as by what lies outside himself, through the tradition of language and its meanings. As such, it contains not a fixed reality but a propositional statement which experiments with the literal. The archetypal motif is largely proleptic. It is useful to us less as an object of belief, as a fixed, systematic item, than as a *transactional fact*, slowly revealing its form only in language and interpretation. It is objective only insofar as it exists as a semiotic item, leading us to link it to other signs and to modify our assumptions about itself and ourselves. The archetype is subjective in that it depends on interpretation for its very existence. This is not to declare an invidious hermeneutic circularity but, again, to assert the necessary *absence* of meaning before meaning can even be discovered. "The most sophisticated cultural experiences," Holland notes in a Freudian way, "go on in a space which is neither inner psychic reality nor external reality (or . . . 'in here' nor 'out there'). They go on in a 'potential space' which both joins and separates the individual and the person or thing he cares about, which originally was the space between the mother and the child separating a self from her."[49]

Holland's space, then, along with Starobinski's, can be defined both in the diachronic terms of an evolution of general consciousness, and in terms of an individual growth-into-consciousness. The child development theories of Jean Piaget, with their dependence on "transformational bundles of thought," can be linked to the theory of the primal gap (signifier and signified, mother and child) and to other contributions to a genetic epistemology, such as Lacan's more metaphoric development of Piaget in the self-other dialectic, or the cybernetic models of Gregory Bateson's "general system," or even perhaps Lucien Goldmann's "genetic Structuralism." It is supposed in all such generalizations that the mind can evolve into an increasing equilibrium between itself and its environment, and succeed at least momentarily in closing that gap. The synchronic is never outside history and process. As Holland puts it for psychoanalysis:

> . . . each man is a scientist, formulating constructs by which he anticipates events and interprets them. He then seeks out experiences to correct his constructs and make them as elaborate and powerful as possible. All such interactions place the person in what Gregory Bateson would call a "general system," his mind being part of a continuing process of generation and feedback in and with his surroundings.

> These theories and experiments insist that people are prehensile animals, actively reaching into their environment for experience. To this general view, psychoanalysis adds the psychoanalytic touch: understanding the organism's activity by taking conscious forces in the present and

from the past, both recent and remote, that shape the
experiences sought and found . . .

In other words . . . "subjective" and "objective" are not
so much predicates as words to describe two different
stances from which to look at the process of experiencing.[50]

What we call "objective reality" is discoverable only by recreating our interiority and distinctiveness from the world
around us (which must include, to repeat my argument, our
way of thinking of our own historic nature metaphorically
and hence negatively). This, in turn, as Starobinski insists, is
always problematic: "For if the notion of interiority makes
sense, it must be conceived not as a receptacle of treasures,
of monsters or of mysterious traces, but as a process—what
we become by virtue of our ever changing relationships with
the other, of our relationship with the *outside*, with that which
we have never been, or with that which we have ceased to
be."[51] Consequently, archetypes in ancient texts exist for us
to bring to light hidden and changing meaning which will
always preserve their "foreignness" and the extraordinary
"opposition between the thing *said* and the thing *hidden*" as
a part of the process of interpretation.

It follows, then, as Starobinski points out, that what we
assume is *the most hidden meaning* (even as the metonym
attempts to duplicate the signifier) is at the same time, paradoxically, a "duplicated exteriority": the location of that
which was once not interior but now is, the rapid shortening
of a seemingly stubborn gap between self and other. Perhaps
this is, within the vast realm of half and relative truths, at best
a temporal coincidence, the mirage of objectivity, declared to
be real in the ecstasy of revelation. But as Starobinski puts it:
"No inside is conceivable . . . without the complicity of an
outside on which it relies. Complicity mixed with antagonism
. . . No outside would be conceivable without an inside fending
it off, resisting it, 'reacting' to it."[52] Not only is the protection
of fantasy necessary and possible only because the object is

detained outside, but, as Starobinski goes on, it is only "through the mediation of exteriority, that hidden part, the dissimulated identity, can become manifest."[53]

The implication for myth and literature studies seems clear. The nature of myth and archetype, since both are revealed as discourse, is surely dependent on the process of interpretation as an endless interchange of the inside and the outside which is in turn dependent on language as capable of creating only a potential, self-duplicating space for the essential to occupy. The archetype is not monistic or a universal sign, but a significance *shared* by subject and object because of language. In a very real sense, myth is only myth because it is discourse. So it is always a mediation and a metaphorical event and never an absolute. But that is not to condemn it to meaningless relativity or to deprive it of metaphysical insight or existential reference for, again, we always seek metonymy *through* the metaphor. Then metonymy becomes the "duplicated exterior." We can insist on the thoroughly existential and *humanizing* function of myth and archetype (out of which a metaphysical meaning might grow), for interpretation, in all its paradox, affirms that man is fortunately limited and inhibited by the language that gives him myth. He is largely in a condition of not-knowing. He is able to understand only by means of projections of his inhibitions onto external events, by his limited foreknowledge, and by the fantasies which the outside stimulates. This process of projection is not a pessimistic one for it can lead to definition of the self as a range of signifiers and to the ordering and transforming of events to be shared in coded systems of language (semiology). It leads us even more urgently than, say, René Girard has suggested in *Violence and the Sacred* to the real reason for surrogate victims and controlled forms of violence in society: namely, as part of our need to systematize human desire, not so much by finding a particular origin for it, but by metaphorically exploiting language to overcome not-knowing and inhibition and to reach a never-changing metonymy. Violence is metaphor; the scapegoat is metonymy.

In this sense, the surreal fantasies of myth are not merely naive association or madness. As the neo-Freudians (such as Lacan, Holland, and Starobinski) have pointed out, our need to systematize our inhibitions is less an overemphasis on our neurotic state, "the disease called man," than it is an acceptance of the unique human virtue of self-regulation through metaphoric language (even as our ritual and "sacred" act of violence). This implies that we accept our freedom to move inside and outside quite arbitrarily. All archetypes, therefore, have their origin in language, for the experience creating the *need* for regulatory gestures, beliefs, and rituals—and for such mediating models of meaning as sacrificial victims, incest taboos, and so on—has as its "primordial" antecedent the very function of language as a *protective barrier* against what Holland has called "the soft inside." (This is rather different from Jung's barrier of consciousness against a rampaging unconscious, for the barrier of language is not so solid a defense, but has its transparent moments, allowing that mediatory movement of consciousness in the dialectic of the "inside" and the "outside.")

Myth, then, reveals the drama of protecting the "soft inside." In Lévi-Strauss's terms, it becomes a matter of locating a system of differences linked to similarities, of finding oppositions. And it does this, we can say, in the face of an *absent*, metonymical knowledge: again, *in order to reduce the non-meaning of the signifier*. Insofar as it is a shared fact between us and the world, language even contains the capacity to nihilate Nothing. Language alone, as Kenneth Burke said, brings negativity into the world. And it alone retains the ability to comment on its own incompleteness. It can assert the necessary presence of absence, even as it implies the absence of a speaker / writer as a meaning is inferred. The arbitrary but interpretative function of language, that is, sanctions mythicity. We can also say that it is the mythicity of language that sanctions myth. Since language must appropriate us as much as we appropriate it, the battle for truth, accuracy, and so on is always fought both inside and outside us at once. Fortunately, neither the subject nor the object alone is the measure of the real; that is found in the paradoxical no man's land of discourse. We are not possessed by archetypes, but our fate is *transacted* in them.

My subjective interest in language, then, is never simply intentional as if what I want to do with language is sufficient to control it, for language has (as even thoroughly subjectivist critics admit) a certain dominance over me, a life of its own determined by its role as the *history* of my inherited metaphors. This domination can even lead us to the conclusion (which Lacan reaches) that the construction of the unconscious itself is in large part linguistic, that not even that most private part of our psyche is free from its touch. That can also lead us to the equally valid possibility that the relationship of myth to man lies in the potentiality of language to make the interior exterior. Plainly, in linguistic and psychological terms, the dynamics of reading and writing—each a complex function of moving the inside out and the outside in—cannot be absent from any theory of myth if it is to be systematic enough to account for its own expressive form. And, of course, an acceptance of that must detract from traditionally essentialist archetypal theory and open up more eclectic versions of the mythicity of discourse. Once the mystically objective status of Jung's archetype as "image" is threatened, and the superstitions about the transition of these images to language are removed, then our nostalgia for myth as something *lost* also weakens. Something absent is not necessarily lost. If a narrative once became myth through the potentiality of metaphorical discourse, then presumably it can happen again.

So there is no reason to discard the term "archetype" as inappropriate. On the contrary, it requires a fresh definition. Signs can now retain archetypal significance for us, in both ancient and modern texts, because they re-enact continually, through the play between metonymy and metaphor, the alternative closing and widening in discourse of the gap between the inside and the outside. They thereby inspire our ratiocination, creative fantasy, and above all, our process of interpreting the world as a sign system. To repeat my earlier point, the archetype as metonym is the rhetorical degree zero of metaphor. It is always the structural operation of the act of interpretation rather than the content of motifs which leads to our sense of the archetypal and, we hope, to a meaning for the unconscious. The archetype carries a necessary exteriority whose interpretative challenge must be met—as metonymy becomes metaphor—or else we lapse into a superstitious worship of the hidden side of its meaning.

The Unconscious as Lack

Deriving the nature of myth from the conditions of interpretation does not dispense with a theory of the unconscious. It can still be argued that no matter how closely we tie mythicity to metaphorical language, we have not altered the fact that versions of the theory of the unconscious origins of desire, art, and myth must be considered. It has also long been widely held that these promptings are intimately linked to a religious essence of myth. For myth studies the unconscious has been somewhat delibidized by Jung, as we see in the work of Mircea Eliade and Joseph Campbell, and has acquired religious connotations in the face of the persistence shown by the modern in rereading and revising Freud's metapsychology. At this stage, it is necessary to review this latter theory and its relationship to language. For, as I noted earlier in this chapter, one of the most important aspects of myth-and-literature scholarship remains the question of whether the mythicity of discourse and the unconscious itself are linked at all, and if so, how.

We have, in fact, reached a point in this preamble where, based on the premise that all meaning relies on interpretation, the "universal" archetype or myth can be seen to be a significant version of the act of interpretation itself. The archetypal motif becomes a triggering device for interpretation which will lead us to some understanding of the absent element in knowledge. It is a constant reminder that there is always something in language as well as in the configuration of the real world, some meaning or implication, which tantalizes us by never being fully known. We have traditionally called this the unconscious, and archetypes apparently turn-up as "proof" of its existence. At this point in my argument, though, the archetype is proof of nothing other than the absent metonymy in the metaphor. That is, the mythicity of myth depends on the highly problematic but exciting suggestiveness which even ordinary language is capable of conveying through metaphor, and to which we are capable of responding. We could locate our response positivistically in some kind of neoscientific discourse. In fact, myth, as Lévi-Strauss has pointed out, can even be called one of the sciences of man. But myth still incorporates the language of creative fantasy. And the lack to which that responds, it has often been said, is discovered in our admission that there are too many questions about human nature to which we have no answers and upon which we must fantasize. The unconscious has become either a mystified wonder-world or, in the now traditional Freudian version, a nexus of unrequited desire, driving fiercely through libidinal energies of a distinctly erotic nature to seek some kind of homeostasis. So, it is often said, too, that the incompleteness of knowledge and language is reflected in our gradual discovery of the unconscious as a neurotic complexity.

It is the Freudian position which seems to me to speak most directly to the anxiety of our finitude. At least it does not rely on a deliberate mystification of the psyche to establish its methods, nor does it automatically sanctify the unconscious, even if its clinical determinism has become as legendary as its cures. But the interesting aspect of Freudianism for myth-and-literature studies does not lie simply in some clever explanation of the significance of the Oedipus story, or of exile and taboo in the nuclear family, and so on. That is, it does not lie in the translation of motifs into some authoritative plot for human behavior. Rather it is relevant for its insights into the very condition of mythicity which we have been discussing as a linguistic fact. Indeed, the impact of linguistics on psychoanalytic theory in the last few years has largely been to demythologize the libido (but not to desexualize it, as Jacques Lacan has shown), even while it has *re*mythologized desire as an *effect* of language itself. The self is no less divided than ever before, but that division is tangibly evoked (even as it is often still admittedly unclear) in the self's discourse.

The question remains: how does the language of discourse function as unconscious activity? I want to argue that it does so most importantly in its struggle to fill the gap between appearance and truth, word and meaning. Language somehow carries the full range of ontological terrors we associate with the absence of identity and knowledge. It is language itself which not only evokes personal, psychological disruptions but institutionalizes them in metaphor. Discourse becomes the pursuit of some absent center (metonymy) for the self, and results in an attempt by the subject to eliminate himself from doubt. Writing acquires a special significance as the intention to create an objective other in the writer's place, an other who wants to be the "I" of speech.

Myth, as we shall see, carries this essential yet disruptive and nihilating use of language. The "violence of the letter," as Derrida has called it after Rousseau (and it is the modern rediscovery of Rousseau by Derrida, Lévi-Strauss, and Starobinski, among others, which has affirmed this theory) lies precisely in the paradox that language would seem to be metaphorical in origin even as it yearns for metonymy. So interpretation itself aims to be literal-minded and self-denying. Derrida, with Rousseauian overtones, offers a flood of praise for the passion of metaphor which, he admits, we always seek to deny in the interests of accuracy:

> In what consists the *precision* and the *exactitude* of language, that lodging of writing? Above all in *literalness* [*propriété*]. A precise and exact language should be absolutely univocal and literal [*propre*]: nonmetaphorical. The language is written, and pro-regresses, to the extent that it masters or effaces the figure in itself.

Effaces, that is, its origin. For language is originarily metaphorical. According to Rousseau it derives this from its mother, passion. Metaphor is the characteristic that relates language to its origin. Writing would then be the obliteration of this characteristic, the "maternal characteristics."

. . . .

Metaphor must therefore be understood as the process of the idea or meaning (of the signified, if one wishes) before being understood as the play of signifiers. The idea is the signified meaning, that which the word expresses. But it is also a sign of the thing, a representation of the object within my mind. Finally, this representation of the object, signifying the object and signified by the word or by the linguistic signifier in general, may also indirectly signify an affect or a passion. It is in this play of the representative idea (which is signifier or signified according to the particular relationship) that Rousseau lodges his explanation. Before it allows itself to be caught by verbal signs, metaphor is the relation between signifier and signified within the order of ideas and things, according to what links the idea with that of which it is the idea, that is to say, of which it is already the representative sign. Then, the literal or proper meaning will be the relationship of the idea to the affect that it *expresses*. And it is the *inadequation of the designation* (metaphor) which *properly expresses* the passion.[54]

But, as I have suggested earlier, it is an oversimplification to insist on the metaphorical origins of language without emphasizing that in its play language has a habit of deconstructing itself and searching for that absent metonymy which reveals the demand for literalness.

The relevant point here is that interpretation must deal with the "proper" yet "inadequate" metaphor. We have to accept our mysterious shortcomings, and our inadequacy in the letter itself. As Derrida rightly insists, we must constantly return to

the subjectivity of the subject and "substitute the phenomenological order to understand the emergence of metaphor,
and the savage possibility of transference." So, especially in
the self-conscious figurations of myth and literature, we must
be in trouble indeed, for there the "savagery" of the linguistic
order of desire is most apparent.

Yet it must also be said, as an aside here, that we are ironically civilized by the disruptions of the letter, not only in
ancient and primitive myth but also in much modern "paranoid" and disjunctive writing (e.g., Barthelme, Pynchon)
where the stylization of desire and patterns of coincidence
seem to dominate and make absent a neutral zone where the
everyday operates. And "savage" is a telling epithet not because
it reminds us of some primitive violence which we have associated with original, sacred, and mythic rituals; it is not
exactly Conrad's primitive terror lurking over our shoulders.
The violence of metaphor can somehow be institutionalized
in even the most sophisticated of literary writing (and as René
Girard observes, in the most complex social systems). In the
modern (to be specific, in the work, say, of Joyce, Lawrence,
Faulkner, Pound, Genet: the list, of course, is endless), the
anarchy of the psyche hovers around the edge of socialized
desire and becomes literary. It can even wrench wish-fulfillment out of wastes of anxiety and apocalyptic feelings. It is
strangely appropriate that such natural paranoia should become literary, for the contortions of the unconscious in the
modern are available to us in the highly self-conscious letter,
not as a fact to be translated into some surreal metaphor, but
as an (often erotic) replay of the timeless effort repeated in
every birth. As self-consciousness increases with more knowledge of language, the hypothetical first moment of acquisition
of language and consciousness together is sought over and
over again. It is this acquisition of language, as psychoanalysis
has told us, which subverts the subject, defines our savagery,
and creates our paranoia. The gap between the subject and
his desire is distinctly homologous to the gap between the
thing and its name: ironically, both are produced by a repres-

sion which is language itself. Since we must return to the *language* of the self, Jacques Lacan's highly original formulations of this fact of psychoanalysis seem to me the most satisfactory description of the accounting of language as lack, which goes on to demand the performance of language as myth. For Lacan, quite simply, the unconscious is that discourse which has "escaped" from the subject, which we produce without knowing why. It is the language which we give birth to, which humanizes us, but which we cannot fully control, and which instead appears to control us.

"It is the world of words," writes Lacan, "that creates the world of things—the things originally confused in the *hic et nunc* of the all in the process of coming-into-being—by giving its concrete being their essence. . . . Man speaks, then, but it is because the symbol has made him man."[55] In a vocabulary which clearly reveals his indebtedness to Claude Lévi-Strauss (and other Structuralists like Jakobson), Lacan raises the problem of our determinism by language. He tries to define the relationship of the logical, cultural overlay of language to the unconscious, not only as a violence but as a "subjective logic" in league with a primal lack:

> The marriage tie is governed by an order of preference whose law concerning the kinship names is, like language, imperative for the group in its forms, but unconscious in its structure. In this structure, whose harmony or conflicts govern the restricted or generalized exchange discerned in it by the social anthropologist, the startled theoretician finds the whole of the logic of combinations: thus the laws of number—that is to say, the laws of the most refined of all symbols—prove to be immanent in the original symbolism. At least, it is the richness of the forms in which are developed what are known as the elementary structures of kinship that makes it possible to read those laws in the original symbolism. And this would suggest that it is perhaps only our unconsciousness of their permanence that allows us to believe in the freedom of choice

in the so-called complex of structures of marriage ties under whose law we live. If statistics have already allowed us to glimpse that this freedom is not exercised in a random manner, it is because a subjective logic orients this freedom in its effects.[56]

Thus Lacan's unconscious is everywhere present in speech. It is structured like a language, and in the analytic moment (for which we can read the moment of interpretation) is itself the absent element fully alluded to; it is the Nothing into which we project our Being:

> It is therefore in the position of a third term that the Freudian discovery of the unconscious becomes clear as to its true grounding. This discovery may be simply formulated in the following terms:
>
> The unconscious is that part of the concrete discourse, in so far as it is transindividual, that is not at the disposal of the subject in re-establishing the continuity of his conscious discourse.[57]

Yet this consciousness of absence (absent meaning and absence of control) that we can call the unconscious is structurally available to us in any discourse as a system of signs creating a semantic structure. Insofar as the unconscious can be understood at all, it must have a history, and Lacan notes that the unconscious is the history of the subject:

> What we teach the subject to recognize as his unconscious is his history—that is to say, we help him to perfect the present historization of the facts that have already determined a certain number of the historical "turning points" in his existence. But if they have played this role, it is already as facts of history, that is to say, in so far as they have been recognized in one particular sense or censored in a certain order.
>
> Thus, every fixation at a so-called instinctual stage is above all a historical scar: a page of shame that is forgotten or undone, or a page of glory that compels. But

what is forgotten is recalled in acts, and undoing what has been done is opposed to what is said elsewhere, just as compulsion perpetuates in the symbol the very mirage in which the subject found himself trapped.[58]

We know, then, of the existence of the unconscious, when the lack is neurotically apparent:

> . . . the Freudian unconscious is situated at that point, where, between cause and that which it affects, there is always something wrong. The important thing is not that the unconscious determines neurosis—of that one Freud can quite happily, like Pontius Pilate, wash his hands. Sooner or later, something would have been found, humoral determinates, for example—for Freud, it would be quite immaterial. For what the unconscious does is to show us the gap through which neurosis recreates a harmony with a real—a real that may well not be determined.[59]

So by revealing itself as the absent element in conscious discourse, the surplus meaning or the blatant lack which we cannot control, which creates our history as much as its own, and which reveals the gap between event and meaning, Lacan's unconscious becomes, as it were, *a myth of the self amid language*. Insofar as language *alone* can bring the concept of negativity into being, so the unconscious emerges in the semantic gap as what Lacan calls the "pre-ontological cut": "what happens there is inaccessible to contradiction, to spatiotemporal location and also to the function of time":[60]

> Impediment, failure, split. In a spoken or written sentence something stumbles. Freud is attracted by these phenomena, and it is there that he seeks the unconscious. There, something other demands to be realized—which appears as intentional, of course, but of a strange temporality. What occurs, what is *produced*, in this gap, is presented as *the discovery*. It is in this way that the Freud-

ian exploration first encounters what occurs in the unconscious. . . .

Discontinuity, then, is the essential form in which the unconscious first appears to us as a phenomenon—discontinuity, in which something is manifested as a vacillation.[61]

Even as every sentence is a temporal pulsation between syntagm and paradigm, so the history of the self is defined, quite literally, as an erotic play in metaphorical language. The gap allows no full belief. The libido is radically alienated, and what follows is what Lacan has called "the paranoiac principle of human knowledge, according to which its objects are subjected to a law of imaginary reduplication, evoking the homologation of an endless series of notaries, who owe nothing to their professional body."[62] (This endless series of homologies is precisely what Lévi-Strauss refers to as the mythicity of myth, and what I have referred to as the mythicity of language.) The fact which allows us to live through the paranoia is that the subject occupies the gap willingly in order to allow metaphorical assimilation to take place, and ideally even the substitution of metonymy. Substitution amid a system of differences is all that establishes essential meaning. So Lacan, in his attempt to break down ego-psychology, sees the subject as occupying a space in time which is no more or less than "the complete, total locus of the network of signifiers, that is to say, the subject, *where it was*, where it has always been the dream."[63] I am a signifier in a world of signifiers, but in the act of trying to make sense of my place in time, I am the focus of those other signifiers and therefore essentially absent from my being. A substitution has taken place *for me*, not only in my imagination, but for all others for whom I am the object.

Again, we can say that all meaning is derived from the structure of the signifier, and the subject himself, in his making-himself-absent, is now "defined as the effect of the signifier." Therefore, the subject actually "begins in the locus of

the Other, insofar as it is there that the first signifier emerges."
Kenneth Burke, of course, has insisted on as much before in
essays (to be found, for example, in *Language as a Symbolic
Action*) concerning the dramatistic nature of language, "negative theology," and the entelechial principle. But Lacan, with
considerably more psychological and linguistic detail, defines
the full irony that for the self to know itself essentially, it must
objectify itself as signifier. The signifier in order to have meaning at all must represent a subject to *another* signifier. The
subject, therefore, is found paradoxically only in the Other—
the field of the Other *is* language—which in turn is much older
than we are and determines us as subjects. We want the Other
to be part of the self. We want to absorb the competition, a
human aggression which dramatically underlies not only our
legal system, but even our need for the sacred archetype. For
since it is only the object which ensures the consistency of the
subject, we have traditionally craved archetypes. Whatever is
essential in experience appears to be Other, and the archetype
becomes institutionalized.

But as Lacan is well aware, the essential is a result of our
signification to ourselves and others in *discourse*, and that
cannot be institutionalized. The lack within consciousness
appears at that moment when the subject is divided by discourse. Lacan maintains the Structuralist fascination with binary oppositions in a most telling way: "when the subject
appears somewhere as meaning, he is manifested elsewhere
as 'fading,' as disappearance. There is, then, one might say,
a matter of life and death between the unary [*sic*] signifier and
the subject, *qua* binary signifier, cause of his disappearance."[64]
And with division comes desire, "established in the field of
the subject by a way that is of lack."[65] Desire itself is—at the
level of metaphorical language—the gap in the interval of
signifiers; it is the metonymy in the metaphor of the self.

"Desire," says Lacan, "is the metonymy of the want-to-be,
the ego is the metonymy of desire,"[66] The metaphor is, as it
were, the symptom of our anxiety for knowledge, while metonymy is a possible substitution of signifiers, a "veering off

of signification," a trope revealing the unconscious attempt to foil both censorship and dissipation, and remain indestructible:

> The double-triggered mechanism of metaphor is the very mechanism by which the symptom, in the analytic sense, is determined. Between the enigmatic signifier of the sexual trauma and the term that is substituted for it in an actual signifying chain there passes the spark that fixed in a symptom the signification inaccessible to the conscious subject in which that symptom may be resolved—a symptom being a metaphor in which flesh or function is taken as a signifying element.
>
> And the enigmas that desire seems to pose for a "natural philosophy"—its frenzy mocking the abyss of the infinite, the secret collusion with which it envelops the pleasure of knowing and of dominating with *jouissance*, these amount to no other derangement of instinct than that of being caught in the rails—eternally stretching forth towards the *desire for something else*—of metonymy. Hence its "perverse" fixation at the very suspension-point of the signifying chain where the memory-screen is immobilized and the fascinating image of the fetish is petrified.[67]

It is, again, metonymy which is really not only the essence being sought after by interpretation, but the organizing principle of the whole process:

> Interpretation concerns the factor of a special temporal structure that I have tried to define in the term metonymy. As it draws to its end, interpretation is directed towards desire, with which in a certain sense, it is identical. Desire, in fact, is interpretation itself.
>
> In between, there is sexuality. If sexuality, in the form of the partial drives, had not manifested itself as dominating the whole economy of this interval, our experience would be reduced to a mantic, to which the neutral term

physical energy would then have been appropriate, but in which it would miss what constitutes in it the presence, the *Dasein*, of sexuality.[68]

In sum, the unconscious is the discourse which escapes the subject, an absence not idealizing itself, as it does with Jung, but rather the gap between signifiers which the subject has to occupy. As speech, it is the metonymy of the self, the location of desire, undercutting all our efforts at understanding. It is the lack we always play off against and attempt to break down, but which we find squarely before us in all our attempts to make a link between self and other. The mythicity of language lies in its control over the self as the site of the unconscious.

We might call this psychology of the self a version of the synchronous dimension of the subject in which one touches fulfillment only insofar as one recognizes that the activity of the self is structured as the language of metaphor. But the Lacanian logic also creates its own history for the subject. It is inevitable that Lacan should attempt to show the stages of human development of the metonymy of desire. This has been traced clearly of late in the work of Wilden and Jameson,[69] so I see little point in going into much detail here, but the relevance of the stages of ego genesis to my argument can be summed up briefly. The essential is progressively defined through stages which Lacan calls "the imaginary," "the symbolic," and "the real." In true Freudian fashion, there is a *gradual subversion of the subject by language*, and the subject's discovery in language of the humanizing of the lack which lies at the heart of self-consciousness. In the imaginary, preverbal stage of childhood, Lacan postulates the discovery of images of the subject's fragmented body: the original differentiation of the inside and the outside, the visual, "mirror stage" of consciousness in which the self is fundamentally alienated from desire. The Other is the nurturing mother, yet an aggressive binarism slowly develops. In the symbolic stage, the "Name-of-the-Father," the signifier as Law and the primal repression, develops around the beginnings of the ego-ideal. This coincides with the acquisition of language and the "paranoia" this brings. The unconscious emerges alongside the growth of cognitive processes necessary for interpretation, which in turn can account for the possibility of an institutionalized negativity and repression defined by language itself. And out of this Law of both Father and Language stem our social obligations and sexual desire:

> It is this moment that decisively tips the whole of human knowledge into mediatization through the desire of the other, constitutes its objects in an abstract equivalence by the co-operation of others, and turns the I into that apparatus for which every instinctual thrust constitutes a danger, even though it should correspond to a natural maturation—the very normalization of this maturation being henceforth dependent, in man, on a cultural mediation as exemplified, in the case of the sexual object, by the Oedipus complex.[70]

In this structurist phase, relations become abstracted—again, a fact available only through the possibility of the linguistic negative. If the signifier and the signified are in each instance in a fixed relation in the imaginary (the gap appears most cogently to the child as existing between signifiers themselves), then in the symbolic phase, slippage takes place of the signifier under the signified: the gap opens up in the sign itself, and interpretation begins to appear as the most essential of all human activities. Here the word's symbolic presence reveals an absence, too, in Lacan's phallocentric vocabulary, signifying penis-envy in women and fear of castration in men.

The final stage of ego genesis is what Lacan calls the real, a highly problematic phase which, as Jacques-Alain Miller and Allan Sheridan have attempted to explain,[71] has changed in meaning since Lacan's early work in the 1940's:

> The "real emerges as a third term, linked to the symbolic and the imaginary: it stands for what is neither

symbolic nor imaginary, and remains foreclosed from the analytic experience, which is an experience of speech. What is prior to the assumption of the symbolic, the real in its "raw" state (in the case of the subject, for instance, the organism and its biological needs), may only be supposed, it is an algebraic x. This Lacanian concept of the "real" is not to be confused with reality, which is perfectly knowable: the subject of desire knows no more than that, since for it reality is entirely phantasmatic.

The term "real," which was at first of only minor importance, acting as a kind of safety rail, has gradually been developed, and its signification has been considerably altered. It began, naturally enough, by presenting, in relation to symbolic substitutions and imaginary variations, a function of constancy: "the real is that which always returns to the same place." It then became that before which the imaginary faltered, that over which the symbolic stumbles, that which is refractory, resistant. Hence the formula: "the real is the impossible." It is in this sense that the term begins to appear regularly, as an adjective, to describe that which is lacking in the symbolic order, the ineliminable residue of all articulation, the foreclosed element, which may be approached, but never grasped: the umbilical cord of the symbolic.[72]

We might refer to this sense of the real as the denotative level of interpretation, the conscious irony of the act of being articulate at all, which Lacan is acutely aware of in terms of the analytic situation: "we always point out that we must not be taken in when the subject tells us that something happened to him that day that prevented him from realising his wish to come to the session. Things must not be taken at the level at which the subject puts them—in as much as what we are dealing with is precisely this obstacle, this hitch, that we find at every moment."[73] This "kernel of the real," then, is very much a fact of interpretation and not simply of a deeply subliminal impulse. Lacan calls it the *tuché*, the encounter, the

unassimilable trauma itself revealed in the fantasy which hides
it.

The real seems to coincide with the impossible, the completely desexualized, the obstacle to the pleasure principle.[74]
It is only at the moment when the unreal has articulated itself
in some elusively metaphorical way that we can call the real
into being: it is the resistance of reality to the imaginary or
to the symbolic, the approachable but never quite graspable.
Into the domain of the real, then, fall not only peculiarly
stubborn analytic problems, but a whole range of ontological
questioning and social compromise that we locate in the area
of art, myth, and philosophy. It is, one might say, the "gap-
ness" or incarnation of absence into which we insert all our
attempts at knowing—again, very existentially, a Heideggerian moment of projecting into Nothing. But the point is that
this is not merely a utopian phase. It is not beyond desire, nor
is it entirely reliable, for it embodies the *symbolic decentering*
implicit in every act of interpreting history. It is, again, the
violence of the letter that is truly metaphorical and yearns for
metonymy. In terms of human sexuality Lacan describes it as
the most primal of all lacks: the death we are all born into
by being reproduced. By the real, we are directed once again
to the subject. The circle is closed. "Everything emerges from
the structure of the signifier,"[75] and insofar as the subject's
history is the history of his coming-into-understanding of his
divided significance, then that which is most real is exhibited
in the pleasure principle and its repetition in desire, which
remains impossible to idealize. So if we seek the essential, the
reason for the need for myth itself, we are bound in a cumulative evolution of the human mind in and out of the imaginary, the symbolic, and the real.

I want to suggest in this study that it is myth and, at times,
literature which reveals the only human discourse embodying
every stage of these efforts at interpretation: from the anxiety
of fragmentation, to the subversion by language, to the encounter with the unknowability of history itself. There we
seek the metonymy which insists on performing as metaphor.

This preamble has been a consideration of two related subjects: (a) the ontological gap between event and meaning, self and other, and (b) the possibility of defining a sense of the mythic as the filling of this gap with signs. It would be presumptuous, at this point, to say it has yielded a completed theory of myth-as-metaphor or interpretation. But I would like to think that in the particular amalgam of contemporary Structuralism (in linguistics and psychoanalysis) and philosophical hermeneutics, some working propositions have emerged which can be further explored in relation to the problem of whether myth is still alive in modern literature. The large question of what Structural Anthropology has to offer to the argument must be examined next, but here I should summarize my position:

(1) The point of departure of my argument can be explained ideologically as a reaction to the deliberate mystification of the essentialist viewpoint on myth and archetype, especially in the work of Jung. This is not to say that myth and archetype will ever cease to be in some way mysterious, but it *is* to say that so long as they are discourse (for the archetypal significance of myth must be a language event), then their mystery and paradox must exist at the level of (i) their medium, and (ii) our problems of interpreting the medium. (By limiting the subject to narrative, of course, we are not precluding dance, drawing, and the other arts of mythology, which have in common with the tale the nature of a semiotic or representational system.)

(2) But I have not yet offered a semiological reading of any myths as such, and this might appear as a distinct deficiency in the argument. If one is writing about myths, then there is no escape from mythology. But so far in the argument, I have not attempted to go beyond the quite tangible nature of myth as a *language event* and the conditions implied by that. This creates the belief that for a narrative to be mythic, whatever the story tells, there must be some concept of mythicity as linked to linguisticality available for discussion. Indeed, in this

whole study, I shall be talking rather more about specific literary works than myths, for I want to show that the mythic conditions are determined by language itself and are just as readily available in literature. Hence the importance of the general question: Are we implicated mythically in the interpretation of discourse? And hence also my affirmative response, which results in the attempt to locate the mythicity of narrative in (i) the central *absence* or *lack* in consciousness which is part of any interpretative act (we simply never know exactly what-is: our consciousness is decentered and decentering), and (ii) the conditions *in discourse* which create and/or verify this lack, beginning with the problematic status of every word as a signifier (semiotics) and moving to the problematic relationship among those signifiers which evokes reference (semantics).

(3) As we slide back and forth from these quite tangible linguistic facts to the nagging problem of what is *essential* about language performance, and what can conceivably make a myth mythic in narrative, then we begin to define the coordinates of the essential in terms of understanding limited by language, yet revealed only in the interpretative act of discourse itself. Any definition of mythicity must concern itself with interpretation theory, which is engaged in terms of (i) the psychological reconstruction we make of a text, (ii) the historicity of understanding, and (iii) the psychological decentering (in the Heideggerian sense) of the Other in discourse. So the universal may very well be only that which is always open to interpretation. The nature of language performance (as syntagm and paradigm) allows only a process theory for the archetype. In terms of the figurative language demanded by our interpretation of reality, the essential emerges as the metaphor's hopeless search to be literal, "achieving" this in metonymy. From the hermeneutical viewpoint, the clue to the essential lies as much in Nothing as the ground of Being—in the history of interpretation theory as dominated by our *inability* to authenticate Being and essence—and therefore in

the metaphor as *lack*. All this uncertainty is determined by language, by the world as a system of signs constantly open to interpretation. Language authenticates its own instability as well as ours, hence the importance of the relatively stable metonymy. Myth, as yet in my argument, is not allowed to be a translinguistic fact, and even if it were, we would not know what it could be without language. So we cling to the essential in myth as an exhilarating play of nihilation and authenticity, all because of and in spite of language. It is in the shared capacity for representation between us and the world that mythicity must reside. Hence the importance of the act of metaphor, the innovative screening of the gap to counter the directness of what the body finds in the world: the "science" of metonymical relationships.

(4) The creation of metaphor raises the question of exactly how we are affected by the capacity for representation, especially in our narrative efforts. Since mythicity for the subject is contained in language and consciousness, and not merely in a motor reaction in awe of some thing, it seems to be productive to concentrate on the psychoanalytic explanation of myth and archetype. This sees metaphor (and, by implication, myth) as a contact surface and a potential space: the "divorcing action" and "duplicating exteriority" of the archetype (in Starobinski's terms) are evident as we seek hidden meaning and choose certain signifiers (and their extension in metaphors) as a systematic protection against our not-knowing, against our "soft inside." So now a further dimension of mythicity emerges: our fate is transacted in the *potential* spaces of language. We are not possessed by archetypes. In language we achieve a certain identity through the repetitive shortening and widening of the distance in discourse between the hidden exterior and our vulnerable interior.

(5) Plainly, this language can carry terror and disruption; that is, we can postulate "primal" fears and hopes in the attempts of discourse, ritual, and other semiotic systems, to close the paranoia-inducing gap between the word and the thing. But the primordial resides *in* language. From the psy-

choanalytic standpoint, furthermore, it is the temporal pulsation of consciousness evoked in language which begins to define the unconscious. The unconscious—the traditional source of all mythic meaning which is still most often revered as the source of absent truths—is now revealed in discourse as the presence of the Other. The Other, that which the speaker leaves out without knowing why, the anonymity of his speech, and the necessary objectification of the self in every genuine act of interpretation. So the unconscious, insofar as it is part of the language of the self, is truly the instigation to myth in that it is the history of our fully existential encounter with the gap between subject and desire, which is now homologous to the gap between thing and name. The essentialized and mythic lies in the unconscious as the *metonymy of the self*. It remains now for us to examine, via anthropology, fiction, and myth itself, the structuring of narrative given these linguistic and psychological conditions for mythicity.

CHAPTER 2

THE STRUCTURAL MODEL: ANTHROPOLOGY AND SEMIOTICS

> Because of the novel's historical position in the evolution
> of literary genres, it was inevitable that it should tell a
> story that ends badly, and that it should now, as a genre,
> be itself coming to a bad end.
> —Lévi-Strauss,
> *The Origin of Table Manners*[1]

> Nothing is more depressing than to imagine the text as
> an intellectual object (for reflection, analysis, compari-
> son, mirroring, etc.). The text is an object of pleasure.
> —Barthes, *Sade / Fourier / Loyola*[2]

CLAUDE LÉVI-STRAUSS AND MYTHIC TRANSFORMATION

Is there a genetic model available to us which fulfills the ontological conditions for myth as discourse which I have just
been discussing? For obvious reasons, one hesitates to assert
that such a model could possibly exist, but it is valuable nonetheless to turn with some skepticism, but a good deal of ad-
miration, to one of the most influential attempts to prove that
myth has some kind of discernible structure. This will give us
an opportunity to examine in more detail the relationship of
the structural model to mythicity. Claude Lévi-Strauss, in
lengthy documentation from totemistic myth drawn mainly
from the two Americas, has provided us with a most comprehensive perspective on the relation of the unconscious to
mythological discourse and on the way mythic thought supposedly structures narrative. What I want to argue is that, in

spite of his apparent lack of sympathy for the continuation of myth into the modern, his theory of the transformational structure of myth is highly relevant to our enquiry.

Furthermore, Lévi-Strauss is a special case for literary studies. He is an anthropological scientist concerned with mythology, the arts, and hermeneutics. Most impressive is his effort to restore a humanistic set of values to the sciences of man, and to insist that modern intellectual development is an interdisciplinary enterprise. Yet his case is a hard one to present because of the interdisciplinary data he offers in the process. He squarely faces the difficulty of understanding myth as concept, code, and language. His science of myth depends on reconciling a theory of reading in which the scientist himself becomes personally involved in interpreting the metaphoric subtlety of a narrative, with a semiological attempt to verify mythic transformations via the structure of plot (described as a genetic binary coding drawn from linguistic models).

In fact, because of this complex motive—seemingly Structuralist *and* phenomenological at once (in spite of his insistence that he does not espouse the latter position)—Lévi-Strauss has had a mixed impact on literary studies in America and Britain since the publication of "The Structural Study of Myth" in French and English in 1955. On the one hand, that essay and most of the works which followed it, have tended to build him a reputation as a meticulous Structuralist working rather abrasively within the French academic tradition. He attacks Levy-Bruhl, opposes certain elements of the Left in spite of his "Marxist" credentials, supposedly resists Sartre's view of dialectics and history, and develops analytic principles (along with Jakobson) in the light of linguistic theory. But, on the other hand, his interest in the structure of myth has become linked with large ontological ambitions which are shown in his persistent attempt to prove that anthropology contributes to an understanding of the workings of the human mind. The way we think, he insists, has always been inherently logical and never primitively animistic. His interdisciplinary emphasis and neo-Kantian premises can even be said to run counter to Jakobson's insistence that linguistics is the dominant Structuralist "science."

We find the first signs of this double intent in *Tristes Tropiques* which also appeared in 1955. When an English translation was published six years later, literary critics in general began to think more fondly of Lévi-Strauss's contribution to modern letters, based on that work's moving personal memoir, its lyrical description of Amerindian society and the Brazilian "spirit of place," and its proposals for the metaphysical limits to the sciences of man—all this in the same breath.

But again, *Tristes Tropiques* ambiguously marks the beginning of the career of a Structuralist. It evokes the very dilemma of that perspective, for it centers on the problematic movement in historiography, art, and criticism, as well as in anthropology, from an emotionally ordered thought to an empirically ordered structure, and vice versa: that is, precisely the transition we most commonly expect fictions to make. For one thing, the Structuralist, like Lévi-Strauss in *Tristes Tropiques*, has first to create his own crisis of consciousness, to establish his own *cogito* and its relationship to the material. This is not only the point of that book, but the beginning of what is perhaps the most important alignment of interpretation theory and social science in modern anthropology: the search for a model for essentializing human logic. There are problems, of course, in following Lévi-Strauss's insight into his own motives—not to mention his documentation of myth as a binary structure—as he turns between an accumulation of formulae for the evaluation of totemistic myths and broad generalizations about the sciences of man which can only remind us of the important influence of Rousseau (as he himself admits).[3] His major work to this date, the *Introduction to a Science of Mythology (Mythologies)*, has unfortunately not made him appear much less formalist than he did in the earlier essays, even to the established schools of formal and empirical criticism in Britian and the United States. But *Mythologies* is probably the most completely documented study of the structure and function of myth that we have; its impressive assembly of exhaustive data and its synthesis of function and structure have made it highly influential outside as well as inside France.

As Lévi-Strauss traces a myth of the Bororo Indians of Central Brazil through "to the furthermost regions of North America," we discover not merely positivistic detail and romantic interest in the sheer abundance of primitive logic, but one of the most ambitious of modern readings of how the human imagination, telling stories about its place in nature and the formation of culture, interprets the world around it in order to reach some understanding of *its own* presence. For always Lévi-Strauss himself is part of the meaning. Anthropology, he has claimed in *Tristes Tropiques*, affords for him the "intellectual satisfaction" of joining "at one extreme the history of the world and at the other the history of myself, and it unveils the shared motivation of one and the other at the same moment."[4] We can compare this with the dilemma of the reader-centered critic seeking to account for the uniqueness of both writing and his own consciousness in the tension between text and context, idiosyncracy and cultural history. Few readers, of course, can be concerned only with a simple impressionism or, on the other hand, merely with positivistic questions about literary sign-making, or about how society alone is manifest in the peculiar nature of the fictions created by those signs. Literary scholarship now returns with relief to the uncertainties of how the reader reads, creating a dialectic between reader and text in order to define accurately the "shared motivation" of author, work, and audience. Lévi-Strauss begins by wanting to define this complex event as an empirically discernible phenomenon.

Literary studies can have in common with Lévi-Strauss's view of myth a theory of interpretation in which the reader-as-outsider has not relinquished the problem of his own consciousness in the search for some essential meaning, and in which revelation of content takes place only in relation to the structural dynamic of the text (determined by linguistic premises). But this "shared motivation" does raise for Lévi-Strauss

unavoidable questions about mythology as primary knowledge. He believes that anthropology is above all about reconciling the problems of metaphysics with the problems of actual
human behavior in society. That synthesis is no less the motive
which underlies all mythology. It is an attractive but elusive
insight, made difficult by the fact that Lévi-Strauss also un-
derstands that in mythology the problem is that of all symbolic
discourse, of contending with *fictions* about human behavior
as well as with the behavior itself. We shall return to this
question of myth-as-fiction or "second-order system" in the
next section, but in order to address it more fully then, we
need first to examine the network of possibilities in which
Lévi-Strauss establishes the Structuralist point of view.

In each of the major studies, he allows time to explain his
sense of vocation, which is quite passionately his starting
point. For example, in "The Science of the Concrete" (*The
Savage Mind*, 1962), in "Ouverture" (*The Raw and the
Cooked*, 1964), and especially in the earlier "Making of the
Anthropologist" in *Tristes Tropiques*, we read that his task,
and that of the social sciences in general, is to find a way
beyond the perpetual manicheanism of the "concrete" and the
"abstract." But his argument only makes sense once he has
acknowledged the manichean nature of reality. His aim is
always to establish how modern man might (as well as does)
think, in light of the way mythology presents us with a history
of oppositional or dialectical thinking. He proposes that a
dialectic between the concrete and the abstract is in fact what
creates the development and also the dissipation of the structure of myths, as human thought attempts to make the concrete intelligible by resorting to the abstract (and the reverse).

But there is a profound pessimism underlying his sense of
how myths do this at the present time which is, indeed, part
of his motivation for writing about myth. Against the brilliant
documentation in *Mythologies* of the endless possibilities of
myth as problem-solving thought, he consistently declares that
as a human enterprise myth has weakened in time through
repetition. So acute is his ontological fear of the present in

Tristes Tropiques, for example, that he is ironically, yet unashamedly, a primitivist in arguing for some mysterious antecedent to life as we know it. The problem is that we cannot restore our "original" vitality, he says, because of all our self-destructive tendencies. But (in a rather Eastern manner), he assumes we can go back progressively "beyond all repetitions," even as we move further away from all traces of "the indefinable grandeur of man's beginnings." We move forward in time, yet imaginatively we must move back to the point of implosion: the way out of the manichean heresy is only available to us in this effort (which he later claims we find in myth):

> As he moves about within his mental and historical framework, man takes along with him all the positions he has already occupied, and all those he will occupy. He is everywhere at one and the same time; he is a crowd surging forward abreast, and constantly recapitulating the whole series of previous stages. For we live in several worlds, each truer than the one it encloses, and itself false in relation to the one which encompasses it. Some are known to us through action; some are lived through in thought; but the seeming contradiction resulting from their coexistence is solved in the obligation we feel to grant a meaning to the nearest and to deny any to those furthest away; whereas the truth lies in a progressive dilating of the meaning, but in reverse order, up to the point at which it explodes.[5]

Unfortunately, in *The Origin of Table Manners* (1968), the statement is clearly made that our "indefinable grandeur" is certainly not recoverable in the novel and that the "progressive dilation" is yet to be found there, an opinion heard more generally in the last few years, though not always with quite the same gloom that we find in the anthropology of Lévi-Strauss. Indeed, in spite of the optimism inherent in his Structuralist premises, whenever he speaks of myths or fictions, he has in mind the fact of human entropy—both physical and imaginative—reflected in the "decline" of mythical thought.

The world began without man and will end without him. The institutions, morals and customs that I shall have spent my life noting down and trying to understand are the transient efflorescence of a creation in relation to which they have no meaning, except perhaps that of allowing mankind to play its part in creation. But far from this part according man an independent position, or his endeavors—even if doomed to failure—being opposed to universal decline, he himself appears as perhaps the most effective agent working towards the disintegration of the original order of things and hurrying on powerfully organized matter towards ever greater inertia, an inertia which one day will be final. From the time when he first began to breathe and eat, up to the invention of atomic and thermonuclear devices, by way of the discovery of fire—and except when he has been engaged in self-reproduction—what else has man done except blithely break down billions of structures and reduce them to a state in which they are no longer capable of integration? As for the creations of the human mind, their significance only exists in relation to it, and they will merge into the general chaos, as soon as the human mind has disappeared. Thus it is that civilization, taken as a whole, can be described as an extraordinarily complex mechanism, which we might be tempted to see as offering an opportunity of survival for the human world, if its function were not to produce what physicists call entropy, that is inertia. Every verbal exchange, every line printed, establishes communication between people, thus creating an evenness of level, where before there was an information gap and consequently a greater degree of organization. Anthropology could with advantage be changed into "entropology," as the name of the discipline concerned with the study of the highest manifestations of this process of disintegration.[6]

So Lévi-Strauss's world view seems at the outset deeply ambivalent. On the one hand, he will go on in the several volumes of *Mythologies* to offer a complete analysis of the actual coding of mythic transformation in the information gap, documenting the changes in a single myth from one tribe to another, and from its concrete references to its growing abstraction (the latter more clearly in *From Honey to Ashes*, 1966). This activity proceeds as if in heroic defiance of entropy. On the other hand, he sees only the tenuous survival of myth in the modern in endless repetition. Myth weakens in transition until finally, transforming into fictional plot, it seems to die in our time:

> The *dénouement* or "fall" of the plot, which from the very beginning was internal to its development, and has recently become external to it—since we are now witnessing the fall or collapse *of* the plot, after the "fall" *within* the plot—confirms that because of the novel's historical position in the evolution of literary genres, it was inevitable that it should tell a story that ends badly, and that it should now, as a genre, be itself coming to a bad end. In either case, the hero of the novel is the novel itself. It tells its own story, saying not only that it was born from the exhaustion of myth, but also that it is nothing more than an exhausting pursuit of structure, always lagging behind an evolutionary process that it keeps the closest watch on, without being able to rediscover, either within or without, the secret of a forgotten freshness, except perhaps in a few havens of refuge where—contrary to what happens in the novel—mythic creation still remains vigorous, but unconsciously so.[7]

Above all, then, we seem to have here another version of the contemporary "sense of an ending," a particularly pessimistic view of how we cannot adequately "fill the gaps with signs," revealed in Lévi-Strauss's involvement with myth. This is one good reason, at least, why our curiosity about this theme in modern literature might lead us to find his position interesting. Yet, we also have to say that he knows that even his apocalypticism has to be genuinely resisted, which surely is the point of his pursuit of the sciences of man. We might remember the final cry in *Tristes Tropiques*—"Farewell to savages, then, farewell to journeying!"—and decide it is easy to see Lévi-Strauss thereafter turning to myth, burdened with the profound second thoughts of a pessimist regarding contemporary culture. Somehow we have come to expect that the modern novelist and poet will act out such a role, but not the scientist or anthropologist, as we demand from the artist diligence in persisting with metaphysical questions (or avoiding them altogether), and from the scientist, persistence with rigorous analysis. But with Lévi-Strauss, we find an attempt at both. What we need to know more pressingly is whether his pessimism is pervasive, and whether it *need* follow from his Structuralist enterprise.

Within the context of *Tristes Tropiques*, it is easy to see Lévi-Strauss as the peripatetic thinker, worn out by travel and by the ways of positivist philosophy and science, and turning with a disaffected humanism to anthropology. But we would do well to remember *all* of the ending of that study, not only for its acknowledgment of the "implacable process" of civilization, but also for its wink at that enigmatic, Baudelairean cat:

> Farewell to savages, then, farewell to journeying! And instead, during the brief intervals in which humanity can bear to interrupt its hive-like labors, let us grasp the essence of what our species has been and still is, beyond thought and beneath society: an essence that may be vouchsafed to us in a mineral more beautiful than any work of Man; in the scent, more subtly evolved than our books, that lingers in the heart of a lily; or in the wink of an eye, heavy with patience, serenity, and mutual forgiveness that sometimes, through an involuntary understanding, one can exchange with a cat.[8]

It might appear that the wink presupposes some knowledge beyond the eternal dialectic of myth, some Hegelian Spirit to the whole transaction. And it seems to me to touch on this without being melodramatic or making a deliberately mystifying gesture. It implies an acceptance of the modern threat of apocalypse and of the limits of science—hence the sanctions of reasonable doubt and the need for "mutual forgiveness." It is a very existential wink which, we have sadly noted, he cannot exchange with the modern novelist, but which does imply at least Lévi-Strauss's interest in understanding, if not explaining away, a great fear of the modern and a hope for a spontaneous, somewhat epiphanic moment of comprehension. This latter need, especially, he goes on to show, *is* available even in the arrangement of incidental detail in mythic narrative.

The curious paradox of Lévi-Strauss's Structuralism is that he invests as much old-fashioned faith in the emotionally intuited "epiphany" to be derived from myth as he does in the "science of the concrete," the terms in which he refers to myth in *The Savage Mind* (1962). But neither the wink nor the epiphany is really a source of full optimism for him. As he explained it in "The Story of Asdiwal," the most one can hope for is a "limiting situation":

> Thus we arrive at a fundamental property of mythical thought, other examples of which might well be sought elsewhere. When a mythical schema is transmitted from one population to another, and there exist differences of language, social organization, or way of life that make the myth difficult to communicate, it begins to become impoverished and confused. But one can find a limiting situation in which, instead of being finally obliterated by losing all its outlines, the myth is inverted and regains part of its precision.[9]

The denouement of mythological narrative is a source of constant irony to Lévi-Strauss. It cannot be generalized, yet he himself can transmit a sense of its latent power. However much he provides the reader with intricate formulae for mythical transformation in the later works, he does not lose sight of the wink of that cat, a wink that never lets him forget the perpetual irony of self-discovery available from engaging other men's myths—and not merely self-discovery but, in the process, the perpetual rediscovery of myths which have not been fully exhausted by translation. At best, we can only receive hints and guesses, as T. S. Eliot has warned us, as to how the human mind works, but Lévi-Strauss knows that he can never explain away those hints, the nature of "involuntary understanding," the quite arbitrary filling of the gap, and the peculiar rhythms of thought seeking revelation, all of which sanction myths as much as their apparently predictable structure.

Consequently, by *The Raw and the Cooked* (1964), Lévi-Strauss must come to see his own work as an orchestration of both empirical evidence (the structure of the mythic narratives themselves) and the continually discoverable mysteries of his own imagination. This is, I believe, exemplary for any Structuralist analysis. In *Tristes Tropiques* he said he was aware of "a structural affinity between the civilizations which are its [anthropology's] subject and my own thought processes." In *The Raw and the Cooked*, he has accepted that that affinity is the very stuff of myth-making itself. So he can move on, in spite of the perpetual possibility of apocalypse, to his *own* myth-making role:

> For what I am concerned to clarify is not so much what there is *in* myths (without, incidentally, being in man's consciousness) as the systems and postulates defining the best possible code, capable of conferring a common significance on unconscious formulations which are the work of minds, societies and civilizations chosen from those most remote from each other. As the myths themselves are based on secondary codes (the primary codes being those that provide the substance of language), the present work is put forward as a tentative draft of a tertiary code, which is intended to ensure the reciprocal translatability of several myths. This is why it would not

be wrong to consider this book in itself as a myth; it is, as it were, the myth of mythology.[10]

Behind Lévi-Strauss's "myth of mythology," then, lies what he calls a "search for a middle way between aesthetic perception and the exercise of logical thought." That middle way, which is perhaps more attractive than ever to contemporary literary studies, finds him continually working over the paradox that human logic seems to have a reason of its own, and creates its own systems in narrative. For Lévi-Strauss, human logic is timeless, but he also indicates that it has no simple, practical function and can provide no permanent examples of systematic thought existing beyond the moment. If anything, myths reveal fully the existential paradox of language itself which I have just been discussing. The "constraining structures of the mind," as Lévi-Strauss calls them, perceive relationships between self and an outer reality, yet these relationships are largely unknown to the speaker until he becomes conscious of them in language. In fact, Lévi-Strauss is always realistically tentative about the ontological status of myths (retreating from their religious significance), for they are, again, only available to us as metalanguage. A myth is never the thing itself, but is always *about* something (idea or fact). It is an attempt to be accurate about a significant absence from discourse. It is appropriative of meaning, but at the same time a generative system, reusable yet tantalizing to us in our search for its relationship to events in the real world. That Kantian dilemma is central to Lévi-Strauss's enquiry.

> Language, an unreflecting totalisation, is human reason which has its reasons and of which man knows nothing. And if it is objected that it is so only for a subject who internalizes it on the basis of linguistic theory, my reply is that this way out must be refused, for this subject is one who *speaks*: for the same light which reveals the nature of language to him also reveals to him that it was so when he did not know it, for he already made himself understood, and that it will remain so tomorrow without

his being aware of it, since his discourse never was and never will be the result of a conscious totalisation of linguistic laws.[11]

So Lévi-Strauss preserves a relationship between the unconscious and mythic thought, but it is much closer, say, to Lacan's symbolic discourse of the Other than to the mystical postulate of Jung's "primitive wonder-world." The unconscious is, again, literally the gap, while the "preconscious" takes care of the idiosyncracies of individual experience.

For the preconscious, as a reservoir of recollections and images amassed in the course of a lifetime, is merely an aspect of memory. While perennial in character, the preconscious also has limitations, since the term refers to the fact that even though memories are preserved they are not always available to the individual. The unconscious, on the other hand, is always empty—or, more accurately, it is as alien to mental images as is the stomach to the foods which pass through it. As the organ of a specific function, the unconscious merely imposes structural laws upon inarticulated elements which originate elsewhere— impulses, emotions, representations, and memories. We might say, therefore, that the preconscious is the individual lexicon where each of us accumulates the vocabulary of his personal history, but that this vocabulary becomes significant, for us and for others, only to the extent that the unconscious structures it according to its laws and thus transforms it into language. Since these laws are the same for all individuals and in all instances where the unconscious pursues its activity, the problem which arose in the preceding paragraph can easily be resolved. The vocabulary matters less than the structure. Whether the myth is re-created by the individual or borrowed from tradition, it derives from its sources—individual or collective (between which interpenetrations and exchanges constantly occur)—only the stock of representations with which it operates. But the structure remains the same, and through it the symbolic function is fulfilled.[12]

The primary law of language revealing the structuring of the preconscious by the unconscious resides in the tension between the diachronic and synchronic status of all utterances. This begins to define the appropriative power of myth as mythic thought. Relying heavily on Saussure's theories, Lévi-Strauss clearly states that myth is a language event revealing both sequence and schemata, chronological order and simultaneous abstraction, dependent on the choice of any number of possibilities to fill a syntactical slot. So the plot of a single mythic narrative, as he explains in "The Story of Asdiwal," is understandable only as a paradigm within a whole series of similar mythical sequences. A myth comprises *all* its versions without simply becoming one myth, and each version can be structurally related to the others in terms of the way the narratives are composed and repeat plot forms.

There are numerous examples of this pattern in Lévi-Strauss's work. The most often cited is one of his first—the controversial reading of the Oedipus myth—which surely does not need full explanation here, though I shall return to it later in another context. The cumulative reading of the myth reduces itself to certain common elements of the plot. These semantic units—mythemes or sentences—can reveal a structure to myth which is both historically conditioned (that is, the history of the myth provides its own context) and metaphorically open-ended (we must interpret it now). The famous "vertical" and "horizontal" reading of the myth, however complex it becomes with its four column headings referring to kinship values and questions of human origin, and however arbitrary its choice of semantic markers, is no more than an attempt to capture the paradoxical *linguisticality* of myth we have just been discussing. Myth is the intersection of learned social and cultural values *and* poetic meaning. The latter seems to interest Lévi-Strauss as much as the former.

All mythical substitutions take place as a science of the

signifier—the replacement of one signifier by another—and that science, for Lévi-Strauss, is therefore a development of synchronic linguistics. Any narrative event partakes of the "storehouse of usage." It reveals language as the "product that is passively assimilated by the individual": its revertible time and its evolutionary and linear social context (metonymy, *langue*). But, on the other hand, language has a dimension of individual expression: the nonrevertible, specific, willful and paradigmatic (metaphor, *parole*). So a linguistic event is always dependent on both its linear function, its place in revertible time, and its vertical function, its specific choice among other possibilities. It can then be said that a myth "always refers to events alleged to have taken place in time [metonymy]. . . . But what gives the myth an operative value is that the specific *pattern* described is everlasting" [metaphor].[13]

The curious thing about Lévi-Strauss's treatment of myth is that his *theory* of what myth can do is distinctly more optimistic than what he actually concludes from his analysis of primitive myths. It is the coincidental intersection of sequence and schemata which provides the suggestiveness and transformational progress of myth. One can align that theory with what I have been discussing in the last chapter. The dialectic of the metaphor insists that the hidden paradigms in metaphor are revealed only because one of the paradigms, at any given moment, exists alongside another, and is discovered in that context. Metonymical relations are established arbitrarily but are at the heart of myth's logic. The metaphors myth makes are able to reveal further paradigmatic possibilities suggested by the arrangement of the evidence found. We are led on, in mythic transformation, by the presence of an exterior with hidden meaning, by paradigm replacing paradigm within a sequence to get to an absent origin. Myths thus combine both functional axes of language with scarcely an emphasis on either since, as Lévi-Strauss explains in *The Savage Mind*, they are a kind of *bricolage*. They are always put together with reference to items at hand, from signs which have no predetermined function in the myth, yet they develop meanings within the context of narrative usage which are in turn open to extension by the imagination of the *bricoleur*. These meanings are built onto each other. Items can be imaginatively rearranged so that new paradigms emerge, and the whole process can appear "timeless" in that it evokes, perhaps more clearly than any other kind of discourse, the paradox of the intersecting synchrony and diachrony of language. Bringing-into-meaning—to receive and project in language—is therefore the primary function of myth. But the question remains: is this a property of language alone, without intention?

Like Jung, Lévi-Strauss believes that language is not the source of logic—it is the unconscious that structures—but unlike Jung (and, with Piaget, Lacan, and Chomsky), he still holds the view that somehow language is grounded in reason and plays a mediating role between unconscious and conscious thought. The central problem for him, then, since he is both open to the essential absence of the unconscious and tied to its scientific method, is in deciding what is meant by "reason" and whether this offers a prospect of salvation.

Lévi-Strauss is empiricist enough to say that the mind follows experience, that reason is after the event. Myths, by implication, are always a struggle to come into consciousness of, and to preserve contact with, the "experienced totality." And the totality, it is emphasized, refers not only to sensory evidence but to some abstract relationship of parts to a whole which is discoverable by the human mind and is implicit in the "unconscious structures" of language. Then the question is: how systematic can a myth actually be? And if it can be interpreted as systematic, does the myth provide us with teleological certainty (even without being reasonable)? But Lévi-Strauss, no matter how much he wants epiphany, is skeptical about this even as his rationalism sometimes gains the upper hand.

In *The Savage Mind*, we learn that primitive thinking is not merely in awe of some metaphysical truth or natural event, but is necessarily analytic in intent. Myths can be said to progress, structurally, in the way that our logico-mathematical structures develop: by integrating previous structures into a broader whole (even via the contradictions we find in the experimental sciences). In fact, Lévi-Strauss's Structuralist treatment of reason—which is perhaps more traditionalist than the functionalism he attacks—is the clue to his whole theory of myth. As reason evolves, so do logical structures and the rules of myth. What is created, in Jean Piaget's words, is a kind of "relational structuralism": "that is to say as positing systems of interactions of transformations as the primary reality and hence subordinating elements from the outset to the relations surrounding them and, reciprocally, conceiving the whole as the product of the composition of these formative interactions."[14]

Lévi-Strauss tackles this problem of interpretation for myth studies by arguing for his view of myth against Sartre's view of history. Indeed history itself, he says, can give us an important clue to the way consciousness and myth work. So Lévi-Strauss finds himself both with Sartre and against him:

> . . . we end up in the paradox of a system which invokes the criterion of historical consciousness to distinguish the "primitive" from the "civilized" but—contrary to its claim—is itself ahistorical. It offers not a concrete image of history but an abstract scheme of men making history of such a kind that it can manifest itself in the trend of their lives as a synchronic totality. Its position in relation to history is that of primitives to the external past: in Sartre's system, history plays exactly the part of a myth.[15]

Lévi-Strauss argues that Sartre overvalues history compared with other human sciences, but he also argues that Sartre is right without knowing it in his description of "synchronic history." History and myth are both intimately linked as code systems, a fact which is available to us by their repetitive function. Because they are available as codes, however, they can provide us with information but no ontological security.

Instead, we have to accept that the attempt to reach a "supposed totalizing continuity of the self" is sustained by the fact that the codes are the result of a community experience—and, consequently, a reflection of the external on the internal, the object on the subject—as well as the result of a teleological yearning. (This might even lead us to assume, as Girard would say, that desire itself is mimetic.)[16] Such a conclusion is available from an understanding of the history of myth, which Lévi-Strauss claims is homologous to the myth of history:

> Even history which claims to be universal is still only a juxtaposition of a few local histories within which (and between which) very much more is left out than is put in. . . . A truly total history would cancel itself out—its product would be nought. What makes history possible is that a sub-set of events is found, for a given period, to have approximately the same significance for a contingent of individuals who have not necessarily experienced the events and may even consider them at an interval of several centuries. History is therefore never history, but history for . . .
>
> History does not . . . escape the common obligation of all knowledge, to employ a code to analyse its object, even (and especially) if a continuous reality is attributed to that object . . .
>
> History is a discontinuous set composed of domains of history, each of which is defined by a characteristic frequency and by a differential coding of *before* and *after*.[17]

In short, we can find in Lévi-Strauss's argument a confidence in the unity and timelessness of human reasoning as a process responding to the demands of both our empirical and teleological needs. As in, say, Holland's or Piaget's epistemology, the human intelligence can aspire to achieving comfort from coded "bundles of transformations," a fact which aligns Lévi-Strauss's epistemology immediately with the interpretation theory I have briefly outlined in the first part of this study.

All creative and analytic attempts with language (and myth, says Lévi-Strauss in his introduction to the analysis of Baudelaire's "Les Chats,"[18] is an "art"), including all sign languages (music, painting, algebra, etc.), exhibit this function. The apparent lack of differentiation between genuinely dialectical history and myth indicates that Lévi-Strauss is concerned not merely with motifs or common themes, or with differences in the rhetorical uses of language, but with establishing how thinking reveals itself in *sign systems*. This is where he seems most optimistic. His subject is as much the structure of historical thinking as it is historiography, mythic thought, and mythology. It is, finally, the nature of semiotic systems themselves. History, for example, has a peculiar relevance for our understanding of myth in that it operates as a function of what we can call, diachronically, "domesticated" as opposed to "savage thought." This does not, for Lévi-Strauss, represent a Sartrean (or Levy-Brulian) dualism of "savage" and "civilized," but a subtle differentiation of coding only: a set of distinctions-amid-relationships. The coding of history exists largely in classes of dates. Myths, as he points out in *The Raw and the Cooked*, can distinguish themselves by the use of codes based on the five sense qualities. In *bricolage*, "all use contrasts between tangible qualities, which are thus raised to the point of having a logical existence." The logic of discontinuous sets, through the discovery of sense properties which they have in common, asserts a continuity that retains differentiation but establishes a system.

Dialectical history, both Sartre and Marx have declared, replaces mythology. But Lévi-Strauss quite successfully argues that dialectical history is itself a version of systematic mythic thought, a fact that should probably allow him more optimism than it does. History and myth both exist on a continuum, as we have just noted, by offering a coding of moments in time. History, therefore, is more than simply a mode of diachronic analysis. Like "savage thought" and myth, the aim of history can be envisaged as the attempt to "grasp the world as both a synchronic and a diachronic totality."

The knowledge which it draws therefrom is like that afforded of a room by mirrors fixed on opposite walls, which reflect each other (as well as objects in the intervening space) although without being strictly parallel. A multitude of images forms simultaneously, none exactly like any other, so that no single one furnished more than a partial knowledge of the decoration and furniture but the group is characterized by the invariant properties expressing the truth. The savage mind deepens its knowledge with the help of *imagines mundi*. It builds mental structures which facilitate an understanding of the world in as much as they resemble it. In this sense, savage thought can be defined as analogical thought.[19]

Since myths, like history, are all semiotic codes, they reveal that the structure of thought does not provide analogies from the "real," nor do myths contain archetypes which are their essence. Rather, myths offer an analogy to the *functions* of the real by acting as interpretation theory itself. A myth is a structure of the human mind at work, solving intellectual and social compromise. It provides a logical model capable of revealing presence and absence and even of overcoming contradictions and suggesting a unity to sequence and schemata. Myth also provides an optimistic diagram of the potential of the human intelligence to recognize truth. In that sense, it is as rigorous as scientific logic, even though the function of the logical model is entirely dependent on the way language works. Mythology—indeed, each myth—Lévi-Strauss is saying, is linguistically a cybernetic system, always providing mediation between its own terms. It is self-conscious form constantly seeking the details of its own justification. As such, it is a coded message from a society to its members—for language is a social fact—and never ceases to keep that message in motion.

The most important fact about mythic structures—which denies them transcendental permanence but also establishes their necessity—is the process of reasonable transformation.

Chapter 2

At the heart of what Lévi-Strauss is saying is perhaps an argument close to the synthesis of mythologic tendencies outlined in the previous chapter. Inasmuch as reason defines the origin of myth as argument, myth can mediate between that which is hidden and unknown and that which it knows about the world. As language, it comes to learn of its own inevitable talents at exchanging the inside and the outside. But myths can be repetitive if they become positivistic and essentialize a metaphor without rejustifying the function of their own terms each time. That is, if myths seek to become one myth, or merely parody the terms of dialectical thought, or else are victims of communication problems, then they will tend to survive only by weak transformations, by repetition of progressively shorter and more discontinuous episodes, all of a similar type. Exoticism, formulae, sets of paradigms—that is, archetypalist categories—work against the progress of myth by replacing the dynamic interchange between signifier and signified with the constant search for one dominant substitution. Lévi-Strauss reminds us in _The Origin of Table Manners_, as I have already noted, that creation can spring from imitation rather than dramatization, and this can progressively distort the interchange between the empirical event and our interpretation of it.

So the distinction between history and myth tends to break down when we center on the demands of dialectical thought. For Lévi-Strauss, myth rigorously tries to make sense of the oppositional nature of sign and thing in an imaginative context and, at the same time, it tries to establish its own presence and historical extension as a systematic event. Mythology, insofar as it is rational, relies on creating its own system based on the possibilities of language, which alone enables it to propagate itself. Lévi-Strauss insists that he is concerned not with how men think in myths, but with how myths think in us without our necessarily being aware of the fact. Above all, he seems to be fascinated by the imperialism of myth as language. Myth operates dialectically because it manages to account for and temporarily fill that gap where there is no end

108

to the give and take between events and their transformation into meaning. A myth's expression determines its mythicity, and by extension, whatever we know about human discourse in linguistic terms becomes centrally important to the whole subject of mythography.

In myth a range of possible human coordinates is engaged, involving both history and revelation, because language itself is its subject. Myth is mythic as a symbolic order of our fear of Nothing at all. A myth is consciously produced as a kind of dialectic between the appropriativeness of language and the intentions a group has to relieve this ontological terror that finds form most clearly in the inadequacies of language itself. Myth prompts the effort of "unconscious reorganization," as Lévi-Strauss puts it, which becomes systematically conscious in language alone and which discovers in language the necessity of the negative. It relies for its meaning on an amalgam of social compromise, problems of understanding, and individual uses of desire. But however much it seems to anticipate an ending, myth never loses consciousness of the impossibility of achieving one. The potential of myth—which I think we can safely say is regarded optimistically in Lévi-Strauss's summary—is one thing; its actual success is another, as we can see in his treatment of its relationship to fiction.

FICTION AS DEAD MYTH?

What exactly does this definition of myth have to do with literature in Lévi-Strauss's theory? To begin with, we have to ask what he has to say about the relationship between fictions and myths in the light of his definition of myth as a narrative form. We have already noted that he sees surprisingly little which is encouraging about the state of either today. In fact, when we move away from his generalizations based on specific analyses of myths to his generalizations about art, we are less persuaded by his existential concerns, and even find that he preserves archetypalist dualisms. In "Charles Baudelaire's 'Les Chats,' " he admits that poetry and myth are "complementary terms," and that "in poetic works, the linguist discerns structures which are strikingly analogous to those which the analysis of myths reveals to the ethnologist."[20] But then he goes on to elaborate a point originally made in "The Structural Study of Myth"[21] which works against the dialectic I have just been describing: "each poetic work, considered in isolation, contains in itself its variants which can be represented on a vertical axis, since it is formed of superimposed levels: phonological, phonetic, syntactic, prosodic, semantic, etc. On the other hand, the myth—at least in the extreme—can be interpreted at the semantic level only."[22]

Myths, that is, tend to reveal the power of the syntagmatic function of language; poetry, the paradigmatic. There are many versions of a myth but only one of a poem. That distinction is expanded in *The Raw and the Cooked* (1964), but there Lévi-Strauss complicates the issue somewhat by pointing out that myths lie somewhere between musical language and poetry. Music "is the only language with the contradictory attributes of being at once intelligible and untranslatable," while "the vehicle of poetry is articulate speech, which is common property."[23] So the problem develops: mythic narrative and literature are forever apart, yet they must have in common articulate speech, language demanding interpretation.

Lévi-Strauss's argument seems to be confusing, to say the least. Poetry is apparently unique, yet potentially translatable; and myth is said to lie between music and poetry. But a poem must surely share untranslatability with music if it has, as Lévi-Strauss says, only one version. Poetry and myth, though, share nothing, yet are supposedly complementary terms. To complicate the matter even more, Lévi-Strauss claims that he himself aims to write a "myth of mythology" on the paradigm of a musical score, by allowing

> . . . the process of analysis [to] take place along different axes: there would be the sequential axis, of course, but also the axis of relatively greater densities which would

involve recourse to forms comparable to solos and *tutti* in music; there would be the axis of expressive tensions and the axis of modulation codes, and during the process of composition they would bring about contrasts similar to the alternation between melody and recitative or between instrumental ensembles and arias.[24]

Both myth and music, he goes on to point out, "transcend articulate expression, while at the same time—like articulate speech, but unlike painting—they require a temporal dimension in which to unfold."

This transcendence is made possible, however, only by the dual axes of all sign systems whether articulate speech, painting, myth, or music. Surely there is no reason to believe that poetry can function for the reader or writer without such sequence and schemata. To complete that tautology: poetry, music, and myth are all structurally definable only in terms of their performance in synchronic and diachronic time. As language systems, they have no alternative. The fact that poetry is not music, and not myth either, is a distinction made only at the more general level of signs creating systems of cultural (and generic) units. But that convention is sustained only by the general theory of signs. The intention of the individual literary work to acquire form can only be a complex experiment in both expression and modulation. (We are reminded, for example, of Eliot's and Pound's theories of the music of poetry, as well as of Cézanne's version of painting as "*réalisation et modulation*").

Lévi-Strauss, while trying to appropriate myth under music, blurs his argument for myth's ratiocinative function. Furthermore, the meaning of a poem, or of any literary event, can never be realistically subsumed under one function of language, but must move between the myth of its own historical function (the history of poetic language in which it exists) and its synchronic performance (the poem's particular statement). It has its own sequence and schemata no less than myth. Performance brings the poem into a dialectic between the mythicity of genre (a poem acts like "poetry") and its intention to justify itself as both uniquely language and part of that genre. So Lévi-Strauss's "untranslatable" poem is an impossibility, for every poem is to a full extent poetry. Whether we refer to the social context of the poem or to its intrasystemic structure, we find the same play between history (metonymy) and moment (metaphor). The uniqueness of the poem's event coincides in time with the universality of its function in developing a received meaning within the conventions of poetry. Even the way in which we interpret a painting (which Lévi-Strauss says does not need a diachronic dimension in which to unfold) must incorporate some link between the language and conventions of the painting and its special significance; its status as painting must be present for us even to be aware of the synchronic moment and to interpret it at all.

Lévi-Strauss cannot have it both ways: if myth looks like history for semiotic reasons, then it looks like art, too, which just as obviously has a semiotic function. In short, if Lévi-Strauss accepts the synchronic and the diachronic as inevitable determinants of narrative meaning and interpretative process, as he plainly does in his semiology of myth as history, then he cannot assume that some narrative codes can escape the dual axes of time and others not. It may very well be the case that a myth tends to function more as a message from society to its members, and a poem tends to function more as a message from an individual to society. But these, again, are qualities determined at the level of the cultural (diachronic) axis alone, for as soon as we retreat to the question of ontological status and analyze the individual poem or myth as writing, we find that its signification is, as always, dependent on interpretation. Hermeneutics, as I have tried to show, is not incompatible with Structuralism. The poem functions as part of the sign-vehicle "poetry" as much as a mythic narrative functions as "myth." But in order to be meaningful, each cannot merely be "poetry" or "myth," but *a* poem and *a* myth. What they have in common is the paradoxical function of discourse which leaves myth and literature on a linguistic continuum. Myth can only develop a plot and approach the condition of a self-conscious literary work. And the poem (or, of course, fiction), beginning from the other end of the continuum with its emphasis on form, must use only received signs, and therefore approach the universal and the condition of myth. Even then, the received sign is never fully absorbed or destroyed. The importance of the social context of myth and literature, which cannot be denied, is entirely dependent on this dialectic. Myths constantly rearrange their terms, and literature constantly redefines its terms—for literature itself is a mythical system—not only within the boundaries of the particular and general in language, but in genre, too. Literature, like myth, can only preserve itself by being vitally self-transforming. So the novel has its own mythology, as opposed to that of poetry or drama, which refers to its performance and its structural intentions.

Now it would be simple-minded at this point to say that all fictions are necessarily myths even if all myths are fictions. But we might accept that fictions are in a subtle but continuous dialectic with their own mythology of genre, and with the mythicity of language itself. It is impossible to create a fiction without *approaching the condition* of myth, without attempting to be tautologous, to complete a meaning, to establish the fiction's own necessity, or to continue a transformation and close an action. The meaning of a fiction is always potentially mythic. It is a matter for literary criticism to decide whether a fiction actually is mythic or not—and that is one of the demands of its unavoidable function as a signifier of literature. As myth inevitably and ironically pushes to its extremes of narrative sophistication (as Lévi-Strauss shows in *Mythologies*) in order to be all things to all men, and weakens its structure in the process, so fictions push to their opposite extreme of aspiring to be as intelligible and universal as myth, by making their structure as tautologous and as minimally "fictional" as possible. They too, no less than myth, have the capacity to aim for some absent truth, some presemiological meaning. This is part of the text's desire to become the object itself, to take over for a moment both the universality of genre and the authority to assign full meaning to it in a particular case, on conditions which a specific text (and only that text) wants to lay down.

The problem with Lévi-Strauss's argument is that it cannot escape his original paradox expressed boldly in "The Structural Study of Myth." There he states that "myth *is* language," but that it exhibits "more complex features beside those which are to be found in any kind of linguistic expression." On the contrary, as I hope I have shown, its complexity can only refer to its origin in its status as language. If it is true, as I have quoted Lévi-Strauss above, that language is "human reason which has its own reasons," even if man can know little about these reasons and is scarcely conscious of them when he uses language, then it is hard to understand why this general truth about the "more complex feature" does not apply to literary language as well as to mythological language. In the same way that myths are repetitive in their constant transformational effort to evoke mythicity, with each version considering itself both complete and yet the start of the next, so when we read poetry we are conscious of the repetitiveness of genre—which is itself a kind of cybernetic system—and the attempt by each poet to essentialize over again the language of poetry.

Yet in *The Origin of Table Manners*, we find the gap between myth and literature growing even wider for Lévi-Strauss. Amid what seems to be a developing pessimism over the survival of the vitality of both myth and literature, there grows a sharp opposition between them. It is assumed by Lévi-Strauss, rather highhandedly, that disjunctions in modern art cannot in any way represent a coded message from society to itself. If anything, he suggests that the modern conjunction of myth and literature lies in the episodic novel as serial romance, where mythical transformation is apparently seen at its weakest. Failure in the transformational function of myth leads to discontinuous literary narratives, and in turn, the very discontinuity of modern narrative form can only kill off myth.

This rather bleak, though doubtless some would say "realistic" view of modern fiction, declares that the novel (presumably in the hands of writers like Faulkner, Joyce, and Pynchon) has overemphasized the paradigmatic function of literature—particularly its habit of creating arbitrary and even paranoid relations—to the loss of our sense of universal sharing in language itself, which myth depends on. It has become almost a cliché that the modern novel has lent itself to Structuralist ideas in its habit of not differentiating genre and incorporating all into self-contained fictions. But, again, the most surprising aspect of Lévi-Strauss's objection to the surrealism of modernity is that he ignores his own most useful premises about "structural fabulation" (to use Robert Scholes's terms) in myth. So we seek Lévi-Strauss in spite of himself. While he does not commit the essentialist fallacy of searching for the immanence of myth in art, he does mistakenly ascribe to the "failure" of myth the radically discontinuous structuring of much modern fiction and art. After acknowledging their broad but mutual function as metalanguage, he will not carry their similarity further. It is understandable that he does not consider that the literary use of prefiguration in myth is lively enough—that it is mere imitation—but it is not the imitation of a particular motif that is important, but imitation itself, as I have been arguing, in the service of urgent interpretation.

But, we can say, as an alternative to Lévi-Strauss's argument from his own premises, that given his terms of narrative as language seeking to prove its own necessity, either mythological or not, there would seem to be no absolute means of differentiating the narrative structure of myths and fictions. The literary imagination, as much as the mythic, is constantly searching for the "third term," or as we more commonly call it, the apt metaphor, the workable fiction. Art, like mythology, seeks to create fictions which *intend* to be essential, not simply in spite of language, but because of it.

The distinction between mythology as syntagmatic and poetry as paradigmatic, then, seems to be an unnecessary opposition. For both, as language, must rely on the fact that *all* meaning in *all* language results from the interplay of syntagm and paradigm, that neither one is translatable without the other. Poetry and myth are, ontologically, complementary classes of discourse: both are definable in terms of language as sign interpretation and as language of the self, as I have been discussing it, which alone allows these genres to perpetuate themselves. The importance of Lévi-Strauss's theory of myth for literary studies, then, lies in his insights into narrative transformation, and not in his pessimism about modern art or his formalist analysis. The models themselves depend on his reliance on interpretation theory and semiotics. We may find that his commentaries fall too easily into the traditional scheme of the superiority of myth to literature, but this results more from his pessimism, his backward glance at the *anima*—and his failure to adopt the same strictly semiological approach to art as he does to mythology—than from the failure of his premises about mythic thought. Let us examine an instance (other than that of Lacan, earlier) in which his semiotic premises have successfully been taken up for literary studies.

ROLAND BARTHES AND MYTHIC APPROPRIATION

Roland Barthes has taken little interest in the revelation of mythic thought in ancient tales or totemistic myth; by "myth" he means something quite different from Lévi-Strauss. Myth for him is both social language and ideological event (in modern rituals, such as advertising or sport, as well as in writing). He outlined his theory first in *Mythologies*, published in French in 1957, which was not translated into English until 1972. The main points of that highly suggestive and now well-known study he has summarized in one of his latest collections, *Image-Music-Text*, in an essay first published in 1971:

> 1. Myth, close to what Durkheimian sociology calls a "collective representation," can be read in the anonymous

utterances of the press, advertising, mass consumer goods; it is something socially determined, a "reflection."

2. This reflection, however, in accordance with a famous image used by Marx, is *inverted*: myth consists of overturning culture into nature or, at least, the social, the cultural, the ideological, the historical into the "natural." What is nothing but a product of class division and its moral, cultural and aesthetic consequences is presented (stated) as being a "matter of course"; under the effect of mythical inversion, the quite contingent foundations of the utterance become Common Sense, Right Reason, the Norm, General Opinion, in short the *doxa* (which is the secular figure of the Origin).

3. Contemporary myth is discontinuous. It is no longer expressed in long fixed narratives but only in "discourse"; at most, it is *phraseology*, a corpus of phrases (of stereotypes); myth disappears but leaving—so much the more insidious—the *mythical*.

4. As a type of speech (which was after all the meaning of *muthos*), contemporary myth falls within the province of a semiology; the latter enables the mythical inversion to be "righted" by breaking up the message into two semantic systems: a connoted system whose signified is ideological (and thus "straight," "non-inverted" or, to be clearer—and accepting a moral language—*cynical*) and a denoted system (the apparent literalness of image, object, sentence) whose function is to naturalize the class proposition by lending it the guarantee of the most "innocent" of natures, that of language—millennial, maternal, scholastic, etc.[25]

Barthes declares that he has not changed this theory in the fifteen years since he wrote *Mythologies*, but now the "science of reading" has broadened the issue of collectivity, a fact I have already tried to incorporate into this consideration of the relationship between myths and fictions via interpretation theory. This important development, as Barthes summarizes it, lies in

> a science of the signifier (even if still in the process of development) . . . [which] has taken place in the work of the period and its purpose is less the analysis of the sign than its dislocation. With regard to myth, and even though this is a work which is yet to be carried through, the new semiology—or the new mythology—can no longer, will no longer, be able to separate so easily the signifier from the signified, the ideological from the phraseological . . . demystification has itself become discourse . . . it is no longer the myths which need to be unmasked . . . it is the sign itself which must be shaken; the problem is not to reveal the (latent) meaning of an utterance, of a trait, of a narrative, but to fissure the very representation of meaning, is not to change or purify the symbols but to challenge the symbolic itself.[26]

This problem is implicit in semiotics, structural anthropology after Lévi-Strauss, Lacanian thought, and the psychoanalysis of reading and writing. There seems little doubt that the once revered objectivity and latent meaning of mythological motifs is strikingly less relevant now to human experience than is the attempt to see myth itself as the state of equilibrium or working compromise between man, society, and nature. The strongest challenge to the symbolic is the insistence that meaning occupies, at best, a potential space. The value of myth, as Barthes explains it in *Mythologies*, lies in opening up signification. In a circular yet progressive form, it can do this only by revealing its own systematic logic (of connotation and denotation) which, in turn, depends on the intersubjectivity of objective events as they are endowed with significance by us in the process of discourse and interpretation.

What Barthes has emphasized clearly about this process is that both myth and literature can only work on objects which already have meaning. So the inversion of culture into nature has a metaphorical function. Unlike Lévi-Strauss's view of myth as probing, rational thought, forcing a negation of its own terms in order to progress, Barthes' mythic thought must first celebrate, and then at best unveil the wealth of potential meaning present in the natural and constructed state of things in the world. The crucial part of his definition is that it takes the meaning of a sign and turns it into form, but it does so to make the meaning transparent, to emphasize its hidden or absent yet natural reference, without suppressing a new meaning. Myth does not "act the things" but "acts their names." It is a gesturing with received meaning but, since it involves all gestures, it is an antidote to Lévi-Strauss's pessimism over the death of meaning in modern discontinuous narratives. For Barthes, it is precisely the discontinuity which is mythic: the structural disjunctions determine value.

Such gesturing, Barthes argues in *Mythologies*, makes for myth's duplicity. It is an open concept and therefore potentially highly acquisitive in its cultural operation, but it functions in such a way that the openness of its concept is never lost. In its cultural use, the potential for meaning is necessarily narrowed down by readers, listeners, and viewers. "Men do not have with myth a relationship based on truth but on use: they depoliticize according to their needs."[27] The irony, then, is that a myth's function is as much to *be* appropriated, as it is to appropriate, for it has no fixity. It naturally courts change (including negation) as part of the inevitably unstable relationship between an event and its meaning. "Myth hides nothing and flaunts nothing: it distorts; myth is neither a lie nor a confession: it is an inflexion."[28] Pure mythicity is the state in which a sign or a system of signs is full and open-ended at once.

If, according to Lévi-Strauss, a myth is a problem-solving event, a dialectic between appropriated terms, then for Barthes it is consciously a compromise forced on us by our cultural roles and it always refers to what must be left out. It is not the solution to compromise, as Lévi-Strauss would have it, but the compromise itself. This, again, is determined by the limits of language:

> Entrusted with "glossing over" an intentional concept, myth encounters nothing but betrayal in language, for language can only obliterate the concept if it hides it, or unmask it if it formulates it. The elaboration of a second-order semiological system will enable myth to escape this dilemma: driven to having either to unveil or to liquidate the concept, it will *naturalize* it.
>
> We reach here the very principle of myth: it transforms history into nature.[29]

But it is, nonetheless, a highly problematic nature, for the moment we use language with the aim of transforming a meaning into form, the form will imply *deformation* and self-destruction—even deconstruction, in Derrida's terms—which is of the nature of language as well. "What must always be remembered is a double system; there occurs in it a sort of ubiquity: its point of departure is constituted by the arrival of a meaning . . . the signification of the myth is constituted by a sort of constantly moving turnstile which presents alternately the meaning of the signifier and its form, a language-object and a metalanguage, a purely signifying and a purely imagining consciousness."[30] The intent of mythic thought is never neutral but never completely engaged either. It remains intimidating and always intent on appropriation. In fact, we can say that appropriation is identical with mythical transformation. In revealing how myth corrupts language in his discussion of many motifs of modern culture from "The World of Wrestling" to "The Face of Garbo," Barthes writes of the morality of myth-making as a dialectic between the form and meaning of the sign itself, made available by the writer's intentions in writing, yet never encompassed by those intentions.

> Myth is a *value*, truth is no guarantee for it; nothing prevents it from being a perpetual alibi. . . . The meaning is always there to *present* the form; the form is always

there to *outdistance* the meaning. And there is never any contradiction conflict or split between the meaning and the form: they are never at the same place . . .

. . . We now know that myth is a type of speech defined by its intention (*I am a grammatical example*) much more than by its literal sense (*my name is lion*); and that in spite of this, its intention is somehow frozen, purified, externalized, made absent by this literal sense . . .

. . . Motivation is necessary to the very duplicity of myth: myth plays on the analogy between meaning and form; there is no myth without motivated form . . . it can give a signification to the absurd, make the absurd itself a myth . . .

The nature of the mythical signification can in fact be well conveyed by one particular simile: it is neither more nor less arbitrary than an ideograph. Myth is a pure ideographic system, where the forms are still motivated by the concept which they represent while not yet, by a long way, covering the sum of its possibilities for representation.[31]

It seems clear that there is an attempt to define the concept of mythicity as *motivated form* which underlies Barthes' ideographic systems. Barthes admits that as much as poetry tries to resist mythology and appears to be different from it, it still wants to surrender to myth in the end. And Barthes, no less than Heidegger, Lévi-Strauss, or Derrida, is rephrasing art's ontological yearnings. He is pushed back constantly to the motives informing the semiological systems of his *Mythologies*. So "literature is an undoubted mythical system" because it is the concept of literature, its self-conscious literariness, which gives meaning to writing and provides its mythic dimension. Modern writing, for example, has struggled against earlier theories of the literariness of literature, only to succumb to new myths of itself. Barthes is more aware of the mythic value of modern experiment than Lévi-Strauss, even as he writes of the moral crisis "modifying the writer's consciousness" in the late nineteenth century, when "writing was revealed as signifier, literature as signification."[32] He goes on: "rejecting the false nature of traditional literary language, the writer violently shifted his position in the direction of an anti-nature of language. The subversion of writing was the radical act by which a number of writers have attempted to reject literature as a mythical system."[33] But, as Barthes has also argued, only new mythical systems can emerge.

The mythic takeover is always linguistically possible even if meaning seems "too full of myth to be able to invade it." Even then, Barthes explains, "myth goes around it and carries it away bodily." This occurs, for example, with poetry. One of the important reversals of formalist argument in Barthes' analysis of mythic performance is the implication that poetry not only uses myth, but that myth uses poetry, too, by taking over its generic conditions. It is curious that, like Lévi-Strauss, he still insists on a distinction between myth and poetry on the grounds of intentionality. Myths are powered by the intention to transfer meaning into form, or into sign systems, while they aim to be factual. Poetry works in the reverse, seeing the world as irreducible and turning signs into meaning with the aim of being essential. Poetry, then, supposedly offers language which is incorruptible, essentialized, a sub-stance for myth, analogous perhaps to Lévi-Strauss's untranslatability. Poetic language, furthermore, even tries to resist being taken over by myth.

> Contemporary poetry is a *regressive semiological system*. Whereas myth aims at an ultra-signification, at the amplification of a first system, poetry, on the contrary, attempts to gain an infra-signification, a pre-semiological state of language; in short it tries to transform the sign back into meaning: its ideal, ultimately, would be to reach not the meaning of the words, but the meaning of things themselves. . . . Hence the essentialist ambitions of poetry, the conviction that it alone catches *the thing in itself*, inasmuch, precisely, as it wants to be an anti-language.[34]

Yet a paradox in Barthes remains in this specific issue of the relationship between literature and myth. Literature is mythic in terms of its function as a systematic cultural performance (which creates the "naturalness" of genre), but it is not mythic, he says, in its particular efforts. This is no more satisfactory for explaining the intentionality of a text than Lévi-Strauss's summary. Surely each literary event, insofar as it treats of specific ideas and feelings within a genre, must again approach and occasionally touch mythicity. To repeat my point: every successful poem has to draw from and contribute to the mythicity of literature, a fact we can reach only by discovering in the poem some adequately completed circle of interpretation. If myth is indeed, as Barthes says, a "type of speech defined by its intention . . . much more than its literal sense," then the speech of myth and the speech of poetry are each open to the same intention to achieve permanent form. The urge to name an event through writing, which we have been most familiar with since the Symbolists, would seem to be one way in which literature takes itself seriously and tries to make itself tautologous. It is the process by which poetry tries to make itself fact *qua* poetry, and by which it approaches the condition of myth, even given Barthes' definition of the latter. Not only does the distinction between "factual" and "essential" seem to be as tenuous in Barthes as in Lévi-Strauss, but we could also argue that the traditional closed rhetorical systems of the various genres, and the gradual breakdown of their untranslatability, must even force us to an expanded sense of the factual.

In discussing the relation of myths to fictions we are constantly confronted with the question of the *penetrability* of reality. To keep to Barthes' terms: in the urge to transform meaning into form, we can either poetically treat the real as irreducible or, if we account for it as history and myth, we can treat it as reducible to coded systems. But either way, we touch on the irony of trying to close the semiological gap. Our relation to reality is always unstable and wordy, even excessively so. Then it is wise to turn back to Lévi-Strauss, whose description of mythic thought as both rational and dialectical seems to ease the pessimism inherent in Barthes' paradox, by emphasizing that the mythic is an interpretative process. Meanwhile, Barthes' "turnstile" of myth relieves the pessimism of Lévi-Strauss's "dying myths." For, again, it is through the cybernetic nature of human reason revealed in each that the connection between literature and myth emerges. In fact, both see the world as, in the end, irreducibly other—both have essentialist beginnings—but that does not stop them from trying to make sense of experience systematically, and so inevitably codifying it in order to return it to fact. That is the paradoxical intention of both poetry and myth, as both are metalanguage claiming much for themselves, insofar as they are systematic and self-conscious. But their intent is always made ironic not only by the sheer excess of reality, but by the instability of metalanguage itself which as a concept makes little sense without some kind of interpretation theory, as I have outlined it in the first chapter, to reduce its potential nihilism.

Thus Barthes' distinction between "factual" and "essential" in terms of a difference of intent between mythology and literature seems not only tenuous but somewhat captious at this point if we accept his premises about mythicity. In the business of signifying our experience of reality, we can see the act of signification itself as essential for one moment and transcended the next, given the highly unstable status of any sign in a metaphor. So we move in and out of myth. Even as mythology breeds myths, and poetry breeds poems, we can only turn back to Barthes' intuition into the concept of mythicity, and hence of literature as a mythical system. It is literary discourse which intentionally guides individual fictions to full literariness. For after all, as Barthes himself puts it, the function of language is not to be real or unreal: "language is a form, it cannot possibly be either realistic or unrealistic. All it can do is either be mythical or not, or perhaps . . . counter-mythical."[35]

Toward the Vanishing Point in Modern Writing

I began this study by saying that much of the energy of myth and literature studies has been generated by the opposition between the archetypalist and Structuralist arguments. Their now familiar positions do not appear reconcilable unless we salvage the term "archetype" and redefine it as a transactional model, a sign open to repeated signification rather than a closed and objective fact. The archetype is universal to the extent that it allows interpretation to take place—that is, insofar as it becomes metaphorically extended. The universality of myth is not a quantitative issue. I am assuming all along that it needs redefining in terms which leave myth open to *re-creation*, and not merely to the reuse of plot motifs in a static way, over and over again. There seems a limited future in self-consciously repeating the great classical tales we have inherited and reworked for some centuries now without allowing their progress into the modern.

Yet the more cynical we become (along with Lévi-Strauss) over the mere repetitions (and weakenings) of the old stories when they repeat themselves in modern writing and preach the sad disappearance of myth, the more we find ourselves engrossed in having to explain our grief at its loss. That ontological gloom itself has achieved mythical proportions, and not only in the work of Lévi-Strauss. To counter this, I have been arguing that mythicity is a potential of language performance, and that myths do not simply disappear because they weaken. We are left, indeed, all the more urgently with the need to define our memory of myth and, more important, to reconstitute it in our time. Mythologies may be ancient, but mythicity surely lives on.

But if archetypalism runs the inevitable risk of becoming nostalgic over a lost unity and seeking a superstitious recovery, Structuralism, on the other hand, especially in Lévi-Strauss's hands, tends to be rather clinical about repetition and cynical about myth's continued existence. So it "realistically" accentuates our failure to recover the "once possible" synthesis of man and nature. Neither Jung's fundamentalism nor Lévi-Strauss's skepticism is an entirely useful attitude. Perhaps Barthes—in Lévi-Strauss's footsteps, but without the ethnologist's religious link to Jung—appears closer to the catholic truth. He attempts to define a universality for myth in terms of its form rather than its content. All signification, he would have it, is potentially mythic. But then this can take the shape of the inflated and rather academic argument that the Citroen can be elevated to the same significance as the Chariot of the Gods, and that Professional Wrestling has the same impact on our imagination as Morality Plays once did. So semiology itself, perhaps the most promising of all attempts to recover a definition of mythicity for our time, would seem to have a problem of expository tact.

Yet I must continue to make some theoretical points about the meaning of myth for literary studies which show a Structuralist bias, for there is no myth without language and system, signifying gestures, and the persistent gap between event and meaning. Semiotics attempts to make sense of myth and mythicity as a function of language as it responds to and attempts to systematize the proleptic nature of interpretation. If myths and archetypes are not primarily language events, they cannot be interpreted with any hope of recovering truth, and if they cannot be interpreted in this way, their universality is meaningless. So literature-and-myth study implies yet again the hermeneutic circle. But having insisted on that, it is equally important to insist that the circle is neither vicious nor imaginary, which is why I have argued for some structural continuity between myth and literature which allows for mythical intentions in fictional form. It is inevitable, simply, that we accept to some degree the imperialism of what Lacan has called the symbolic order of language, but also, the transparency of that order *as* language, as transparent as the unconscious which needs it to bring desire into being.

My discussion of myth as narrative, then, has been for the moment theoretical, and for a good reason. We must not begin with mythological motifs but with interpretation theory, more precisely with the problem of understanding mythicity. Then the fate of myth is, of course, tied closely to the psychological fate of reading, listening, and seeing, and to the accompanying task of making sense of what we are doing. We can too easily forget that central dialectic between the inside and outside of consciousness which defines mythicity and, under a more formalistic emphasis, we can lapse into the theory that myth is above all available to us objectively as "deep structure." That deep structure is never a simple transformational formula, but the metaphorical play of the absent element as the "duplicated Other." The structural facts about myth as a type of speech are first noticeable for their challenge to the *interiority* of readers. There is a dialectic between the transparent but significant order of language, and the transparent but significant order of the reader's unconscious becoming conscious in reading. The fact that myths are (or are so close to being) universal makes sense only in that they are able to reconcile this opposition with some authority. They are appropriative because they demand open interpretation even as they propose closure, and make that evident by explaining the logical necessity of their own terms in the development of a plot. Mythicity exists, therefore, not only because there are readers, listeners, and viewers with their own appropriative ambitions, but because human experience can only be defined in language. We can go from this to Lévi-Strauss's terms for the universality of a story as dependent on its "shared motivation." At the same time, this is only possible because its expression in a plot is an "open concept," as Barthes points out. So the mythicity of language allows the creation of some marvelously suggestive potential spaces we can occupy in the world, the successful interrelationships of our inside and the world's outside; a careful unveiling of possible meaning in story-telling is itself natural and part of the history of discourse.

But even if interpretation is essential to get us to this point, we need some theory of signification to take us a step further, which is why I have turned to Lévi-Strauss and Barthes for clues to a further link between myth and literature. Their semiotic premises do not forget interpretation theory even if they do not always develop the optimism inherent in such an approach. The nature of narrative, and our entry into it, is the meeting point between myth and literature, whether we see it as metalanguage acting out social compromise and teleological need (Lévi-Strauss), or as ideological appropriation (Barthes). I have wanted to show that Lévi-Strauss writes with impressive scope about the rational nature of mythic discourse, and with a quite traditional respect for "epiphanies," in spite of his pessimism over modern art. He is semiologist enough to demystify archetypes, but not to deny the unconscious. On the other hand, his analyses of the function of reason in mythic narrative provide an approach to the phenomenology of writing which literary studies might usefully bear in mind. While Jung seems to stop short of a full emphasis on the hermeneutic intentions of myth, feeling that archetypes are not rationally assimilable, Lévi-Strauss emphasizes the reasonableness of myths through their plot structures, and through the way they logically go about the business of becoming problem-solving thought. The ongoing impact of myths for him is that they are narrative projections *onto* experience—"myth for"—without which we have no understanding of what happens to us.

Barthes also emphasizes an intentional factor defining myth: myth is the incarnation of ideological intent. He is aware of the powers of a myth to subsume a reader's needs, largely because this must be based on an open concept as a give-and-take between event and meaning. That is, he is aware, above all else, of the mythicity of language as its own imperial system. He therefore operates more fluidly between cultural meaning and the textual unit. If Lévi-Strauss is perhaps too rigid by defining mythology and poetry as separate ideas, Barthes, even though he wants the distinction maintained, seems to believe that anything can be a myth. In other words, mythicity amounts to appropriation itself. While Lévi-Strauss nostalgically declares that dialectical realism can be and often is lost in the negative forms of myth which are found in modern fictions and art, Barthes, with a little more optimism, follows another insight of Lévi-Strauss and treats the weakening as inevitably derived from myth's motivated form, which even includes a systematic self-negation.

I would question whether, in the best modern writing, there is any weakening at all, and that is the point of my discussion of Joyce, Eliot, and Lawrence later. But for good traditional reasons, both Barthes and Lévi-Strauss are wary of bringing literature and mythology too close together, and both turn more to myth than art as a lively form. My point has been that their views are not entirely consistent either with the definition of myth as a superior act of interpretation, or with their semiotic principles. For if myth is indeed appropriative, then there is no reason to believe that as metalanguage, it cannot allow its dialectical reasoning to continue in or exist separately as literature—let alone criticism—which also has its own problem-solving and naturalizing intentions in discourse. Whether we see myths and fictions as opposite ends of a continuum, as Lévi-Strauss does, or second-order semiological systems straining in different directions, as Barthes suggests, we can postulate a relationship between the two based on their mutual need to make their own logic of necessity available to us as narrative. We can say that literature frequently intends to acquire the status of myth (a) by exploiting language itself, (b) by becoming a cultural document—dependent still, of course, upon language, and (c) by offering a genuine attempt to think through a social compromise as an interpretative process.

In this sense, in spite of the inconsistencies of their argument, the insights of both Lévi-Strauss and Barthes seem to me to be central to any connection we might offer between myths and fictions, because they develop the structural contingencies of language performance: in short, they draw our attention—however single-mindedly—to myth and fiction as metalanguage. Once we have decided on the mythicity of language, we must rely upon the ironic claims made by a text (or a mythic event, as in Barthes' *Mythologies*) to being limited in this significant way. The text is always a second-order system and the reader a third-order system. The ironic possibilities are endless for, again, language establishes itself as neither realistic nor unrealistic, but as a form of the real or unreal. Even if it follows that a sense of equivalence between myth and literature can be based on the fact that both as metalanguage must see the world as constantly open to signification, still we must add that they both evoke the dramatic irony of the excessive absence of meaning which demands the form narratives take.

For that dramatization we can emphasize—via Lévi-Strauss's description of essential, problem-solving thought as dialectical—that the pessimism which might develop from Barthes' hermeneutics of excessive reality need not appear inevitable. What we are dealing with in both myth and literature, and their attempts to make sense of reality, are the ironies created by readers resisting yet having to enter the semiotic function of language. It is the combined event of reader-in-text, or text-in-reader which defines mythicity, and not the text alone. Language at its most suggestive, and, we can say, at its most lively, is endlessly transforming itself and its readers. The transformations are not simply from a slowly unfolding essence within the consciousness, as Jung would suggest, though the unconscious, without being institutionalized into collective captivity, may be a convenient repository of what we do not know but gradually learn about ourselves. Rather the transformations result because we intend to go on giving meaning to the available forms of our experience. This intent, well represented even by the subjectivism of Holland's introjected fantasy, helps close the gap between myths and fictions; for the aim of literature, as well as of myth, is to go on in some way forever giving meaning further meaning. It can only do this by allowing the reader room to play. As with mythology, poetry cannot go on forever unless it encourages more poetry, unless it finally does not essentialize anything more than poetry itself, and helps to create poetry in the reader. That depends, of course, on the existence of readers who are aware of the interpretative paradox we have been discussing.

All this has a very special signficance for readers of modern literature, not merely as an applied theory of reading, but as the theory which much modern writing has evolved about its own status. A desire to establish a mythical system for literature seems to lie at the heart of the modernist aesthetic which Eliot, Lawrence, and Joyce—to name only three familiar figures—made the very subject of poetry and fiction. James Joyce's intricate handling of evolutionary, cyclical history and fluctuating, punning time becomes, for example, a way of seeing revealed as ironically limiting and modifying what is seen, fixated with the world as a sign system. *Ulysses* and *Finnegans Wake* are both narratives of plot implosion: the layers of simultaneous meaning they offer take the fact-finding out of the art of reading, however much we strain for the precise reference Joyce seems to be making. The simultaneity and coincidence of meaning is, in effect, the open-endedness of mythic thought, available in a development from the epiphanies of *Portrait*. The novels belittle linear and cyclical time. The sense of plot and character which we want them to impose, which provides the illusion of freedom we have traditionally needed in the novel by quantifying time and space, breaks down under the effect of Joyce's use of epiphanic puns and plot repetitions with subtle disjunctions of time and place.

Eliot's *Four Quartets*, one can briefly add, are nothing if not a grand hermeneutic for poetry, a display of the poet's concern not simply with watching himself write, but with summing up the fate of poetry as the fate of language and reading. The *Quartets* do not merely use the myth, but seem to operate as myth themselves, at least at the semiological level Lévi-Strauss emphasizes, with the specific intention of recovering some sense of the numinous in the guise of "the still point of the turning world." The function of the poem's narrative is to carry a message in patterns which are repetitive, dialectical, even cybernetic, for the patterns are constantly evolved as functions of the reader's consciousness of the poem and of the limits imposed on poetry by language.

That is, as we shall see in later chapters, both Eliot and Joyce offer homologies for mythic thought: constantly self-transforming sets of signs which reveal the urge to discover reasonable and progressive form. What is narrated are not simply events in a plot but signposts to the process of thought which will not give up, which constantly seeks the third term to every set of contradictions. In Lawrence, too, inherited mythology (primarily theosophist) contains no more than the coordinates for thinking, is neither implicitly believed in nor really a sacred mystery, but is dependent on setting up the probing of human reason within an inheritance of dualistic thought. In his case, this is concerned above all with establishing the mythicity of the novel as "the one bright book of life": a document which is reasonable, open-ended, and erotically the site of his play. He too seeks the return of words and, by implication, the unconscious to the central existential fact, the body, in order to restore not so much specific sexual myths (Christian and pagan) but the breakdown of the body-mind dualism.

In short, the discontinuities, the esoteric references, the play of nihilation, and the radical disjunctions of time and place in modern writing would seem to want to force the reader to reconcile the extremes of full and empty living. Such a profession of dialectical strain tries to make us proficient at myth-making ourselves as a way out of the strong possibility of apocalypse and the transitoriness of the numinous. This process, finally, is a rational one in much the same way that Lévi-Strauss describes mythic thought as rational: "so much addicted to duplication, triplication or quadruplication after the same sequence . . . repetition has as its function to make the structure of myth apparent . . . (for the purpose of myth is to provide a logical model capable of overcoming a contradiction)."[36]

Art, one wants to say, no less than mythology, is a search for greater accuracy in what can be said. There is nothing more misleading than the study of aesthetics in a vacuum, isolated from other attempts to account for human knowledge. For what Piaget has called the modern necessity for an "interdisciplinary epistemology" is surely in part the attraction of modern literature. The aim of literary writing has often been described as to restore the numinous to language, to recover the ecstatic, hortatory, or vital origins. This is not a process of mystification, but of psychological deconstruction and reconstruction which is the aim of mythic thought. The search is for the surface of contact between the concrete and the abstract, the inside and the outside, the present and the absent, and all those very existential opposites in all their coded analogies. Modern poetry, after all—not to mention its predominantly New Critical readers—has long been fascinated by what Eliot saw as the struggle between the man who suffers personally and the man who creates objectively, trapped in a world of psychological needs which assume both ontological proportions and vast social significance. Eliot's distinction is usefully preserved by a desire for the anonymity of the poet in the poem, the universality of the experience. That very paradoxical relation between feeling and creation— for it is little more than paradox in Eliot's writing until *Four Quartets*—reminds us of Barthes' "transparency" of myth, or Lévi-Strauss's statement that myth depends on the disappearance of an author. If the universal reasonableness of myths can be justified by the fact that no author *need* be found, then in a sense the very intelligibility of a poem depends on the disappearance of the poet and the reader. In much modern writing, the radical manipulation of signs in constant movement between form and meaning must lead to the vanishing point of an author's *cogito*. One must go over to Lacan's paranoia of language in order to create at all.

We know that such disappearances in reading and writing are never final, and that is something which Structuralism does not let us forget. Consciousness of a directed, coherent understanding comes and goes in time. We search to recover the text when anonymity threatens. Writing and reading are

dialectical, for identity can never be simple. And the epistemological problem would seem to be, as Paul de Man has
expressed it so succinctly, that "knowledge of the impossibility
of knowing precedes the act of consciousness that tries to
reach it."[37] That existentialist paradox is familiar to the modern reader. The act of interpretation in poetic language can
be seen to contain in itself the inevitability of dissolution
which, Lévi-Strauss says, is just as true of all mythic narrative.
Criticism, goes on de Man, "thus becomes a form of demys-
tification on the ontological level that confirms the existence
of a fundamental distance at the heart of all human experience."[38] Myth for us must be above all the imaginative leap
over that gap, even while the phenomenology of desire is
preserved. The mythic possibilities of much modern writing
lie always in a tension between consciousness constantly reflecting on itself, and no less intending to reach "the center
of things," and the fact that at the "center" of consciousness
lies a void of desire according to which the discovery of essential meaning can only be a repetitive act. Myth, like poetry,
is produced out of not-knowing, determining the necessity
only out of a repetition of experimental probes by which
events become "known." Consequently myth is not so much
weakened as dissipated in the modern. As I want to show in
the next chapter, *it is abstracted to a sophistication that only
literature can handle.* The large implication is that myth itself—as mythological narrative—is not any less significant
now in modern writing than it ever was. Such are the structural
pressures on myths to preserve their mythic status in the modern that it is perhaps largely in the fragmentations of modernist experiment that the increasing abstractions of myth can
survive.

So in both art and myth we are dealing not simply with sign
systems but with sign systems in the process of transformation
through the intent to interpret: a "science of the concrete"
expressing itself even through increasing abstraction and anonymity. What gives any narrative life, be it mythic or literary,
is its ability to maintain that interpretative paradox, to dram-

atize the relationship between any number of problematic and pressing opposites of meaning, involving self and society, nature and culture, words and things, and so on, in a way that makes their contingency, their mere *bricolage*, seem necessary and dependent upon interpretation. Then the presence of an author is incidental, for writing has seemed to demand its own increasingly abstract and, I believe, its own increasingly mythic necessities.

CHAPTER 3

MYTHIC INVERSION AND
ABSTRACTION: JAMES JOYCE

God becomes man becomes fish becomes barnacle goose
becomes featherbed mountain.
—Joyce, *Ulysses*[1]

. . . mythic thought transcends itself and, going beyond
images retaining some relationship with concrete experience, operates in a world of concepts which have
been released from any such obligation, and combine
with each other in free association.
—Lévi-Strauss, *From Honey to Ashes*[2]

THE NOVEL AS MYTHOLOGY

In the last two chapters, we have seen that there is a progression from the ontological conditions of myth as language
to more functional terms for its existence. Mythicity may be
revealed in the play of language, but it is also a systematic
attempt to grasp the world as fact and metaphor, as a synchronic and diachronic whole. We can see the relevance to a
theory of myth of Saussure, Gadamer, and Lacan, on the one
hand, and Lévi-Strauss and Barthes on the other. The theory
of myth and mythicity embodies a necessary link between
interpretation theory and Structuralism. But a practical question remains. If myth suspends the "I" of discourse in its play,
and offers instead a series of coded bundles of transformations
in which language perpetuates itself as form, then what, again,
is the relevance of myth to literature, that most personal of
intentions in discourse?

The answer we have already touched on involves the linguistic origin of the gap to which all myth and literature refers—a relatively positivistic discovery—and the emphasis on the mythicity not only of language itself, but of linguistic form, of literature and its types. As we adjust our perspective from the text to texts in general, attempting to identify literary history, then we can speak of the mythicity of *genre*. The field remains complex in this category, but let us examine the novel alone in this chapter—and specifically the work of James Joyce, for the novel, as much as any other genre, has often been associated with mythological longings.

It matters little how we sum that up: perhaps in Georg Lukacs's phrase that the novel is the "representative art-form of our age," or in D. H. Lawrence's statement that it is "the one bright book of life." Both Marxists and less ideological readers have assumed that the novel's literariness is a function of the middle class in all its universally ironic duplicity. Whether that means that the novel reveals a sociologically absurd ontology or the desirable and necessary compromises of social democracy, it really makes no difference to the mythic nature of the novel and genre. The novel always implies some set of assumptions about the nature of the divided self in society and about the problems of its discourse. The concept of the novel, that is, is positively mythic in scope even before classical, religious, or totemistic mythologies lend its plots their meaning. In fact, it would seem that mythologies could not enter the novel, and be something more than merely functionalist motifs, unless the novel as a genetic system had a history and a set of appropriative needs of its own, allowing a repetitive attempt to get beyond history and, like a true "science of the concrete," accommodate everything to itself.

So to say that myth is an *intentional structure* in a novel is not to say that novelists are free simply to borrow, or rewrite, or juxtapose great stories (because they are worth retelling), but that the novelist finds himself forced into the transformational modes of mythic thought and into the appropriativeness of language and genre whenever he tries to make sense of his human material. We can speak of these generic transformations as "logical," not in any sense that the novelist merely celebrates or produces an argument that could be outlined as well in expository prose but, I want to show, because there is an essential logic to the plotting of good novels which lies not in mimetic faithfulness, but in the ordering of mythic form. Modern novels, individually, are not myths. Perhaps in some future time they will be, but there is no argument that we can allow even so consciously mythopoeic a work as Joyce's *Ulysses* that status yet. But beyond all the conditions of language itself, a novel can be said to have a mythic (and not simply a mythological) intent (a) because it is written within the myth of the novel's own mythology or genetic system, and (b) because whatever mythological motifs the novelist may use are just as effectively taken over by the novel, to the extent that (c) the intrasystemic functions of the plot can be said to keep alive mythic narrative in the modern.

Myth reveals logic making itself apparent, venturing to prove its own existence out of concrete beginnings, a logic which manifests itself in what literary convention calls plot. But, we must not assume that that logic need be syllogistic. In the first two chapters, I have argued that it is the logic of deconstruction, a transformation around an absent center because language cannot contain its own origin. The modern novel often relies more on a firm *cogito* than on exploiting the infirmities of consciousness. Indeed, one of the more traditionally enigmatic functions of story-telling is that inversions of the real can be intensely serious accounts of human experience. By definition, all fiction, however much it looks like reality, is a refusal to accept that the real world is ever quite enough. We need it in more vicarious, even abstracted forms, for it to be fully alive. With both the naturalistic and symbolic novel, we have no difficulty establishing direct lines of reference (to anthropological, religious, or psychological theory). But with the more surreal efforts (of a Joyce, a Barthelme, or a Rulfo) we have traditionally been less sure of its overall value. Understanding surreal performance by translating it into more realistic terms is one thing, and it has been accomplished by literary scholarship with great imagination in the last few years. But evaluating the surreal, declaring its worth as something more than a Freudian source book or an entertainment, has been very much harder.

We have had less trouble accepting such formulations in mythology than we have in the novel, so perhaps that is where we should start. Here, then, is Lévi-Strauss on the subject in "Four Winnebago Myths":

> There must be, and there is, a correspondence between the unconscious meaning of a myth—the problem it tries to solve—and the conscious content it makes use of to reach the end, i.e., the plot. However, this correspondence is not necessarily an exact reproduction; it can also appear as a logical transformation. If the problem is presented in straight terms—that is, in the way the social life of the group expresses and tries to solve it—the overt content of the myth, the plot, can borrow its elements from social life itself. But should the problem be formulated upside down, and its solution sought for *ad absurdo*, then the overt content can be expected to become modified accordingly to form an inverted image of the social pattern actually present in the consciousness of the natives.[3]

Now we can easily recognize the *ad absurdo* mythologizing about modern society in twentieth-century fiction which transforms reasonable expectations into negative forms (dystopia, black humor, etc.) in order to free us from mere ideology and mere wishing for utopia. The forms of modern fiction, it is well known, resist endings, are suspicious of transcendence, and replace chronological development with a world in flux, often barely proximate in space and time. We can see this "upside down" formulation, this lack of mimetic faithfulness, quite clearly in Joyce's fiction. The plot in *Ulysses*, for example, does not simply develop; it thickens in detail as it proceeds, as if deliberately to avoid a conclusion. It indulges in a kind of arbitrary richness of event. And it is not simply a matter of the plot picking up speed or gathering force in a single direction. So complex are the inversions of the original odyssey myth that we are confronted by absurd correspondences which confound the evolutionary nature of the quest with a systematically ironic treatment of many of its paradigms.

In other words, we undoubtedly have *The Odyssey* in mind as a working analogy for *Ulysses*, which is what Joyce intended, and Stuart Gilbert, T. S. Eliot, and everyone else confirms. We are not disappointed to find that Joyce's novel reflects, residually at least, the "archetypal order" of the geography of Ulysses' quest. Bloom wanders from home, a failed lover and a frustrated father, seeking adventures which will return him refreshed to his starting point. But the repetitiveness and circularity of that attempt are strikingly ironic, for the mythological motif of the quest appears anything but consistent in the details of its reappearance. Knowing the myth, we quickly admit, is only the beginning of the process of reading *Ulysses*. Herioc Ulysses in heat on Circe's island, for example, becomes mock-heroic Bloom, stumbling through the perverse wetdream-world of Bella Cohen's whorehouse. The point emerges that Joyce's novel both is and is not Homer's *Odyssey*, or any other related quest paradigm. The function of the myth is itself necessarily problematic—it is both in and out of the text at once—mainly because what we expect from its order and structuring is clearly unfinished in *The Odyssey*, and temporarily in the process of being completed in Joyce's novel. The function of the mythicity of narrative is preserved, I want to show, by the transformation of particular myths into fictions, absurdly yet vitally.

The mythic imagination reveals itself as something more than the amazing ingenuity unearthed in Joyce's prose by critics who see the business of reading as that of fitting together motifs and archetypes into a solution to a giant puzzle. That has been the bent of most Joyce scholarship since Gilbert. The puzzle, though, is always ironic in the way it incorporates events, not to mention reader and text. We know *The Od-yssey*, we say at the outset, but we do not know *Ulysses*, and irony abounds as we discover through the latter that we did not really know the former either. Heroic Ulysses does not merely happen to become the highly complex and mock-heroic Bloom for comic-epic effect alone. Instead, the myth, on one level, seems to appropriate the novel for structural aggrandizement. It is as though Ulysses must change into Bloom in order to save the meaning of the myth in this antiheroic age. Bloom, on the other hand, must look like Ulysses the hero to preserve his identity, as someone other than the thoroughly mundane figure he could so easily be. Although Bloom's Dublin odyssey is the center of attention, the Greek odyssey and all other questing remain alive. That is, Homer's tale and the quest myth are transformational; in a sense, the myth "writes" Joyce as well as the reverse. Not only does *The Odyssey* reveal the overlap of myth and fiction, it transforms each in its reappearance in Joyce's novel. *The Odyssey* is not simply a paradigm for *Ulysses*; it is, insofar as Joyce intends to preserve its importance, myth regenerating itself by *ad absurdo* inversions in order to keep the probing of the mythopoeic mind alive.

The problem, then, is not simply to note the coincidences between Greek myth and Irish novel, but to find the common intentional structure, which would seem to be an increasingly abstract and peripatetic process of making sense of the real. The myth is plainly unstable in its details, and not the single set of events of self-evident value that it is often thought to be. But the instability of the Greek tale leads to the fact that the "original" myth, in repetition in Joyce's novel, can exist in a more abstruse and even comically negative form and still live. Whatever we think about the enticement of a particular myth as a complete, essential story, important for our understanding of the deep structure of literature, we have to allow that it goes about the business of preserving itself in the minds of men in a most ironic and self-negating way, and is not to be entirely trusted. It is largely mythicity which prevails—not a particular story—and then only in structural intent. The literary critic, too, cannot trust the conventions of "modes" of literature (comic, epic, tragic, and so on), but must refer to a logic of specific forms: that is, to the way in which comic and other elements relate between comparative versions. In the case of *Ulysses*, for example, the function of Bloom is homologous to that of *The Odyssey*'s hero. A relationship, however increasingly abstract, is discernible, and we reach a sophisticated level of myth-making which Lévi-Strauss has described in *From Honey to Ashes*:

> If this tendency towards abstraction can be attributed to mythic thought itself, instead of being, as some readers may argue, wholly imputable to the theorizing of the mythologist, it will be agreed that we have reached a point where mythic thought transcends itself and, going beyond images retaining some relationships with concrete experience, operates in a world of concepts which have been released from any such obligation, and combine with each other in free association: by this I mean that they combine not with reference to any external reality but according to the affinities and incompatibilities existing between them in the architecture of the mind.[4]

As readers, of course, we know that even if the "tendency to abstraction" is "imputable to the theorizing of the mythologist," but can still be located in the text, then the point is made. The reader (I hope I have established) is after all myth-making in his reading as much as the writer in his writing. He can assert, by entering the play of the text, that he wants to bring the text to a close too, that coincidence occurs not merely between text and sources but also between text and reader. My approach to Joyce in these few pages is to outline only baldly this superstructure of mythic intent, which is discoverable in Joyce less in a craving for archetype than in the need to abstract events, seemingly in free association, but really in a manner that suggests that, no less than Homer, he was intent on preserving a sense of the mythic. It is this

142

condition of mythicity which we engage in fiction—its logic
of form—and the fact that the modern novel chooses to move
away from a naturalistic empiricism and a mimetic responsibility to concentrate on that logic is not a sign of aridity in
the modern imagination. Rather, it is the inevitable and necessary step for myth in an analytic age.

For Joyce, the abstraction, the consciously mindful configuration of events, is not merely surreal. The forms of his fiction
may require careful analysis, but he has already engaged us
with the metonymy of events, the apparently discrete moments
suddenly unified, the drama of compromise (sexual, social,
and intellectual) which engross Stephen, Bloom, and Finnegan, and which force the writer, the characters, and the reader
into abstraction only *after* the event. In Joyce's world, as in
the world of myth, reality is a set of facts which have a life
of their own, insofar as a sign is inevitably a pun, a self-
transformation which strains to be tautologous even while it
insists on more than one meaning for itself. Abstraction, then,
results from the intent to proliferate fact. It accompanies myth
naturally as a means to transformation, and links the world
of the novel to the world of myth through the language of
metonymy shifting in and out of metaphor.

EPIPHANY, STASIS, AND THE PROOF BY ALGEBRA

In *Dubliners, Stephen Hero,* and *Portrait of the Artist,* the
major effort of Joyce's art-activity is to reach "epiphany." In
the first two books, the epiphany is described as the sudden
emergence of some moment of truth. In the well-known words
of *Stephen Hero,* it is "a sudden spiritual manifestation,
whether in the vulgarity of speech or of gesture or in a memorable phrase of the mind itself":[5]

> This is the moment which I call epiphany. First we rec-
> ognise that the object is *one* integral thing, then we rec-
> ognise that it is an organised composite structure, a *thing*
> in fact: finally, when the relation of parts is exquisite,

when the parts are adjusted to the special point, we rec-
ognise that it is that thing which it is. Its soul, its whatness,
leaps to us from the vestment of its appearance. The soul
of the commonest object, the structure of which is so
adjusted, seems to us radiant. The object achieves its
epiphany.[6]

In *Portrait* and the *Paris* and *Pola Notebooks*,[7] the explanation that an epiphany is achieved in the apprehension of a
unique relation is examined further in the famous outline of
the theory of *stasis* and *kinesis* in art. Here is found Joyce's
understanding of the structure of perception itself, in which
the "beautiful" creates a sensory "stasis," and "truth," "a
stasis of the mind." Didactic art does not allow art to be an
end in itself, and therefore is kinetic. But the key word in
Joyce's aesthetic theory is stasis, "called forth, prolonged and
at least dissolved by what I call the rhythm of beauty."[8] Such
a "rhythm" refers to the tautologous and self-regulating language of an aesthetic event. The state of equilibrium is further
related to an ideal homeostasis in man: a fusion of purpose
between language, thought, and body. Stephen's bastardized
Aquinas—"Pulchra sunt quae visa placent" ("These things
are beautiful the apprehension of which pleases")—sums up
the tension which Joyce defines as essential to the naming of
the beautiful. The tension incorporates both viewer and object, arresting the movement of perception, creating a moment
of acute awareness, and thereby achieving *katharsis*. The act
of apprehension, then, is clearly homologous to the act of
creation.

It is probably safe to say that most critics of Joyce would
assert that the epiphany is either a part of a Scholastic theory
of knowledge, or symbolic of a breakthrough of an unconscious state of mind. But the epiphany as a psychological state
is only part of what is meant by epiphany in art. It is also
part of the function of literature as metalanguage. In literature,
the "revelation" is symbolically institutionalized in the text
and cannot necessarily be relied upon to provide an apodictic

experience for the reader. We are aware, in reading literary epiphanies, of writing *about* a way of seeing, as well as *from* a momentary revelation and, as readers, of having to recreate the moment of heightened perception.

S. L. Goldberg's definition of the epiphany has so far come closest to what I want to say without being entirely accurate. "It is a constructive act, a creative *making*. It is also the expression of a personal attitude on the part of the maker. It is also insofar as the thing made has signification, the expression of an intuition, *an act of understanding* or apprehension. Or we may place the emphasis differently and think of the structure of the work itself as objectifying and thus *revealing* a structure, a meaning, in *reality*. These are not separate elements of functions, but simply different aspects of the one complex activity."[9] To carry this argument a little further, I would add that the epiphany is of central importance in the modern novel because it is a *problem-solving* act (at once a making and an understanding), not only revealing a moment profoundly lived in, but resolving the terms of thought itself in the persistent search for understanding. It reaches no conclusions and does not symbolize anything at all—not even as the "constitutive symbol" Goldberg suggests elsewhere that it might be—for the thrust of its presence is to create a potential space to move in. It contains the tensions in the moment of knowing itself, so that we learn more about thinking, perception, and the limits of consciousness than we do about a specific conclusion to be reached.

In that celebrated scene in *Portrait*, for example, where Stephen gazes upon the girl in the strand, caught in an almost static, photographic pose, we are presented with a key moment in his life not because he has realized the meaning of anything—his outburst of "profane joy" is involuntary and phatic and related to seeing clearly rather than to understanding—nor even because we know he is caught in a rare moment of achieving a union between sexual fantasy and the tangible presence of an object fulfilling that fantasy. However great the rapture, the imaginative release for Stephen, we are shown quite clearly how he is sharply aware of the limits of transcendence and of the questionable absolutes of knowledge. Confronted with the possibility of saying everything, of indulging the moment, Joyce gives us only a spare, even impressionistic description of the presence of the girl, holding back on the expansion of Stephen's consciousness while the implication is that expansion is precisely what must be taking place as he discovers the other. Assuming the possibility of saying how the world can interpenetrate in limitless ways—which is the position both Joyce and Stephen are slowly moving to in the later fiction—Joyce describes selectively, in a Symbolist manner, how the girl, the clouds, Stephen and, by implication, the reader and the author, all have a metonymic rather than a metaphorical relationship. That is, Joyce does not want to tell us what to believe, rather he reveals the structure of apprehension; he states our proximity to each other and nature as a means to pointing out context and similarity, to defining the site of play, but not equivalence.

The point is this: all the events in the epiphany are simultaneous and open-endedly significant, left so open-ended, in fact, that the meaning becomes deliberately impoverished and provoking, and not merely understated. The Joycean epiphany comes into being through a problem-solving consciousness, homologous to the logic of mythic thought, constantly trying out its terms and holding them in a tension, "resolving" them only momentarily, for the terms change. Epiphanies always bring an alteration of consciousness which can, ironically, only offer its own disintegration, as the image of the girl on the strand fades before Stephen. An epiphany inevitably breeds other epiphanies as part of the frame of reference.

In order to get to the inevitable circularity of such constructions, there is always a dialectical prelude and build-up to the epiphanic moment in Joyce. In this case, the section containing the epiphany at first finds Stephen restless, impatient to capitalize on his mortality after refusing the priesthood, and ready to accept his inevitable fall. He finds the first rhythms of freedom in what Joyce calls "fitful music," an "elfin prelude"

summoning him to "escape by an unseen path," to obey "a
wayward instinct." But as he becomes caught up in this lyric
play for freedom, he is set back (humorously) by the "uncouth
faces" of the Christian Brothers who pass him on the bridge.
Stephen is guiltily reminded of his fallen Christianity and so
turns to an old defensive standby, his "treasure" of poetry,
and tries out a purple passage to exorcise his guilt—"a day
of dappled seaborne clouds." But this is not enough. It is itself
an epiphany of sorts that he realizes that he cannot really
trust, as Joyce says, "the contemplation of an inner world of
individual emotions mirrored perfectly in a lucid, supple, pe-
riodic prose." Joyce ironically leaves us peering through a
crack in the armor of Stephen's solipsism, the aesthete's celebration of himself and nature as merely self and other. Even
when the "cold infra-human odour of the sea" calls up a
heroic vision of a possible fatherland in Europe, it is the murky
view of Dublin and the name-calling of the boys swimming
which negate those terms and force him to turn away, to
question his distinctiveness. He tries to soar upon the meaning
of his own name, learned ironically from the swimmers, and
through a careful elevation of style we enter Stephen's now
deliberately inflated consciousness. "As never before," says
Joyce, "his strange name seemed to him a prophecy," even if
it is a prophecy which becomes deflated for us by the banter
of his friends at play. For all the mock-heroism of Stephen's
"instant of wild flight," though, we do take him seriously
because we are watching the rhythms of his very real thought,
his attempt to come to terms with the contradictions of his
experience, the inevitable failure of establishing an unrelated
cogito. His are truly the workings of a mythopoeic mind,
however adolescent, as he tries to construct the new, more
mature relational "idiom" of himself. The young Stephen is,
in this sense, learning to be a mythmaker.

Stephen the Daedalus with "a lust of wandering in his feet
that burned to set out for the ends of the earth," wades up
a rivulet in the strand, "happy and near to the wild heart of
life." That deliberate overstatement might make us wary of

his progress. The embroidering of emotion, the preciosity, could be a prelude to further deflation, yet Stephen suddenly confronts the girl on the strand, who is magically transformed. He is momentarily taken out of his indulgent stream of consciousness: the other and his relationship to it are clearly established. All his efforts have succeeded in his reaching what he calls later a stasis, a suspended moment, paradoxically the condition of anonymity, and he can only let out a cry of relief at the confrontation with the girl. The rhythms of Joyce's prose at this moment lyrically outline the sensual contours of the girl's body and the quiet flow of the stream, until Stephen's cry of "profane joy" turns again to more overstatement and a pre-Raphaelitish swoon with nature, just to remind us of the adolescent limitations of his ecstasy and the pressing solipsism of his claims for selfhood. The spring of his consciousness is uncoiled for the first time, but his outburst reminds us that it will have to be rewound over and over again.

The point about any of the epiphanies in Joyce is that they are moments of awakening (in T. S. Eliot's words, an "intense moment isolated") yet they offer no final redemption. They are quite spasmodic moments of realization, resolving only momentarily the terms immediately preceding them and forming a version of understanding in the novel which, again in Eliot's well-known words from *Four Quartets*, shows us that "history is a pattern of timeless moments." This rhythm of language, seeking at best momentary resolutions which are understood to be open to further development, is precisely what Lévi-Strauss says myth as narrative depends on. Epiphanies above all help to establish a rhythm to Joyce's prose which is really a constant duplication and expansion of Stephen's consciousness: establishing thinking as a process rather than specific thought in the way that I have described it in the first chapter. For example, it is no surprise to find Stephen, shortly after the incident on the strand, obsessed with the notion of beauty as an aesthetic ideal which can be defined, as he tells Lynch, at its best in its *dramatic* nature. The dramatic is the highest form of art for Stephen—as well as for

Joyce—because it recreates tensions via constant repetition, and encourages a refining of the play between perception and imagination ("life purified in and reprojected") to a composite "image of beauty."

Joyce's faith in the dramatic based on epiphanic awareness underlies the fact that his art is achieved in irony and constant interplay, and deeply involved in the world as an endless system of signifiers. Stephen, in his impatience, becomes an appropriate consciousness through which to evoke a sense of the real itself as open to mythic interpretation (i.e., the real as endlessly signifying and transforming), for we are very much aware of the irony of his early haste to indulge in naming the world. But by the end of *Portrait*, and throughout *Ulysses*, Stephen comes to learn as the young artist that whatever is meant by "meaning," "truth," and "beauty" makes sense only with the acceptance of language as necessarily arbitrary in its naming, and so able to leave the world open to significance. Hence the literariness of his references, for art is the most self-conscious and arbitrary of all sign systems. Epiphanies, then, are those moments in the text when, through Stephen's groping for terms, we learn that what can be grasped is not simply a succession of new names and meanings, but, as Roland Barthes has put it in *Mythologies*, in relation to myth, "the correlation which unites them [the terms] . . . the associative total." In semiotic language, this leads us to insist that the novel offers above all the science of the signifier. Each epiphany, from the build-up to the apotheosis, to the fading away, is a nexus of signifiers. This energy of the novel lies in the epiphanic style, for it is the value of the epiphany occasionally achieved, and the nature of the writer as *bricoleur* which seem uppermost in Joyce's mind. As simple-minded as it may sound, Stephen's constant act of intending to interpret the signifier, even while he remains more in awe of locating it, lets us approach Joyce's writing as we would a Symbolist poem.

Signs, of course, always slide into other signs, for knowledge is a constant mosaic. But epiphanies are those moments when we can *pause* and accept the associations implied before the action starts again. They are incidental, uncontrived, and essential to genuine understanding. They hold Stephen, for one—and he is the privileged consciousness in all of Joyce's fiction—between openness to mystery and naming it, and that responsibility to remain open is what he comes to accept as the artist's task by the end of *Portrait*. It is not a sense of the mythic as transcendence or borrowed from mythological motifs that Joyce points to in the epiphanies. Like those statements in myth which have the potential for transformation (for being essential means being able to expand terms), Joyce's descriptions of Stephen's awe at the mysterious beauty of the world reveal subtly expanding but thoroughly existential coincidences (and not equivalences) between Stephen and his context. Stephen is most self-consciously a *bricoleur*. If there is a release in myth from the unsatisfactory compromises which make up daily living, then what is revealed to Stephen is literally his full place in the world, based on the primacy of perception, and not a sudden revelation of transcendent truth. Stephen's life in *Portrait* is described as an endless attempt to re-create these moments in a world which simply opens itself to signification rather than having only a few essential meanings. Stephen is compounding coincidence, creating interpretations, and encouraging the repetition of experience which, he would have us believe, is the character of life as well as of fiction.

"A horrible example of free thought"

Stephen's very abstract musings in *Portrait* about art, the self, and the relationship of both to the empirical world, create the conditions for his performance in *Ulysses*. In this novel, Stephen becomes in his own words, "a horrible example of free thought," dedicated to the creation of himself as a free thinker. This is our entry into Joyce's distended world of fiction-making. Stifled by the folktale telling of the Irish, as well as the "exhausted whoredom" of his age "grasping" for its god, Stephen finds himself condemned to speak excessively about himself if he is to speak at all. For *Ulysses* is centered on the grand premise, as Stephen explains in the novel, that "life coexists with art as a representation of the self." And art, as a creation of the idiom of the self, is necessarily an unstable medium. In their separate ways, Stephen and Bloom realize that creative acts can and must be excessive insofar as they repetitively and cloyingly seek progression. Stephen's consciousness compounds meaning with a high degree of ratiocination. Bloom lives anecdotally and fitfully at many intersections of events in Dublin. Joyce himself seeks through both of them to create a talkative sense of the self which responds but is not left vulnerable to the fluctuating world awaiting the senses. Stephen, especially, carries the burden of translating experience into meaning in his protean imagination. His stream of consciousness is the main vehicle for abstraction by which the Greek myth enters the novel and finds itself as myth again. Of course, his is by no means the only abstracting intelligence at work: in a less convoluted manner, Molly and Bloom perform this way as well. But it is the closeness of his thought to Joyce's intentions with myth in this novel that leaves Stephen at the center of the organization of the book.

Stephen's trust in his protean imagination allows less of the preciosity that we find in *Portrait*, and is more a trust in being able to discover a logic to the everyday nature of events, a logic entirely based on the necessity of seeing clearly and interpreting imaginatively. *Ulysses* is a much more worldly book than *Portrait*, but what we find out about the epiphany in the earlier novel alone makes the latter possible. Now, empirical facts, however discontinuous (in fact, because they are discontinuous) are celebrated fully as the signifiers which they are. Yet at the same time, no character is in a vacuum, nor is Joyce's world purely one of endless, metaphorical relativity. The controlling intelligence of *Ulysses* is one in which fact (so meticulously faithful to Dublin) is turned to fiction in the imagination of the major characters, yet can be retained somehow by the reader as fact, for we are very much aware that the surreal will allow interpretation only while the signifiers instigating it remain intact. The reader is obliged to enter a novel dealing ostensibly with the trivial, everyday, and low-mimetic, a series of cultural and even psychological common-places. But by dramatizing the world as signifier so richly, and giving us clues to its interpretation in the figures of Stephen and Bloom, the author is able to convince us that the nature of the everyday itself is, as it were, a totemistic and certainly a fetishistic event. The author constructs the idiom of the reader as either the anecdotal but earthy Bloom or the imaginative Stephen. As readers-of-the-world, Joyce seems to be saying, we can attain a sense of the mythic, once, like Stephen especially, we confront the compromising limitations of perception and have to reason our way out of it.

What *Ulysses* is so conscious of is the problem of knowing anything with certainty. The novel does have a social significance in that it is constantly turning itself over to a community of readers, for it so emphasizes the multiplicity of the signifier that it demands a group reading. It is the kind of fiction that heightens the problematic nature of reality by showing that stories "explaining" the real are so difficult to write that they are impossible to complete, and can only refer over and over again to their starting point: the self's compromising position in the world, thanks to language, which Stephen has discovered in *Portrait*. The most we can hope for as reader is a kind of equilibrium, the same equilibrium Stephen searches for in *Portrait* and *Ulysses*, as he tries to prove that his aesthetic theory describes not simply his role as artist, but his growth into maturity of thought. In *Ulysses*, that fact is taken for granted, as Joyce treats the creation of the self and the creation of fiction as one.

This leads to an anonymity of authorship such as we find in myth, for we are dealing not simply with rounded characters (Stephen, Bloom, and Molly are surely fully drawn in any realistic sense), but with the process of thought, the necessity of interpretation to which they become almost subservient in the novel. After all, we identify in myth not with specific characters but with ways of seeing and thinking that are in some sense universal. Joyce goes on to remarkable lengths in *Ulysses* to create a hint of a universal consciousness behind the text. Meaning in this novel, though not as radically discontinuous as in *Finnegans Wake*, is dense enough to appear to have thrust aside a single controlling intelligence, an assertive *cogito*. Events are related by their proximation in time (one day) and space (Dublin) in such a way as to suggest that the problematic nature of experience does indeed lie in an unconscious totally in the control of language. The dominant figure of the novel—as with the epiphanies in *Portrait*—is, again, the coincidence of metonymy. There seems to be little metaphorical development allowed to the characters beyond their own stream of consciousness, for they are compressed by both cause and effect and coincidental events. But the play of consciousness in each character, their high degree of awareness of fact and the constriction of the self by fact, results especially in revealing repetitions of the same events. For example, what actually goes on between Boylan and Molly is anticipated and replayed in the consciousness of Boylan, Bloom, and finally Molly herself, each time making possible more of a sense of redemption for Bloom in his acceptance of his role as cuckold, and for Molly in her acceptance of her role as wife-mother-lover. The pleasure of the text lies not only in the rich scope of relativity, but also in the coincidences which occur endlessly as characters contemplate the same events, cross paths, and develop parallel actions. Metonymy, by its very compounding, seems to have demanded, if not equivalence, at least some sense of insisting on the grounds of interpretation as strictly empirical and coincidental: a constant modification of preunderstanding. It is as though Joyce distrusts the metaphorical transformations of which Stephen is capable, and demands that the reader, like Stephen and Bloom, be responsible for making connections.

To the extent that metonymy actively controls the richness of meaning in the novel, I must qualify my earlier assertion that it is Stephen who is the major myth-making intelligence, for his ratiocination would be much less effective within the scheme of things without the peripateia of Bloom, who reminds the reader of the concreteness of Stephen's location in Dublin. Bloom contemplates events insofar as he identifies with the action of Dublin as a whole, even when he is an outsider (as in "Aeolus"), vicariously living out the role of the citizen with a finger on every pulse, in order to acquire identity. Bloom is defined primarily by action, and only later by contemplation. He may be parodied as the voyeur throughout, but he alone lives out the myth of *Ulysses* actively questing for himself through various roles: at once comic, erotic, unashamedly excremental, impressionistic, and brave enough to descend into Hades. Stephen, on the other hand, contemplates possible roles, is concerned with what the structure and sense of unity might be behind all the changing events. He is a careful and witty analyst of superstitions and sexual compromise, for example, in his parables of the two fifty-year-old virgins atop Nelson's Column and of Shakespeare as androgyne. All, he plainly tells us, cannot be what it seems. Yet to go deeply into things must lead not to nihilism but to negation and the thrust of transforming fact. So Bloom lives, however badly, and Stephen thinks, however convolutedly, and each comes in the last chapters of the book to teach the other his specialty. The novel operates through a kind of parallelism of event and contemplation of event, often disjunctive, but always drawing us into an enormously abstract yet coherent arrangement.

A related factor emphasizing the coherence of the novel, its insistence on occupying a present and pressingly universal time, is the intersection of events and the use of coincidence. The linear pattern of events, fully summed up by the Gilbert and Linati Codes and aligned along the quest motif, intersects with the many incidental motifs which complicate it (from Bloom's soap to metempsychosis). For the reader, intersections are pauses, ambiguous or distracting signposts to the action, which can actually tell us the direction to take, if we are prepared to store away possibilities for future reference. And we are rewarded because facts do recur (like the ironic appearance of Bloom's soap), and paths will cross on a rerun. The sense that we are never quite seeing the end of an action emphasizes the text's fascination with alternative paradigms, which suggests the continuous present time of the novel, which in turn, like mythical time, aims to become a full history. But it must be admitted, of course, that we tend only to be wise to that after the event of reading, and in contemplation (that is Stephen's example), for the compression and intersections are so complex as to demand an almost impossibly syncretistic awareness of the text. Yet, ironically, as the reader cannot really cope with the whole pattern of happenings, cannot hold the complexity in his mind, so we are not surprised that Bloom cannot either, nor can Stephen unite them after the event, in spite of his ingenious parables. Each combines to make a very human reference to the syncretism of mythic thought and action.

Let me reemphasize that the compression of time and event through the consciousness of Stephen and Bloom is nothing less than epiphanic for the reader. The plot moves not by guaranteeing that something will happen, nor particularly by arousing our expectation. We do not really expect Stephen to return home or leave Dublin again, nor Bloom to leave Molly or take revenge on Boylan, nor Molly to grow tired of Bloom. Rather, we are constantly reminded that we are likely to see some piece of information about these characters, some accurate perception, fall into place more completely than before, and as if for the first time. This may appear more like an anagram than a myth, but the narrative works throughout by repetition to achieve this effect. The plot is always commenting on itself as well as on the real world. And, of course, after a while, it becomes very difficult to tell the plot *apart* from the real world. The plot evokes meaning by offering other plots similar in structure to those we have learned. We quest, transubstantiate, fornicate, descend into hell, and rationalize our way out of things again and again. Plot, that is, depends on our memory of previous patterns of explanations and intent. The familiar intent is to reach epiphany, to discover the way events simply come together in clear proximity and coherence. No less an intention spurs on Bloom and Stephen, both needing, in different ways, to gain release from guilt, general inertia, and the failure to come to consciousness. The characters, simply by being immersed in the great sign system which is Dublin, learn exactly what the reader learns: that there are, optimistically, many ways of establishing the self in an event.

What of these events, though? What does the enormous range of motifs amount to in the end? In scholarly discussion of *Ulysses*, we are most often treated to translations of the text, and even justifications of the realism of the novel in terms of possible walking times from A to B in Dublin, Joyce's faithfulness to sight and sound, and so on. Mimetic responsibility for Joyce did begin by making sure that he had the right signifiers at the right time and place. But the sign remains to be completed. It is true that Bloom, Stephen and Molly are alive and open to change (in the conventional psychological sense), that the novel is a celebration of Dublin, and that Joyce does indulge his infinite delight in variety. In as realistic a way as literature can manage, Bloom and company are real Dubliners, and for that matter, even Finnegan / HCE is a recognizable picaresque variant in the *Wake*. But there is not real permanence to experience for these people, except for the guarantee of ongoing transformation, of more information to be gained, and of interrelationships to identify. Nature and culture, that is, sanction the signifiers themselves, but not what happens to them. What we might be interested in is how they are interpreted. The epiphanies the characters all seek may be moments of truth, but such truths were never so likely to change.

In other words, the epiphany becomes something even more profound in its implication in the later work than in *Portrait*. There it had been a naming of an event and a dissolution of its terms. That is, it had proven that the world signifies— opens itself to signification—but does not signify any one thing permanently. The event was full, yet quickly emptied itself of its presence as the vision left Stephen who had, anyhow, first stumbled on the girl on the strand as arbitrarily as she disappears. Yet in *Ulysses*, interpretation appears more fully mythic in that it offers a constantly compounding coincidence. As the Symbolists and the Cubists realized (ironically, saving myth for our time), and as Joyce translated it into prose, only a discontinuous world can be lived in fully. Continuity is mere impressionism, seen too exclusively from one perspective. But in lively experience, there is no neutral space to be found. The effect of Bloom's and Stephen's discovery that there is no neutral space in Dublin is that the reader learns to trust epiphany, for the infinity of possible relationships emphasizes that we can only move in and out of apprehending and trying to name events.

So no event is named but once in *Ulysses*; no single character is entrusted with a single reference, nor is any single reader spoken to. Fiction becomes the environment created in harmony with the consciousness of freedom, a freedom, as Joyce understood it, which lies in an acceptance of the contradictory and transformational, and a trust in the problem-solving imagination, as we follow Stephen and Bloom in having to name our various positions in our passage through the novel. The dramatic in *Ulysses*, then, has more *abstract* implications than its use in the aesthetics in *Portrait*, for in the later novel it undercuts any attempt to name the world consistently. All it sanctions, to repeat Barthes, is the *paradox* of myth: "the meaning is always there to *present* the form; the form is always there to outdistance the meaning. And there never is any contradiction, conflict, or split between the meaning and the form: they are never at the same place."[10]

Joyce, that is, is not merely tantalizing us with oblique references; he is making an epistemological point. The more consciously the novel aims to "say it all," the more open the chance of transformation, but ironically too, the more difficult it is for the reader to return from the peripheries of his search for meaning back to a center. So myth, and in this case *Ulysses*, have that strange effect of guaranteeing our future, ensuring the changing meanings of the nature of reality while demanding that the present, defensively, never be abandoned. *Ulysses*, strictly speaking, needs no history—the *Odyssey* is there, but ironically does not seem essential—for the reader feels strung out in time, trying to grasp the aphoristic present in Dublin, which he learns to discover is very much like that which he has been living in all along. Hence a reading of *Ulysses* is a distending experience, but not a schizophrenic one. The attempt in the novel is to move away from history and continuity as neurosis: to awake, as Stephen says, from the "nightmare" which is history (merely metonymy) and to establish discontinuous events in the endless transubstantiation of the present.

So the rite of transubstantiation in the Mass is a continually repeated event, humorously parodied throughout the novel, from Mulligan's shaving bowl ritual to Molly's menstruation into the chamber-pot. But even in its negative and comic form, it is as serious as all the protean images which Stephen conjures up. Transubtantiation is parodied in the enthymeme of "Aeolus," the masturbatory fantasies of "Nausicaa," the parable of Shakespeare as androgynous father of the race, the grotesque metamorphoses of nighttown, the duplicities of coincidence in "The Wandering Rocks" and "Eumaeus," the birth of Rudy the Saviour at the end of "Circe," and in the variety of exalted prose styles in "Oxen of the Sun." The changing of roles—Stephen as Hamlet / Christ / Parnell, and Bloom as Ulysses / Wandering Jew / Moses etc.—and the numerous mythological connections between the characters and events of the *Odyssey* and *Ulysses* also offer an affectionate yet ironic perspective on the scope of self-transformation, and on the lengths to which the imagination can be trusted. The list of references to transubstantiation is far longer, but it should be clear that Joyce is reminding us, as myth does too, that the unlikely is seriously part of the likely, even if it offers a completely inverted structure. Things are never what they seem, so we must always try to get at that "ineluctable modality." This can be achieved, as Stephen learns in *Portrait*, not by pursuing one's destiny "ardently," but rationally. In *Ulysses* we find that the negation of particular myths, the inversions of fame and authority, still reveal, even in the obverse of the heroic *Odyssey*, the constructivist, rational intentions of the "original" version of the quest myth.

The seriousness of Stephen's intent is nowhere more clear than in "Proteus," where we are given a direct look at our fate as readers, and Stephen's fate as artist, according to the extent to which he can resist imprisonment by the world of changing signifiers. The protean world is not merely in flux; it is, in the full meaning of these very current terms, deconstructed and depoliticized. Signs empty and fill themselves in Stephen's world with startling rapidity and could (and momentarily do) reduce him to lapsing into the rhythm of cloyingly anxious, eternally present time. But they do so in order to build again. In that surrealistic scene when the two midwives descend the steps, one with a dead baby trailing its navel cord in a travesty of birth, Stephen is acutely and humorously compromised into grappling with the problem of the ontological meaning of events, given that we exist in a dialectic of sequence and simultaneity. Discovering the intersection of patterns of time past and time present (as Eliot was to do later in *Four Quartets*) is the beginning of Stephen's effort to think through his crisis. The whole chapter rests, with all its sprinkling of mythological motifs, on the issue (at once intellectual and a matter of simple survival) of grasping the coincidence of appearance and reality while preserving the "ineluctable modality," the sense that a meaning does reside in ever-changing forms. It is that potential, surely, which is the bedrock of mythicity.

That is, Stephen is rephrasing yet again the central problem which had been with Joyce since *Dubliners*, that of finding epiphany in the midst of eternal flux and metamorphosis. Since we are trapped in a universe of signs, Stephen realizes, to name is only to name an inflection. In effect, we can only *re*name, for nature is protean—affirming and denying at once. Stephen enters the spirit of such a shifting reality by a series of metamorphoses of himself (including his change into Aristotle, Adam Kadmon, an "unfallen" androgyne, Jesus Christ, Arius, Hamlet, William of Ockham, a drowning man, a monster hatched from an egg by a snake, and so on). Amid images of change which are symptoms of his own "decay," Stephen is forced to recognize his own temporality and corruption (humorously, in his mucous hardening and micturation). He seeks a solution, with mock pomposity, in the Arian heresy that the Father, Son, and Holy Ghost are not consubstantial, and blasphemy (negation, again) gives him freedom to assert the imagination's ability to transubstantiate reality. *His intent is to empty signs of meaning, however temporarily, in order to be free to rename them.* So the frequent reference to transubstantiation in *Ulysses* implies not simply the mystery of change, but the consistency of it, even of the act of negation. We may not be able to predict that change reliably, but it forces on us the need to discover its underlying common sense. What more is myth? As such, the word implies, as it does for Stephen in "Proteus," that we must offer the imaginative fact of our own reasonable metamorphosis in order to discover truth.

Thus Stephen plays out his myth-making role with an awareness that the function of mythic thought lies in the rational effect of thinking through our very compromising fate in a world always open to signification. Stephen can stop the action in his protean world, but must inflate the pause which will start it again. He will not be immobilized by the hundreds of mythological motifs which rush through his head, with their pretense at universal order and prototypical knowledge, but turns for a brief but salutary moment to the freedom of persistent associations, which sanctions mythology with the utmost irony. *Ulysses* begins with borrowed mythology which becomes modern mythicity. It is quickly incorporated into the myth of the novel's literariness, keeping the motifs alive in a world which has no respect for fixed meanings, which will always bring us back full circle again to Stephen, picking his nose in Dublin Bay.

Roland Barthes has an interesting comment on myth in

Mythologies which seems to capture something of the onto-logical limitations Joyce realized to be part of its function. "For the very end of myths is to immobilize the world: they must suggest and mimic a universal order which has fixated once and for all the hierarchy of possessions. Thus everyday and everywhere, man is stopped by myths, referred by them to this motionless prototype which lives in his place, stifles him in the manner of a huge internal parasite and assigns to his activity the narrow limits within which he is allowed to suffer without upsetting the world."[11] This is the extent of Stephen's discovery of his new idiom in "Proteus"—a deeply ironic but powerful inversion of activity. As he plays out his roles, he is able to escape into transubstantiation even while he is imprisoned by change. Hence he is "condemned to speak excessively about reality," in effect to make myth as much as Bloom lives it, in order to prove that he is free.

A Footnote on the *Wake*

I have suggested that an important aspect of the development of Joyce's art from *Portrait* to *Ulysses* has been the increasing autonomy of the text (the disappearance of the author) as linguistic transubstantiation becomes more complex. This has been established by the function of the epiphany in *Portrait*, and borne out by the experiments in narrative transformation in *Ulysses*. In the epiphany, we can see a tendency to stop and start the flow of consciousness suggestively by avoiding metaphor for the play of metonymy. In *Ulysses*, the stopping and starting is speeded up by the author's constant interplay of motif and by Stephen's increased talent at making connections. But the metonym remains the key figure, and historic development the primary axis of meaning. Diachrony dominates plot. In both *Portrait* and *Ulysses*, the fictional technique aims above all to create a persistent, rational pressure which is both a symptom of myth and the mainstay of Joyce's art. In all his work, we are conscious of being in the presence of a mind vigorously pursuing its own construction through close

reference to the real and its re-creation in the world of signifiers.

In other words, the sense of a narrative's mythic form lies
precisely in that play between consciousness and the limiting
presence of the outside world as sign, a play which is analogous to the reader's attempt to extend his or her consciousness, even within the limits the text insists on. As Joyce and
the French Symbolists realized (and the semiologists have been
reinforcing), the play is not between form and meaning as *a
priori* dualistic, but between forms of the real which interrelate
and provide the basis for further development. It is only structures which can be common, not contents. Form is always the
content for other form, and every content is the form of what
it contains. The novel at its best entices us into the consciousness of the artist intent on proceeding via these rhythms of
real thought, allowing his or her terms systematically to work
out in the plot their affirmation and negation. Joyce is very
much aware that fiction, like myth, can never actually show
us the perfect form, nor convince us that the essential is all
there is, but it can at least tantalize us as we seek a comfortable
reading, by compromising our assumptions about naming the
world, and so, as Roland Barthes has said, by bringing to a
"crisis" our "relation with language."

The most complex version of this phenomenon of discom-
forting form in the modern novel, especially in what we can
call its radical plot implosion, is probably *Finnegans Wake.*
The *Wake* aims to work beyond the *closed* form of moment-
by-moment plotting by reproducing the structure of thought
as operating simultaneously on diachronic and synchronic levels. The few comments I am going to offer on the *Wake* refer
to this quite conscious intersecting of time, and presuppose
that we accept Joyce's experiment as a logical continuation
of the pursuit of the mythic which is implicit in the earlier
fiction. His attempt to integrate massive amounts of data with
many structural variations into the necessity of history, leads
not to a sense of facetious or gratuitous embroidering of a
naturalistic plot, but to a genuine continuation of his exper-

iment into how the novel seeks to solve the compromises of language and form. Of course, my comments can only be a mere footnote to the *Wake*, but my point is not necessarily reinforced by lengthy explication.

Of all the extended studies of the *Wake* in the diachronic mode, Clive Hart's account[12] of the relationship of structure and motif seems to hold the most true, as he ingeniously sums up the rhythmic patterns of the novel while leaving them free to expand further. On the other hand, one needs to go beyond the merely diachronic readings and point out that the *Wake's* formal implications are indeed more complex, and certainly more mythopoeic. One can only agree that the difficulty of the *Wake* lies in the interrelationship of structure and motif, not in its syntax. It is the effect of the interrelationship, however, that I am concerned with. The limits of the more realistic plotting of the *Wake* (the adventures of Finnegan, the history of Ireland, and so on) seem determined by the two patterns of time and knowledge that Joyce claimed he "used for all their worth": the cyclical, spatial structure of history outlined by Vico, and the dualistic patterning of Giordano Bruno's gnosticism. All of Joyce's critics have commented on his use of these patterns, so there is little point in merely offering another elaborate arrangement of the novel's many plots to fit that mold. Suffice it to say that Hart's, anyway, seems to fit as well as any. All the themes of the novel, from the metamorphoses of Finnegan to Earwicker and from Dublin to World City; the conflict between Shem, Shaun, HCE, and ALP; and the story of the creation of the race, Ireland, and the world, the fall, and the quest for rebirth, are all subsumed by the Viconian evolutionary pattern. Yet this spatial structure seems to have the function of parodying the repetition of all myths, since what Vico so brilliantly located (as Joyce realized) is the myth of repetition itself. But what lies beyond merely saying more of the same—for it is not uncommon to point out that there is little original material in the *Wake*—is a pattern of conflict involving each event which reveals Bruno's influence on Joyce's belief "that every power in nature must

163

evolve an opposite in order to realise itself, and the opposition brings reunion." These two patterns, of course, are apparently contradictory, yet the implied determinism of Vico's cycles coexists in the *Wake* with a need to interpret the flux of reality. There is nothing unusual about this, for all language works that way. What is unusual is that Joyce is consciously taking on the ontological limits imposed on fiction by writing itself.

Hart has shown just how complicated even that Viconian circling can be, working its way in counterpoint to other cyclical views of time in the novel (Blavatskyan, Christian, Buddhist and so on). The three major Viconian ages of Birth (Book I), Marriage (Book II), and Death (Book III) contain many lesser circles making up a "four-plus-one quasi-Indian progression which Joyce has counterpointed against the three-plus-one Viconian scheme."[13] He notes, too, that along with the evolutionary and repetitive cycles (the Eliade scheme of myth) come three Dream layers integrated by an anonymous dreamer into a penetration of the unconscious. Books I and II contain the largely "alcoholic dream cycle" beginning and ending in the public house; in Book II we find Earwicker's dream of Shaun; and in Book III "the Dreamer's dream about Earwicker's dream about Shaun's dream."[14] But against the cycles and related dream patterns comes daytime thought: the concern for intersections of meaning, correspondence between motifs, and an even more bewildering set of transformations than in *Ulysses*. The use of leitmotifs, synaesthesia, punning, polyphonic patterns, song rhythms, and epiphanies, as Hart says, has a unifying effect: all is "caught up in a whirl of reincarnation," often seemingly by "remote control." I have hardly done justice to Hart's argument here, but the point is to raise the question which he does not answer: what does all the circularity, relativism, and *pointillisme* (Stuart Gilbert's term, after Seurat, for the style of the *Wake*) imply about the author's sense of creating a new idiom for the novel and himself?

Plainly, linearity, circularity, and epiphany meet in *Ulysses*, and epiphany and linearity in *Portrait*. But what happens in the *Wake* is a logical development of the early attempts to define but not take to its limits the intersection of history and moment. Here Joyce's imagination discovered a structure for mythic narrative in the epiphany extended into endless metaphor. The *Wake* is clearly the most metaphorical of all his fictions, the most intent on creating transformations before it can insist meaning has been reached. Action is suspended in a mass of empirical data which is quite literally protean. In the *Wake*, Joyce planned to operate within a complex of signifiers which never stay still. What is narrated is the structure and process of real thought which involves countless highly oblique versions of the significance of events. The irony is that we are abruptly returned to metonymy to discover any meaning at all. Mythopoeic creation, that is, encourages us to live *entirely* through the novel as epiphany, to be proficient at myth-making ourselves, and to occupy only a world of signifiers. Whereas, in his earlier fiction, Joyce was very conscious of using myth to structure his work (though myth also uses Joyce), now he is concerned to alter fiction entirely in pursuit of the synchronic and diachronic whole. Imploded plots are not merely complex, multilayered structures; they faithfully reflect the need for multilayering because the essential can no longer be simple. The novel, in other words, in the best tradition of powerful myths, has totally appropriated reality. There lies behind the form of *Finnegans Wake* a rational resistance to mere linearity or any simple version of epistemology. This is seen in the constant search for analogy, for new information, for new terms for worldly compromise which might offer a clearer version of the way we must enter a world continually open to signification.

The plot of *Finnegans Wake*, then, is repetitive; it is not a collection of incoherently scattered incidents, nor merely associative logic or the structure of a dream, although Joyce called it his "night book." Most readers of Joyce have quite monotonously taken his comment about dream literally and, seeking the recognizable repetition of Jungian archetypes and Viconian cycles (as even Hart tends to do), have spoken of the novel as creating the patterns of the mind dreaming, and of myth and archetype as the content of dream. They have even spent time wondering who the dreamer is, as if he or she must be only one person: ALP, Finnegan, or Shem, or Shaun. But my point is that it is not merely in the reconstruction of the unconscious promptings of our dream life, or in the repetition of quest or other ancient mythical motifs that *Finnegans Wake* gains its mythic quality. Rather, it is through the creation of the mythical plot as a mode of argument—in this case, one which is a deliberate and highly comic parody of the sequential, historical imagination. By simply providing us with too much information, Joyce ironically deflates man's progress and optimistically celebrates the life of the imagination, destroying mere linearity but *recreating* dialectical thought which, of course, is still dependent on history.

To supplement the diachronic and early Freudian studies of the *Wake*, which not surprisingly outnumber all others, we need the more recent development of the synchronic analysis of the novel. Margot Norris, in *The Decentered Universe of "Finnegans Wake"*,[15] has provided the most useful of these to date, and her study bears mentioning here for its interest in Lévi-Strauss's theory of myth, Lacan's theory of the unconscious as discourse of the Other, and Derrida's related notion of deconstruction. But the *Wake* is still a Freudian dream book, she insists, for dream and myth are homologous structures, and the narrative of the book reveals the compulsive and associative patterns of the unconscious as language: its repetitions, protean forms, and obsession with the mythic model of the family, guilt, ancient crimes, infantile traumas, incest, "perversions," and so on. Everywhere the psychoanalytic interests tend to prescribe translation into myths. Characters are not differentiated; patterns of collective guilt (etc.) emerge in their place. Identities are interchangeable. The self is self-deluded and inauthentic, moving in a closed circle of mythic guilt, "transferring the arena of self-knowledge from the epiphany to the dream, where the self knows itself not through brilliant flashes of light and insight, but through laboriously constructed labyrinthine puzzles."[16] The language of dream, furthermore, is not univocal but decentered: full of free-play, displacement, condensation, distortion, doubletalk, imitative form, and bricolage.

As important as this commentary is, there is a serious problem with the exclusive synchronic approach, which lies in the fact that no discourse yields meaning from one axis alone. No reading can be simply or exclusively synchronic or diachronic. Norris's version of the world of the *Wake* makes sense only in conjunction with the linear flow of the book, or else it ends up merely as a compression of the same fact, which is disturbing to the reader who in the simple *act* of reading cannot live in all places at once. So, ironically, Norris herself is forced to say that the *Wake*, read with an unrelenting zeal for vertical paradigms, presumably can only be "inhuman" after *Ulysses*.

But there is more to the *Wake*, and to Structuralist analysis, than this pessimism. Again, I must beware of simplifying Norris's argument, for it is true that she does say that "the results of critical efforts are not important in the *Wake*, but rather the compulsions and motives of the questors, their styles and methods, their quarrels, their self-justifications, and their own implication in the object of their study. Hermeneutics is an important issue in *Finnegans Wake*."[17] She is right, too, to point out that any "authentic" interpretation of the *Wake* is doomed to be destroyed by the punning of the book. But specific interpretations aside—and I have no intention here of offering anything other than an approach to the discourse— one can argue with her that the novel is so decentered as to demolish plot. As decentered as it is (and that, after all, has been my point about the epiphany in *Portrait* and the style of *Ulysses*) we are still aware of many plots, as layered as they may be. Decentering, as I have tried to show in the first two chapters, does not necessarily mean nihilism. Many specific incidents are both memorable and quotable—such as ALP trying to awaken HCE from his sexual lethargy, or the tale of Jarl van Hoother, or the incident in Phoenix Park—and do not diminish even an old-fashioned sense of character as they allow figures to live on in a world of dramatically increased information and value. Furthermore, myths and dreams may very well be homologous, but they are not necessarily identical in intent or performance, for myth is consciously a problem-solving act, and even a neoscientific use of language; dreams refer us again to the unconscious discourse of the Other. Joyce is actively constructing a fiction, the truism bears repeating, and not merely allowing free associative play. However much he does deflate linear progress, he does not forget that he has a story to tell, namely that of HCE and ALP, and a metonymic responsibility to keep up. Characters in the *Wake*, that is, do live in a world dominated by the mythic, not merely as an old-fashioned Freudian analog (dream), but as a synchronic and diachronic whole.

Myths repeat themselves in the *Wake*, especially the cycle of birth-death-rebirth, in order to transform and not to weaken. The concept of myth I have been discussing, there-fore, allows authenticity and the guilty extinction of the self, dream, and consciousness to interchange, as we know they always must. Nondifferentiation is a function of our being overwhelmed by fact, but at no point are Joyce's characters so blurred. One can hardly prove the point simply by quoting one well-known example, but the reader of the *Wake* will know that it does not represent an aberration in style. When the washerwomen move up and down the banks of the Liffey (I, viii) gossiping about HCE and ALP, we are first made very much aware of two quite faithfully low-mimetic characters (the washerwomen), as Frye might say, with recognizably sa-lacious interests, fascinated in a voyeuristic way by the strange behavior of two equally low-mimetic Dubliners. These are character types, however much they become myth-makers and HCE and ALP become primordial figures in the tale. Whatever the symbolic implications of their talk—and it is, of course, highly suggestive and, as always, punned to satiation—we do have a time, a place, and indeed, a metonymical basis for interpretation. We go, literally, from soiled underclothing to primordial sex.

What we find at any point in the text is that the diachronous flow of narrative does indeed follow the circular Viconian monomyth of birth, death, and resurrection (even, as Norris points out, in inverted form)[18] but it does so in a highly ironic manner. The myth implies a structural unity historically: the picaresque movement of Finnegan as primordial man, ALP as primordial woman, the founding of Dublin, the birth of the sons, the growth of civilization, and so on. But there is also the *psychological* analogy of the symbolic passage from birth to consciousness and sexual battle, to internal conflict, to guilt, anxiety, taboo breaking, expiation, and calm which constantly dominates the lives of HCE, ALP, Shem, and Shaun. And there is a *dream* analogy, emphasizing the arbitrary, coincidental nature of all the events, allowing a certain surrealistic license in the performance of the plot. Finally there is the *aesthetic* analogy (developed from Stephen's discussion of aesthetics in *Portrait*), dealing with the cycle of mythopoeic creation itself from lyric cry, to epic, to dramatic / dialectical form which, as we can see in the transition from *Portrait* to the *Wake*, in practice means a movement from epiphany (metonymy), through metaphor, back to epiphany.

So amidst the necessary linearity of the plot, analogs develop: a constant, synchronous compounding of meaning, a perpetual lyric recall, mainly through punning and superimposed or intertwined tales. This works against the possibility of reading the book consistently on any one level of analogy, such as the versions of the circular quest, or the psychological and aesthetic phases. For example, the well-known incident (I, v) where the Hen (Biddy, Doran, ALP) digs up a letter (defense of HCE's slandered name after the Phoenix Park incident and Shem's parody of literary criticism, *Finnegans Wake* itself) from the dungheap (Dublin, literary scholarship, Shem and Shaun's slander of their father) = a parody of the literary scholar (reader and writer) searching for meaning in the text = parody of HCE as fallen hero searching for his potency = parody of questions about birth, death and rebirth itself = a self-parody by Joyce of his own writing = a parody

169

of the novel's frequent use of quest motifs. And so on. Of course, this summary is a drastic oversimplification, but what I am trying to say is that instead of establishing a recognizable form for the novel, these ideograms of meaning ironically break down the Viconian monomyth under the sheer weight of multiple motifs, yet still rely on it and preserve the necessity of the metonymy in the metaphor—perhaps not so absent here. It is always possible to trace some kind of circular patterning in the book, but the immediate experience of reading the text emphasizes its amazing ability to synchronize, to allow substitution for events in time. Each sentence is a "self-regulating transformation." We exist in the novel in networks of information for which a linear or even cyclical pattern is not sufficient but nonetheless necessary. All that we have to tell us the time is the sense that experience develops its power from the tension between an immediate, unconditional reference to the concrete (metonymy) and an earned development of the plot which involves prodigious acts of memory and abstraction (metaphor).

Joyce's novel at all times maintains this *openness* of mythic creation, a sense of consciousness constructing itself. Synchrony does not cancel out diachrony; it depends on it and makes it richer. The spatial form proposed by Vico is attractive since time appears measurable and controllable. We can create an illusion of freedom by quantifying and compartmentalizing time and experience. But the effect of Joyce's unique confrontation of time and experience in pun / analogy, plot repetition, and variation is not that of plot degenerating but of the freedom of endless transformation. The epiphany of the pun becomes a layering of simultaneous meaning that belittles an *a priori* metaphysics and a simple sense of history. And this literally occurs in every line. Joyce—as Wallace Stevens described his own poetic aim—wanted the old metaphysics (here so clearly treated ironically in the use of Vico) taken out of fact-finding, so that facts might make their own metaphysics.

CHAPTER 4

THE MYTHIC
AND THE NUMINOUS

. . . we constantly drift between the object and its de-
mystification, powerless to render its wholeness. For if
we penetrate the object, we liberate it but we destroy
it; and if we acknowledge its full weight, we respect it,
but we restore it to a state which is still mystified. It
would seem that we are condemned for some time yet
always to speak *excessively* about reality.
—Barthes, *Mythologies*[1]

PREFIGURATION AND INTENTION

We cannot answer the question of what makes mythology so
attractive to writers and readers of modern literature if we
remain with structure and semiotics alone and ignore myth's
talent for arguing for the numinous signifier and the validity
of the supernatural. But, not surprisingly, that has been a
much avoided question in modern literary criticism. The safest
way of showing the relationship between the sacred and art,
for example, has long been to emphasize art's reference to or
use of religious and mythological (meaning archetypal) motifs.
Art becomes the transition between the numinous and the
everyday. But as I have been arguing, the problem lies in
locating the mythic, and now the sacred. Mythology, including
religious mythology, is a body of myths, which means that we
are dealing at best with hypothetically comprehensive narratives made up of all the variants of each myth. The motif
is a transformational fact; the archetype must be part of a
process theory of art. We cannot be sure of the coherence of
myth, the singularity of the motif, or the stability of the nu-

171

minous, since each is a matter of interpretation. Not only is authenticity always in doubt, but we may very well not have all the known variants. Even if classical and Biblical mythologies have been more popular than the totemistic for establishing the presence of mythological motifs in a literary text, they too are no more unified than any other.

So we must ask ourselves how religion and mythology can be important to the writer in spite of their unreliability as precise thematics. There are parallels between mythic and literary form, given their linguistic basis, but the nature of writing's intent to recover the numinous remains a difficult question, and one set apart from motif usage. One answer which has been traditionally offered is that mythological motifs are universal aspects of the religious sensibility. Myths are sacred in their irrational, ritual function, at best dramatizing pressing ontological questions, and evolving unconscious archetypal behavior. Given the hypothesis of the primacy of ritual behavior, it has been said (by W. H. Auden for one) that poetry itself becomes a ritual response, thereby turning the artist into a shaman, at one level, and art into a form of incantatory performance. A more empiricist response to the problem— consistent with the position I have been taking on myth—is to admit that the religious directly refers to some unanswerable questions about human nature which myth and art also address, but the authority of myth as a sacred document refers less to a fundamentalist interpretation, or a literal meaning, or even to its expressive possibilities than to its openness to interpret experience. Apart from the problems of the archetypalist position already discussed in the first chapter, it bears repeating that scarcely every writer interested in religion wants to take the authority of myth for granted. Many of those who do have not turned to myth with the idea that the questions have been solved adequately in ancient texts, but rather that the questions have been posed with unavoidable relevance within the limitations of human discourse. The link between literature and religious and mythological motifs, themes, or forms is available to us not because writers need actually believe in myths, but because both myth and literature function within a general theory of fictions. More precisely, language makes the sacred possible.

The most important aspect of myth studies for literature lies in returning myth to its existential origin in human conflict and compromise, which is where we define the ontological limits of language, and in aligning myth and literature in carrying out this mandate. Myth needs literature to maintain that ritual effacing of its origins in language, and modern literature, for its own survival, is only too keen to adopt some of the methods myth uses to show it is in some way a narrative of origins, and so acquires mythicity. But does this mean that myth is not effectively *demythologized* of its sense of the numinous by literature? Apart from Lévi-Strauss, Mircea Eliade and the neo-Jungian school of myth study would say it is:

> . . . in modern societies the prose narrative, especially the novel, has taken the place of the recitation of myths in traditional and popular societies. More than this—it is possible to dissect out the "mythical" structure of certain modern novels, in other words, to show the literary survival of great mythological themes and characters. . . . From this point of view we could say, then, that the modern passion for the novel expresses the desire to hear the greatest possible number of "mythological stories" desacralized or simply camouflaged under "profane" forms.[2]

At least for Eliade, the desacralization of myth in literature fulfills some human purpose, however profane that can only be. "The novel does not have access to the primordial time of myths, but in so far as he tells a credible story, the novelist employs a time that is *seemingly historical* yet is condensed or prolonged, a time, then, that has at its command all the freedoms of imaginary worlds."[3] So reading literature, he goes on to say, encourages a "revolt against historical time," and "preserves at least some residues of 'mythological behavior.' "[4] Similarly, Lévi-Strauss's theory of the weakening of myth into the novel, although it is more accurate about the function of "the primordial time of myths," is pessimistic about future acts of understanding.

But if I am to be consistent with the argument outlined in the chapters before this, I must be more optimistic than Eliade or Lévi-Strauss and say that it is precisely the function of language determining the mythic which cannot allow myth or literature to be desacralized. To consider the novel as largely profane in that it implies a "revolt against historical time" is to misinterpret its link to myth, and to say no more about myth today than that it is a mere nostalgia for our "real" origins, a dream about *alcheringa*. Nostalgia it may be, but so peculiarly stubborn that it tantalizes our reason as well as our ability to create vicarious structures of pleasure in art. As we have seen earlier, myth does not necessarily have a different form from the novel, and if that argument stands up, then the condition of being mythic, even as a semiological fact (after Barthes), must offer some sense in which literature can also be termed essential in the attempt to close the gap between event and meaning. The requirements of our interest in structure and interpretation must insist that this sense be, as always, an existential fact, no matter how closely it can be linked with the sacred.

Clearly, the question of the relationship between "the religious / sacred / numinous" and literature offers distinct problems to be solved. The first is to decide what is meant by "the religious / sacred / numinous," and the second is to explain how this condition plays a role in and beyond the sign: that is, how its intentionality might be defined. Both these issues are notoriously difficult to answer, but it can be said that there are two options for describing the sacred. First, the sense of the sacred refers to a presence occasioning awe beyond the text, implying some absent event, mysterious, resisting understanding and only accessible to further *synonyms* for "the numinous," as Rudolf Otto has put it.[5] In this case, the sacred is beyond connotative language, and so truly originary that we can only retreat before it. But under very unusual circumstances, some examples of discourse (most notably devotional texts) may be said to capture and even instigate awe and require reading to be a kind of heightened revelation of truth. The alternative is to insist that since all texts must use language and narrative form, the absence which makes the sacred grow fonder for us is implicit in the very mysteries of language itself. The sense of the sacred is created both by the human failure to name and understand experience *and* by the conditions language determines for assigning meaning: that is, it refers to the perpetual play in the ontological gap.

The problem with pursuing the first alternative is that it presupposes some faith in the numinous qualities of a *non*-human fact, since all human facts immediately incorporate the problem of language. But I do not want to presuppose that the holy is beyond all expression in order to prove the importance of myth. Instead, I must acknowledge that once language is said to be in any way part of our understanding of the sacred, we are left not simply with an irrational accretion of terms for the "*tremendum* and *augustum*" (as Otto would have it), but the very elusiveness of words put to such a task. The mysterious absence, that is, which occasions our sense of awe at the arbitrary nature of meaning, becomes above all a hermeneutical problem. It exists in the paradoxical always-interpretable-but-never-closed gap between event and meaning.

In order to come to grips with this problem, it is not surprising that we have often associated the supposedly pure representation of myths, their tautologous nature, and even their function as sacred texts, with the tautologous nature of religious belief itself. Because of that, the gap has become a kind of pathetic fallacy, and has even been anthropomorphized into a human context which can only become desacralized. It is, after all, a commonplace that the more religious man is, the more he turns to paradigmatic models for that mysterious absence (or presence, once it is turned into God) and insists on a literal fusion of language and desire, image and event, in text and icon. Eliade quotes Malinowski, who has summed up this supposed magic of myth and religion as well as anyone, in the attempt to indicate how magic becomes universal authority once its transcendental origins are asserted.

> Studied alive, myth . . . is not an explanation in satisfaction of a scientific interest, but a narrative resurrection of a primeval reality, told in satisfaction of deep religious wants, moral cravings, social submissions, assertions, even practical requirements. Myth fulfills in primitive culture an indispensable function: it expresses, enhances, and codifies belief; it safeguards and enforces morality; it vouches for the efficiency of ritual and contains practical rules for the guidance of man. Myth is thus a vital ingredient of human civilisation; it is not an idle tale, but a hard-worked active force; it is not an intellectual explanation or an artistic imagery, but a pragmatic charter of primitive faith and moral wisdom. . . . These stories . . . are to the native a statement of a primeval, greater, and more relevant reality, by which the present life, fates and activities of mankind are determined, the knowledge of which supplies man with the motive for ritual and moral actions, as well as with indications as to how to perform them.[6]

Of course, mythological narratives function as religious beliefs and intend to be significant, precious, and exemplary in that way, but they also reveal the unavoidable paradox of such intentions: namely, that such understanding can only be described as an interpreted process, even once it is a moment of illumination. The nature of narrative form is such that myth can only hope to communicate as a closed plot, a finite system offering its own coding in the midst of a world of negative knowledge and open-ended signs. Even before it is a sacred text, myth must make its point as a necessary "science of the concrete." Furthermore, the mythological tale and its practical suggestions must appropriate the sense of the sacred, must make it in some way realistic, part of an exchange system with nature and culture. That very need to essentialize narrative can even find fulfillment in the novel, not as an escape from historical time (which, as Lévi-Strauss has shown, is essentially mythic time, anyhow), but in the survival of plot itself, and the continuing attempt to give meaning form in discourse.

In other words, there are some very practical and discursive issues concerning the play of the sacred in the mythic. On a superficial level, the more we learn about the form of mythic plots (largely via Structural Anthropology) and the poetics of the novel, the more we might see that myths and fictions share plots of similar shape. Without turning to the complicated issue of comparative poetics (Greimas, Todorov, Kristeva, Culler, and so on), I have offered in previous chapters some broad coordinates for the status of that shape, whatever we decide it actually looks like. If mythicity is a function of the ontological status of language, the point to discuss now is how mythic and literary form functions in such a way that we may attribute to it a sense of the sacred or the numinous. Is it the case, again, that myths are by nature sacred and believed in implicitly, while novels are not, and for that reason myth and literature will always remain apart? The reader will know by now that the argument has been that myths are not believed in literally but symbolically. Myth is an expanding contextual structure rather than a recurring motif, a logic of reconstruction against compromise. Because the crises occasioning myth by definition do not disappear but produce further myth, all that can be believed is the power of the human intelligence to persevere in its logical struggles in the face of nonmeaning. Again, our starting point must be that the fate of literature is tied up with the fate of myth as language. For if literary plots look like mythological narratives, then the literary qualities of myth and the mythic qualities of literature must be allied. That surely must be the result of an argument for the link between myth and literature based on the theory of the mythicity of language. But to resort to a theory of fiction is not to make it necessarily easier for us to define the numinous. However we locate mythicity in the nature of language, the apparent interest that myth shows in religion remains largely a mystery, taking us between the world as signifier and as numinous quality, always evasive and resisting generalizations about the way it works. Beyond the phenomenology of the writing, drawing, dancing, music and so on, by which the mythic makes itself known, we have only the fact of the human need for sign-making itself on which to establish the status of religious yearning. Myth, like Lévi-Strauss's "unity of human reason," has its own reasons about which we know very little.

Does this mean that if myth is a blanket term covering all the thousands of attempted tautologies which have been produced to explain human experience, only a theory of the imagination, or of the intelligence, or of reason can emerge to explain the sense of the sacred, depending on which faculty psychology one intends to pursue? It would seem that this is the case, and at least that one must be careful not to allow automatically a superstitious ranking of myth and fiction, nor to fall into the trap of assuming that myth lies beyond human intelligence and must stay there in order to be myth. This would place little faith in the human imagination and implies an anthropomorphic approach to our subject. My point is that a theory of myth and the sacred is in part a theory of how the imagination creates fictions given the conditions of language. And there lies the value of myth: not in discovering the origin of fire, but in asserting the power of the human intelligence as it pursues such large questions. In fact, beyond what we know of the linguistic basis of myth, *intentionality* is all: the intention especially to confront the unanswerable. It is impossible for us to tell whether the totemistic myths Lévi-Strauss analyzes have the same function for the primitive mind as, say, Garbo's face or the professional wrestler has for us, at least according to Roland Barthes. It does not matter, though, that the process of aiming for ultra-signification, for fullness of meaning, is the same in each, and the same in all myth. In Barthes' words, which can summarize my earlier argument: "truth is no guarantee for myth; nothing prevents it from being a perpetual alibi. . . . The meaning is always there to present the form; the form is always there to outdistance the meaning."[7] In this sense, then, a myth must point to the ongoing intention to be valuable because it is full of meaning, whatever its particular motive. So in terms of the religious significance of myth, its reference to the ineffable, the real issue is not whether myths perpetuate themselves because they successfully embody the sacred as an objective fact, but whether they offer a lively enough argument to enable us to interpret the numinous—whatever we think that is—in the world of signs. It then becomes the business of myth studies to devise a theory of fictions which reveals the possibility of this activity of myth. And, no less, it is the business of literary criticism to devise a theory of fictions which expects nothing short of mythic activity in literature and can evaluate works in terms of how they transfer meaning into form.

This still does not answer the question of how myth may be logical in its search for the sacred origins. Again, any variety of transformations does not explain logic, and Geoffrey Hartman has suggested that Lévi-Strauss has not really found a logic for myth with his theories: repetition is only a "venture."[8] Perhaps adventure would be more appropriate, for Lévi-Strauss finds in myth little that is different from poetic play. The logic of myth is a logic for metaphor in that each myth (like each good literary work) authenticates itself by revealing its mode of interpretation as aiming for ultra-signification. The intention of the myth may very well become "frozen," as Barthes would say, by the arbitrariness and literalness of its terms, but nonetheless, myth is not merely anecdotal or phatic, but aims to carry a message which can only appear essential or universal because the logic of the plot is available to us in terms of radical self-authentication. Structure and intent are thereby inseparable; one reveals the other.

John White's interesting study, *Mythology and the Modern Novel*,[9] has tried to avoid this problem of myth and its logic by insisting that we are only safe in using the term "mythological motif," for myth is impossible to describe accurately.

His influential idea that mythological motifs prefigure literary images has all the empirical sanity, but also all the fear of ontology expressed some time ago by the New Critics. One can hardly disagree with him that the novel uses myth as a prefiguration, and in various ways: to renarrate a plot, to juxtapose a motif with a fiction and, through inference and innuendo, to develop a complex and suggestively ambiguous meaning in the fiction itself. But the problem still remains that we do not find out what that prefiguration intends, and why the earlier stories seem more essential than the later. There is no easy answer to that question, but it is not one to be ignored either. I have been arguing throughout this study that the future of myth criticism lies less in the identification of motif in literature than in the attempt to follow the phenomenon of the writing of myth and fiction as each tries to suppress the void of consciousness, the failure to understand fully, which always lies behind the fictional proposal and its closed plot. A fiction never ceases trying to be real, even while it must always be largely metaphorical. Neither mythologies nor novels can exhaust consciousness or language, and it is the intention to go on in the business of making the world transform into further meaning which may very well be all that we can understand by "mythic thought."

Thus it is not a reusable plot, spare but clear in its development of intent, which makes myth mythic and which literature admires. If we could find such plots, perhaps that would be true, but mythic progress in narrative is subtle in its turns and, if anything, the novel—as I have tried to show with James Joyce—imitates myth's highly ambiguous and suggestive reasoning rather than borrows its motifs. It is true that myth appropriates via plot, but it is not the plot alone which is reusable, but the logical intention of the plot to make the arbitrary coincidences of experience seem somehow coherent, to maintain compromise amid contradiction, even to create tautologies and full meaning. If we say simply that the motifs of a few mythological narratives turn up again and again, and that this unity alone allows myth to perpetuate itself, then the pleasure of the text is little more than a constant repetition, eventually of one plot. A theory of prefiguration needs to go beyond simply the irony of immanence (where White wants to leave it), and to argue for mythology's intentional logic of form rather than content, which is what conveys myth to the novel. Or else it must seem that myth prefigures while the novel merely configures and, some people would also say, disfigures.

It is persistent mythic intent to "say it all" which drives on plot transformation and leads us to the sense of the sacred. Mythologies are not merely documents of the religious and other beliefs of another time, and of historical interest only, but statements attempting to withstand time because of the universality and thoroughgoing nature of their logical pursuit of imaginative coherence. We sense as we read Homer and Vergil, for example, or Lévi-Strauss's transcriptions of Amerindian myths, that the narratives not only tell a story but create a closed, self-sustaining argument. Aphorism itself is a kind of ultra-significance. Language pulls us to literalness and facticity even as it flounders in reference; the human condition and the awareness of time bring us to the realization of questions we cannot answer. The impossibility of ever really solving this tension is temporarily banished by the workable fiction, the reasonable and energetic effort to think a compromise through. But such fictions have no hope of surviving unless they encourage further effort by their internal logic.

So it would seem that even in trying to formulate the preliminaries for a definition of the sacredness of myth, one must still argue for myth as a reasonable structure rather than a repeatable motif, however much it reaches for the ineffable. If we assume that the origins for myth are in the unconscious or in a "unity of human reason," we do not have to prove the rationality of mind or its irrationality to agree with Lévi-Strauss that mythological tales, whether they have only a few variants or are quite ubiquitous, attempt to show that they are self-sustaining. What can be more sacred than absolute self-containedness, a condition that is hoped for in the excessive speech of myths? Myths must make continual but arbitrary reference to the real world and that is our stimulus to see in myth something more than a glib scientism. Like fictions, they have a matter-of-factness, even when the implications are quite supernatural. But they attempt to recover the numinous as a logical possibility in closed plots which are solutions to compromise. Myths can only use events and objects which already have meaning, so they are self-consciously metalanguage, but they argue over and over again that metaphor for the real (which is nothing less than the overriding reality of metaphor) has implications beyond the empirical.

Even as they can aim for their sense of the sacred through ultra-signification, myths are transparent and duplicitous. Men make myths intentionally, but once made, myths have a life of their own in their collective and individual function. If we live with them, and they demand we do, they try to immobilize us, to become prototypes in the imagination. Only the moment we take them seriously and start to believe in them, they either weaken, or they take over other events and force us to argue further with them, sometimes totally inverting the original proposition. Furthermore, this appropriation is not reserved for supernatural events alone nor for those metaphysical questions which are so large as to seem meaningless. Myth does not shy away from the unanswerable, but it has a devious way of making everything seem appropriate to questioning and available to closure and to the numinous. Therefore, it is intimately related to art as the most symbolist of all *bricolages*. Dragons, teeth, and lameness all have something to do with Oedipus' plight. And soap, liver, lotus flowers, nose-picking and chamber pots have everything to do with Joyce's *Ulysses*.

APHORISM, OEDIPUS, AND DECONSTRUCTION

How does this intention to say it all inform structure? The more we examine the numerous arguments for the nature of the mythic form (Functionalist, Archetypalist, Structuralist, and so on), the more it appears that myths are doomed to feed on their own terms. Yet, that is perhaps their main attraction: they are an embodiment of the hermeneutic circle. One of the things we know about myths—whether we believe they function in binaries or not—is that they attempt to close the semiological gap and aspire to be tautologous. They have been believed in and used; they are locations of infinite metaphorical play trying to solve the social, sexual, and psychological compromises which create our civilized nature. But we still do not know exactly why their terms are chosen or if perhaps they choose themselves. The events of their fantastic plots engage us, not simply because they are exaggerated, but because they are so arbitrary, matter-of-fact, and self-contained, and we are not. In effect, what we engage in any myth is a persistent existential crisis and the allegorical neatness of the solution.

Here is a familiar example. We know that the Oedipus story, thanks to Greek Drama, Freud, and more recently, Claude Lévi-Strauss, is an important myth, telling us something about incest taboo, sexual identity crisis, kinship structures, and above all, suggests Lévi-Strauss, human origins. When society holds the belief that we originate from one, implicitly from "out of the earth" or nature itself, then the belief exhibits itself in a myth which attempts to reconcile that origin with the more tangible evidence that we are born out of the union of men and women. In this case, the myth creates a self-conscious contradiction between superstition and empirical evidence even as it makes a metaphorical fusion between the two. Beyond Freud's obsession with the psychological determinism of the story lies an even more persistent problem of deciding how the race came to be and of deciding, in effect, how far reasoning can take us with that question. The story of the man who unwittingly kills his father, slays the sphinx, marries his mother as a reward, and dooms his sons to fratricide and his daughters to murder is more than a cautionary tale, or a repository of archetypal behavior, or a set of binary oppositions. Behind the fatalism of the incest taboo lies the whole question of why there is such a taboo at all. Where do we originally come from and how can our sexual conventions be justified? Lévi-Strauss makes it clear that, in his interpretation, the difference between nature and culture, and the possibility of their symbolic exchange, is dependent on the mystery of the incest taboo, that ultimate law of difference. Its exact origin remains magical even if it gives rise to elaborate kinship structures.

As we have seen, Lévi-Strauss's controversial interpretation of the Oedipus story emphasizes the division of the plot into its mythemic or aphoristic units (for example, the founding of Thebes by Cadmus, the killing of the dragon, the planting of the teeth, the birth of the Theban race, Oedipus' actions, the suicide of Jocasta) and their contrasting implications (patricide / fratricide, rape of sister / rape of mother, death of dragon / death of sphinx, and so on). All these elements, and the rest too numerous to elaborate on here, are in a highly arbitrary relationship deriving from the incest law. In fact, the problematic nature of myth becomes clear when we ask why sex is somehow connected to chthonian beings born lame in Thebes. Or, what is the relationship between Jocasta's suicide and the deaths of her daughters Antigone and Ismene? There are no final answers to these questions and all the other issues of the plot, though we suspect they are related. The incidents may be systematized, but the problem which the myth dramatizes, related to the origin of incest, kinship, and teleology, cannot be solved, and the myth is conscious of this. Instead, what it provides in the plot is a kind of "logical tool which relates the original problem—born from one or born from two?—to the derivative problem: born from different or born from the same?"[10] In myth we find problem begetting problem in a repetitive way. Oedipus, for example, denies his origin (by sleeping with his mother and by killing the chthonian sphinx), which seems an unconscious act on his part but can also be said to result from his failure to reconcile superstition to fact, fate to freedom of will, nature to the supernatural. But the myth cannot end there with that statement, nor can it go "back" to a pristine moment when this reconciliation did take place. For it is plain that, although experience contradicts superstition, it can never remove the thinking that leads to superstition. It can also never avoid the fact that it depends on metaphorical language, which is itself unable to contain its own origin, and thereby breeds superstition.

I do not want to raise the much debated issue of whether Lévi-Strauss's four-column vertical and horizontal reading of the plot fragments is adequate, since it is not his actual methodology that is of interest here, but only the implication that no matter what model we use to analyze a myth, we can only find a contradiction and an oblique, arbitrary structure which confounds any simple solution and in fact raises our whole need to be superstitious even while we try not to be. What is evident from the Oedipus story is that the line of logic which argues for our sexual origin ironically works alongside the line of logic which argues for our supernatural origin. These apparently contradictory arguments are structurally related. Each is a *bricolage* of fact which refuses to consider any references outside its own system, and each possibility is coherent in its argument for cause and effect. What is missing is a unified consciousness arranging these facts. So again, although experience contradicts cosmology and the supernatural, the myth proves, as Lévi-Strauss points out, that we can still argue for the supernatural as a logical possibility. Although each set of terms (natural and supernatural) is self-sufficient, it is impossible for them to remain that way. Whatever the problem dramatized in a particular myth—kinship, the relationship of man to the Gods, the origin of fire, and so on—it is always the problem of superstition and teleological need in conflict with experience which is somehow the real subject of the myth.

In other words, there is a logical intention in myth to fill the gap with signs, to explain the origin of its own terms, apparently arbitrarily chosen, and then to reach for an answer to the problem of reconciling origins with the present, word with meaning. The fact that myth uses terms which are current and at hand—items from nature, society, other legends, and so on—to document the logic of its own intention does not necessarily mean that the solution to a myth lies somewhere outside itself. But it does mean that myth, being after all a condition of language somewhat frustrated by its own referential talents, will at least try to find a solution to its origins symbolically, by attempting to draw a tentative conclusion from outside evidence. This open-endedness of myth leaves the Greek tale of Oedipus (as it is found in Sophocles, for example) still rather more powerful for us, perhaps, than Freud's version. For Freud seemed to want to see a clear conclusion to the Oedipus myth in the "fact" that young men are tempted to sleep with their mothers, perhaps because they want to return to the womb / earth, or because early child development through polymorphous or undifferentiated sexuality must linger past puberty. This is an attempt to close the myth through the mistaken view that one can definitely close the gap. On the other hand, Lévi-Strauss can say: "although experience contradicts theory, social life validates cosmology by its similarity of structure. Hence cosmology is true."[11] It is that condition of myth as analog which allows the Greek tale to perpetuate itself, and ironically allows Freud to substitute another structure for cosmology (in his case, metapsychology) and to reinterpret the myth to prove that that is true as well. For the power of a myth is expressed not in any literal reference, since there is no literal meaning to be found (only the myth's metonymical constituents drawn from the real world: mother, father, teeth, lameness, other myths, etc.), but in the open-ended repetitiveness of the relationships it creates between items.

Myths tend to look alike because of this talent for substitution and not because they declare the superiority of the supernatural. Not every reference to the supernatural is a myth, but the supernatural remains one of the mythical possibilities. If we accept that myth comes to us above all as language, as plot and narrative, then we can locate the motive for myth in the conditions of language itself, and especially in the fact that language is a system of substitutions allowing the indefinite play of signification and the possibility of proving how inevitable are "superstitious" thought and symbolic solutions. As Jacques Derrida has observed, it is only the infinite play of the word in language which allows us to think the essence of God. This in turn relates, as I noted earlier, to the Structuralist implication that all language involves substitution in terms of equivalence (metaphor) or proximity (metonymy). And so on, into the more complex varieties of semiotic analysis, which eventually leave us with Roland Barthes' idea that if we are to be consistent in our substitution theories, then, since a myth is a system of signs, anything can be a myth which appropriates meaning through form. So Greta Garbo's face, striptease, the futuristic Citroen, and steak and chips are also myths.

I said earlier that the semiotic position does have a problem of expository tact but that the theory is still central to our understanding of myth since it concerns itself with the open-endedness of meaning. Then what, for example, has steak and chips got to do with the great quest for self and society through love and war and the wrath of the Gods? The question is not as ludicrous as it might seem for Joyce, for if that modern Odysseus Bloom does not eat steak and chips, he does eat pig's cheek and cabbage, kidneys and bacon with grand but humorous significance: "In liver gravy Bloom mashed mashed potatoes. Love and war some one is."[12] On every page of *Ulysses*, however deliberately comic, metonymy is contiguous with metonymy, the parallel logic of oxymoron abounds with a telling and suggestive irony: the chalice and the shaving-cup and the chamber pot; the "snot-green sea" aligns with the "sigh of leaves and waves, waiting, awaiting the fulness of their times"; the "isle of Saints" contains "Dirty Dublin"; the Christian is a "chewer of corpses"; the "old shrunken paps" produce the "milk of human kin . . . the honeymilk of Canaan's land."

Via semiotics, we can come up with endless circumstantial evidence for explanations of mythical significance. In fact, all we can ever find is circumstantial evidence, for all events with meaning reveal an arbitrary relationship between the event and its meaning. Aphorism itself is born of that, and myth is nothing if it does not aim to be an aphorism even while it knows it cannot. A myth has an arbitrary beginning in the world of signs, a fact it never lets us forget although it has high ontological hopes and lures us into intricate explanations of experience. It is precisely that metonymical arbitrariness of a myth, the implication that it is only a function of the real, an analog by substitution, which ironically is what justifies its reference to the supernatural and guarantees its transformation into other myths, or versions of the same myth. No mythic narrative can be said to have a necessary beginning—an ontological simplification by us as readers—for then the anxiety of human thinking can be resolved in some fixity of form, some paradigm for reality. Such clear beginnings, middles, and ends cannot be determined in mythic plots, for myth aims to express the continuity of human thought amid the discontinuity of meaning. Where, after all, is the true beginning and end of the Theban race in the Oedipus story? Stages in a mythic plot are mainly ironic signposts to temporary closures, to pauses that only anticipate further compromise, so transformational is the nature of a powerful myth.

Yet this want of a definitive origin for myth outside itself—though many have claimed to have found it—has not stopped myth from achieving for us, especially in its powerful classical tradition, a certain superstitious sense of security. The irony is that we too often forget that myth is a structural network, a value system even, but not an absolute truth. It is concerned with the very nature of ontological questioning and the anxiety implicit in human reasoning, but not with final answers. For again, there is no absolute beginning, middle, or end to myth except in a very self-consciously symbolic way, or else we would not be able to retell the tale of Ulysses, Aeneas, and so on, in fiction. The apparently closed plot of myths, the inflexible will of the Gods, are deliberately paradigmatic and therefore heavily ironic. So the world of mythology is a rationalized, logical world, yet it is one which involves a questioning of rationality itself. It offers an allegorical explanation which by its very starkness can only have the effect of pushing us beyond the tangible to the possibility that a particular narrative is providing us with reasons for saying that there is something beyond language responsible for how the human mind and body work, and how culture makes its exchanges with nature. We identify in myth, not with specific characters, even if psychoanalysis or wish fulfillment might push us to see ourselves as an Oedipus, or a Ulysses, or an Aeneas. Usually the deeds of the Gods and mortals with the attributes of Gods and access to magic are too distant from us for that kind of sympathy. Rather we link up with their circumstantial tact and compromising equations, with their aphoristic and vicarious solutions to human compromise. In myth we enter the therapeutic of sheer inventiveness.

Myths are not only arbitrary, they can be long-winded as if in justification of their uncertain beginnings. They strain our logic in that way too. They have a habit of taking the oblique way round in their explanation, like Ulysses' tour of the Islands. They self-consciously nurture their own imaginativeness. If the mythic model, as I have been arguing, is troublesome in its ontological status, its function is relatively easy to describe if not explain away: it is tied to language as endless metaphor; it operates as a language ritual; it plays an exemplary role for the imagination; it has its own self-contained systems and, above all, it is an explanation we would rather not do without because it reveals the very importance of human reason as a means to find answers to impossible questions. Myth, that is, cannot help but substitute the supernatural for the empirical even as it is a constant reminder of our human failure to understand why we should need to do this at all. Even if we do not take translinguistic fact as an *a priori* to myth, a ghost still emerges from the mythical machine, for we cannot conceive of myth and its ambitious answers without creating an ontological crisis, implicating religion and talk about God as the One or the Many, and without introducing some concept of a hoped-for transcendence of mythic function, beyond ordinary language, which allows the unanswerable to be answered.

My point has been that the tension between an event which is the subject of compromise and the explanation of that compromise is preserved in myth. Cosmology is one of the substitutive structures, and the ineffable may even be the teleological end of myth as well as its vague beginning "before language." But again, we have to keep contact with the linguisticality of the narrative and a theory of imagination, without which there is no myth at all. It is most unwise to forget that it is humans who make myths and not the Gods. Even though we cannot escape the sense that ontological questioning has always sanctioned myth, still we know that it is a very down-to-earth human wisdom, methodical yet unstable, which has attempted to discover essential meaning. Clearly, under the influence of mythology attempting to say it all, we are condemned to speak excessively and hopelessly about reality and even to continue to attempt to discover the numinous: a fact which I think writers like Yeats, Pound, Eliot, Joyce, and Lawrence understood from their fascination with ancient, classical, and (in Lawrence's case) totemistic myth. The modern paradox, as I have quoted earlier, is clear: "if we penetrate the object, we liberate it but we destroy it; and if we acknowledge its full weight, we respect it, but we restore it to a state which is still mystified." The paradox of myth is the semiological one. Myth is metalanguage, yet it cannot help but be Oedipal and propose questions of origin. It is a second-order system which constantly intends to get back to primary order. But the fact remains that unless we are prepared to accept the "primitive wonder world" of the unconscious as proven, then all we can guarantee about myth is that it will remain discourse among men, intending to make the most careful of attempts to fill the gap between event and meaning and to create a universal opportunity for interpretation which does not deny the supernatural.

Whether, like Levy-Bruhl, we try to show that myth is the

result of the "primitive intelligence" or, like Lévi-Strauss, that it can only refer to the unity of human reason, we are still none the wiser (as Lévi-Strauss has made clear for his own thesis) as to what that unity really is; for we live in a world of fundamental discontinuity of reference "solved" only in tautology. What always remains is the fact that the human mind pursues a course of proving itself to be reasonable and tautologous—as Lévi-Strauss insists it does in myth—but its failures to prove the mind's self-sufficiency and close the gap creates also cosmological structures. Myth may exist in response to some condition outside the linguistic event, but so arbitrary are the details of that condition that a myth can only hope to show that there is a similar structure between cosmology and social life. The aphorism of myth is not really an aphorism at all, for it is always a compromise generated by the semiotic function of its own terms. It does not matter what terms are chosen, for all will reveal the arbitrary relationship between signifier and signified.

With this problem of the sacredness of myth as a linguistic issue have we reached a point where literary theory fears to tread? A common criticism of Structuralist theory, for example, is that it can tell us what a work of art looks like, and can even lay down the limits to understanding imposed by language, but it cannot tell us what a text means, let alone how language can be said to refer to the numinous. Since this seems to be a serious criticism, I have been making the argument throughout the study that without incorporating an active interpretation theory, a hermeneutical exercise of the imagination, into structural analysis, the latter will swiftly return us to mere formalism. There is no strain in linking a theory of reading with a theory of structure. Form itself demands interpretation by forcing on us its own absence of meaning: the elusiveness and relativity of its signification. This, we have seen, is especially apparent in the form of myth, where the dialectical and ironic patterns of recovery which a plot makes to reach a resolution of its terms serve to heighten its intent to acquire meaning. Not only can the gap between structure and meaning create endless progress, but the Structuralist enterprise, especially in anthropological and literary studies, becomes the science of analyzing and interpreting discourse in order to fill that gap and supplement the text: it is analysis *for* as much as analysis *of*. It is supplementary mythic activity. Paul Ricoeur has suggested this function: "Structural analysis does not exclude, but presupposes, the opposite hypothesis concerning myth, i.e., that it has meaning as a narrative of origins. Structural analysis merely represses this function. But it cannot suppress it. The myth would not even function as a logical operator if the propositions that it combines did not point towards boundary situations. Structural analysis, far from getting rid of this radical questioning, restores it at a higher level of radicality."[13]

The "boundary situation" is both inside and outside discourse. Within the text we can recede to the point where we never lose sight of the arbitrary nature of the sign and the systematic opposition of elements in mythemes / sentences. But all the inversions, negations, and protean forms that metaphor makes in trying to bridge the gap between signifier and signified make sense only by playing out that drama in real life. The semiological gap is available only from the experience of living in the world and trying to understand it. It is the task of interpretation theory then to make sure that Structuralism never becomes inhuman, overtheoretical, and positivist— never simply an end in itself, but posing its own demand for the recovery of existential reference. On the other hand, the endless oppositions to be found in experience: of life and death, nature and culture, intention and reality, and so on, do not acquire meaning for us without the logical function of myth and art. The opposites need a mediation which never loses sight of their arbitrariness of presence. Thus the hermeneutical interests of Structuralism and post-Structuralism are unavoidable.

But no matter how clearly we can show that myths validate cosmology, still we have not explained away, nor do we want to presume to explain away, the sense of the sacred and the numinous, those ontological yearnings which drive mythology on and sustain religious belief. A reference to language in order to find God in the play of significance need not be incompatible with the Structuralist argument. This has become more theoretically valid perhaps as Saussure's assertion that word and thing are never univocal has infiltrated contemporary literary thought, along with Heidegger's attempt to free language from the notion of the fixed origin. So talk about God is hermeneutical talk in which "God" is inscribed in the question, and the meaning of "God" only makes sense in terms of the difficulty of the hermeneutical exercise required to describe the concept. Then one is especially led today to Jacques Derrida's thoroughgoing work on "deconstructing the transcendental signified."[14] To treat the sacred with a certain semiotic profanity, it can be said that the sign—in Derrida's terms—is the location of essential difference between "the other of the signified" and the "subtly discrepant inverse or parallel . . . of the order of the signifier." The implications of this for myth studies I have already suggested in the first chapter, and again, as we approach the central problem of myth and the sacred, it should seem of undiminished importance. We have been fascinated since the Symbolist aesthetic by the fact that the possibility or the impossibility of writing lies in the hypothetical fusion of signifier and signified, a "unity of language throughout time." The essential meaning modern literature has sought since Mallarmé spoke of the orphic function of art is of this order. But for that intimate revelation to be meaningful, the sacred must appear unbearably appropriative and demand not simply endless paradigms (after Eliade, Malinowski), or endless synonym (Otto), but the very removal of itself from its hypothetical origin: the split in the sign. That is, like myth itself, the sacred may depend on the fact of metonymy, but for it to be known, it can never be other than elusive metaphor. Derrida:

> What is intolerable and fascinating is indeed the intimacy intertwining image and thing . . . to the point where by

a mirroring, inverting, and perverting effect, speech seems in its turn the speculum of writing, which "manages to usurp the main role." Representation mingles with what it represents to the point where one speaks as one writes, one thinks as if the represented were nothing more than the shadow or reflection of the representer. A dangerous promiscuity and a nefarious complicity between the reflection and the reflected which lets itself be seduced narcissistically. In this play of representation, the point of origin becomes ungraspable. There are things like reflecting pools, and images, an infinite reference from one to the other, but no longer a source, a spring. There is no longer a simple origin. For what is reflected is split *in itself* and not only as an addition to itself of its image. The reflection, the image, the double, splits what it doubles. The origin of the speculation becomes a difference. What can look at itself is not one; and the law of addition of the origin to its representation, of the thing to its image, is that one plus one makes at least three. The historical usurpation and theoretical oddity that install the image within the rights of reality are determined as the *forgetting* of a simple origin.[15]

The existential return to writing by myth as it appropriates modern fiction and poetry emphasizes that the mythicity of myth is conditioned by this split in the word. Words mean in their absence of meaning. And being cannot precede existence; it can only be, as Derrida puts it, "Being-of." But at the same time language, in asserting Being, defaces / erases it at once even as it cannot help leaving a residue for interpretation. So the transcendental signified never exists outside a system of differences, and "God" becomes either the residue after erasure or a concept of infinite play itself, romantically preserved as one of the God-concept's necessary conditions. The most sacred words create, as Edmond Jabès has implied in *The Book of Questions* and Eliot in the *Four Quartets*, the most thoroughgoing absence of meaning: that is, the absence of

God. The Marquis de Sade has shown this inversion, on the side of profanity, for human sexuality. It makes no difference whether the intention is to be sacred or profane: the structure of the sign is determined by the split in itself, the other of discourse which it must always grasp for. This is, again, the interplay of the inside and the outside which I outlined in the first chapter. In effect, we can only find an existential meaning for the sacred in that gap between event and meaning, and in the negative knowledge which defines our intentions (which Derrida calls the "trace" of the signified). This implies that whenever the gap operates—as it always does in the intent to give meaning form—the sense of the numinous is potentially available.

We are talking, therefore, not of sensible qualities for the sacredness of myth, nor of a God of ancient or contemporary religion, but of the peculiar way in which discourse *deconstructs transcendence yet perpetuates ontology*, because a language context can never be saturated. That is, we are talking of the only way we can make the numinous intelligible, which is in language, specifically God-talk. "From the moment that there is meaning there are nothing but signs,"[16] Derrida explains. The trace represented by the signified both destroys and rebuilds ontology, but not as a metaphysics of presence. Rather, as I have been saying all along, myth is a *metaphysics of absence implicit in every sign*. The aphorism actually destroys itself. Interpretation pivots on the paradox that it is only such an absence which perpetuates meaning. This pure trace Derrida refers to as "differance":

> Although it *does not exist*, although it is never a being-present outside of all plenitude, its possibility is by rights anterior to all that one calls sign (signified / signifier, content / expression, etc.), concept or operation, motor or sensory. This differance is therefore not more sensible than intelligible and it permits the articulation of signs among themselves within the same abstract order—a phonic or graphic text for example—or between two or-

ders of expression. It permits the articulation of speech and writing—in the colloquial sense—as it founds the metaphysical opposition between the sensible and the intelligible, then between signifier and signified, expression and content, etc. If language were not already, in that sense, a writing, no derived "notation" would be possible; and the classical problem of relationships between speech and writing could not arise. . . . There cannot be a science of differance itself in its operation, as it is impossible to have a science of the origin of presence itself, that is to say, or a certain non-origin.

> Differance is therefore the formation of form. But it is *on the other hand* the being-imprinted of the imprint.[17]

The crux of our problem with myth and its relation to literature is emphasized here. We cannot simply announce that mythological or literary narratives refer to the translinguistic, for we know too much about their existence as sign systems. And, as I have already noted, to say that the "holy" is merely aphoristic or tautologous does not help much either. What is indeed a metaphysics of absence is available only in the coming-into-being (imprinting) of this absence which is nothing less than the existential act of writing:

> . . . it should be recognized that it is in the specific zone of this imprint and this trace, in the temporalization of a *lived experience* which is neither *in* the world nor *in* "another world," which is not more sonorous than luminous, not more *in* time than *in* space, that differences appear among the elements or rather produce them, make them emerge as such and constitute the *texts*, the chains, and the systems of traces. These chains and systems cannot be outlined except in the fabric of this trace or imprint.[18]

This brings us to the question, "How is the numinous interpretable in literature?" with the answer largely implied.

The sacredness of myth is a condition of discourse, an aspect of our awe at language overwhelming its referent yet never quite capturing it. But how do we define this intentionality as a general condition in literature? In the same way as with myth. Again, we return to our familiarly elusive "origin." What a text means to say depends above all on our obsession with the discontinuity of experience and the necessity for rescuing meaning from its absence. This works with telling irony in art, as we saw in the case of James Joyce. The disjunction between subject and object must drive the writer to a hermeneutics of literary discourse: the gap is enforced anew between the writer's mind and the writer's words, between words and meaning, between meaning and understanding, and so on. The prospects, not surprisingly, must be regarded with a degree of pessimism. To inhabit the gap necessitates, first of all (as with Joyce), our acceptance of the need to find the originary metaphor, which is no particular figure but metaphor itself. To inhabit the gap is in large part an essentially irrational act which the writer struggles to rationalize through experiment, by moving on from one way of filling the space to another. For to dwell reflectively on one is to realize the necessity of the next. This may indeed lead us to despise the so-called sacred moment and return us to a "pragmatic charter," and this is partly true for Joyce's Stephen. But then he ironically proceeds to discover a distinctly religious theory of literature, moving from one epiphany to the next, trusting entirely in the aesthetic of *consonantia, integritas,* and *claritas,* which he learns from the Jesuits. But Stephen is not so foolish as to force experience into this mold. The numinous for Stephen, as we have seen, is a condition of not-knowing, of trusting in the clear metonymy of fact, and of allowing the world to fall into place. And this too, as we shall see, is the case with T. S. Eliot.

The intent to deal with the essential in literature must, then, reveal this trust in anecdotal relations. But of course literary intention is never simply what the words say but is also related to the preunderstanding of the reader: it is made, that is, by reader and writer, which leads us back again to language. Intention cannot be made clear unless there are spaces for both reader and writer to occupy, and for that reason, the sense of the sacred is engaged by the starkness of aphorism and sharply compromising juxtapositions, by indulgence in the process of forming impossible links as myth has shown the modern can do. The sacred, we insist, must be interpretable. It relies not on taking the word of the writer as truth, nor on any fusion between word and thing. It does not involve any simple one-directional shift from poet's awe to poet's words, or poet's words to reader's mind. Rather it is an arbitrarily reversible process: a dialectic in which foreknowledge is confirmed or altered, seeking totality or synthesis. The uniqueness of poet, poem, and reader is retained, while meaning becomes possible only as a mediation between each. Any sense of unity between them depends on mutual acceptance of the ontological limitations of writing itself.

What I am saying is that given the temporal gap between event and meaning, the sacredness of myth and the numinousness of the literary work are potentially one, and then not as a matter of infinitist metaphysics, but as the result of a very existential grasp of what can be said in and of writing, as well as what cannot. It is a transformational event, as Stephen learns from the epiphany. It is not an abstract point, but a living principle, dependent on the phenomenological fact that the world is what we perceive—not an idea, but an event which is lived through. Stories about our sacred origins are above all explanations of what takes place in the gaps between events and meaning.

RECOVERING THE NUMINOUS:
D. H. LAWRENCE AND
T. S. ELIOT

The novel is the highest form of human experience so
far attained. Why? Because it is so incapable of the absolute.
—D. H. Lawrence, "The Novel"[1]

We have a mental habit which makes it much easier for
us to explain the miraculous in natural terms than to
explain the natural in miraculous; yet the latter is as
necessary as the former.
—T. S. Eliot,
"Virgil and the Christian World"[2]

ALLEGORIES OF INTENT

From opposing ideological positions—familiarly translated as
vitalist-theosophical on the one hand and orthodox Anglo-
Catholic on the other—D. H. Lawrence and T. S. Eliot have
been considered important in our modern tradition for their
effort to reinstate some connection between religion and art
in a literature aggressively shorn of religious thought. If we
think of early twentieth-century writing as occasionally turning to some prescription for spiritual health, then we do think
of Lawrence and Eliot. But what prescriptiveness there is—
and it is perhaps less pronounced than criticism would have
it—is not the affinity between these two writers that I want
to emphasize. Their modernist sensibilities are clearly different, and their plans for salvation often contradictory. Yet they
are prepared to make writing, however paradoxical it is as an

activity, the ground for a persistent attempt to confront trans-linguistic fact, even to the extent that reaching the unspeakable becomes the primary object of writing itself. Their religious interests are less a matter of devotion than of developing (in contrasting ways) an interpretative medium which aims to rediscover the nature of the mythic and the numinous as the motive for the literary experience.

We know that this motive provides a very serious and complex mandate for art, going beyond specifically ideological terms in any sense of a faith behind the text—although both Lawrence and Eliot grapple with ideology—to an extraordinary faith in the therapeutic act of writing itself. The meeting point for Lawrence's and Eliot's literary versions of the mythic lies not in any agreement on what "the religious" is objectively—there is no chance of the chapel congregationalist meeting the baroque Anglo-Catholic—but in their mutual acceptance of writing as the process of recovering what Rudolf Otto first called the "numinous consciousness." For Lawrence and Eliot, literature is an interpretative act which intends to deal with questions which cannot be answered. It is this intentionally self-conscious factor which is important, an intent which drives writing to fold in on itself as it pursues the impossible task of proving its self-sufficiency. If there is essential meaning available somewhere in art, then Lawrence and Eliot believe that it can only be the result of making literature a hermeneutic exercise. They are conscious that in writing it is not possible to ask questions about meaning without eventually questioning the literary question itself, and the means of asking the question. For Eliot especially, an endless circularity awaits the writer, allowing words only to be experimented with and reconstituted over and over again, in the face of uncertainty over all hypotheses of fact, numinous or otherwise.

Now there is nothing new for the modern about writing as a secular hermeneutical exercise, but the question of how this can preserve the link between religion and art in modern literature without resorting to devotional clichés remains very real for Lawrence and Eliot. All writing has to give form to meaning in order to justify even temporarily the need for fact, and writing with a religious motive especially finds that a problematic matter. Not only is the condition of the numinous highly controversial, but the intention to recover it is a defensive undertaking. This is revealed in some conventional gestures from Lawrence and Eliot. Both at times attempt to re-create the arcane text. One thinks immediately of moments of ideological indulgence in Eliot's "Ash Wednesday" and *Four Quartets*, and Lawrence's *Apocalypse* and metaphysical essays like "The Crown" and "The Reality of Peace." Furthermore, they sometimes argue with a quite obvious utopian intent, as with Lawrence's physiocracy and heterosexual love ethic, and Eliot's post-Conversion euphoria, especially at the end of *Four Quartets*. But they also are both very much aware that there can be no such thing as an "unmediated vision," for all must be mediated in discourse and live on particulars in the everyday world. The visionary text gains authority only because a relatively confident existential center to the "numinous consciousness" can be established by the writer. However much this center shifts in and out of focus, it must appear to be constituted by the text and be justified only by the text. Writing becomes a way of diagramming teleological yearning, of presenting its phenomenology. Lawrence and Eliot emphasize, I will make a point of showing, that one cannot discuss myth, religion, and literature without in some way dealing with the primacy of language: its inevitable deconstruction of fact and its talents for substitution in order to mediate vision. Their respective world views offer up an attempt to show that the moment of illumination is discoverable in the effort of discourse to give meaning to form.

I have put this simply, without repeating the phenomenology of absence or presence as outlined in the first chapter, which may now be seen not simply as an *a priori* to reading or even as an unconscious condition of writing, but as something the text may itself create as a theme. Let me begin, though, by offering generalizations about those themes before showing how they may be found in the work of Lawrence and Eliot. Perhaps it is reactionary, indeed, to attempt to do so by returning to Eliot's Anglo-Catholicism, or by referring to Lawrence's "religion of the blood." But it is not necessary to treat either of these ideologies solemnly or literally in order to show the peculiar relation of writing to religious and mythical intentions. Again, we must acknowledge that the strain of writing from and for revelation in Lawrence and Eliot occasionally gives way to ideological arrogance, which exhibits itself in a fixity of religious paradigms, a refusal to let substitution go on, as in Lawrence's "leadership" theory (in *Kangaroo, Aaron's Rod,* and *The Plumed Serpent*) with all its totemistic revivalism. It is found, too, in the mystifying determinism of his discussions of the relationships between men and women in the essays on love, education, aristocracy, and democracy. On Eliot's part, we find a solemnity of tone touching on conceit which "justifies" the writer as Christian, and society's values as the same (in essays like "Virgil and the Christian World"), together with the assumption (which is implicit in the short prayers of *Four Quartets,* the litanies of "Ash Wednesday," and the Choruses from "The Rock") that prayer is axiomatically poetry. And we cannot forget that there are more than casual hints in both Lawrence's and Eliot's works that the Christian world view can lead to anti-Semitism and clearly authoritarian gesturing, as they are carried away by the "preach," as Lawrence called it, of what writing and society should be like.

But the perjorative aspects of Lawrence's and Eliot's beliefs have been well covered in recent years,[3] and do not bear repetition in these notes. They do not necessarily follow from the writers' awareness of the self-consciously linguistic conditions of their writing. So, in discussing their religious motives and their self-consciousness over religious values in writing, one must concentrate on their general intent to locate the essential in language as its own theme. If poetry is created out of the felt tension between something signifying and something signified, which strains to express some dominant significance and locate the emblematic and the significant cluster of facts, then Lawrence and Eliot accept this as a profession of strain necessary to define any meaning at all. Furthermore, whereas Joyce is fascinated with the displaced narrative structures of myth, with the unbridgeable nature of the gap between signifier and sign, for Lawrence and Eliot there is a hoped-for ontological equivalence between the language event and the states of consciousness and feelings which produce it. Writing takes place literally with the hope of producing the unproducible text. Lawrence's theory of the novel as "the one bright book of life," as the place where all human motives and actions can be dramatized amid the flux of living without disturbing that fluidity, moves toward keeping art as an essential category of reality. The novel for Lawrence must become Bible. Eliot, too, is directly concerned with the numinous in his use of the "objective correlative," which slowly moves from its attachment to the object and its emotional status in the early poetry to the religious value of the sign in *Four Quartets*. This transition is revealed in the move from a constant early reliance on metonymy rather than metaphor—to the extent that poetry not only attempts to become the thing itself but the embodiment of a desire to achieve higher understanding—to a trust in metaphor. The ideological motive for both is always discourse on the character of the literary act itself, and the continuous struggle to define an authentic viewpoint on the nature of the sacred, even while the "language of the tribe" makes full authenticity impossible.

This is the self-conscious problematic of both Eliot's and Lawrence's art, even as each accepts the inevitability of that highly publicized and now secular modernist sickness, the "dissociated sensibility." Their attempt to recover the numinous consciousness begins with the conviction that the world is patterned on manichean principles, and there lies an important aspect of the mythic in the modern. Both Lawrence and Eliot have contributed much to making an awareness of that "disease" quite endemic. Lawrence constantly preached the impossible reconciliation of mind and body, and Eliot himself reinvented the phrase "dissociated sensibility" in order to emphasize the split between the man who "suffers" and the man who "creates." Ironically, their idea of a cure has often seemed from a contemporary perspective to take a superstitious line of defense: an attempt to rework Christian belief, an unscientific awe of metaphysical truths, a neo-Romantic wonder at nature which somehow reveals its "spirit of place" as inscrutable. We seem to go beyond the empirical to the magical in Lawrence's reverence for the holiness of sex, or Eliot's attempt to reach understanding through prayer. But it is not simply a matter of superstition breeding art. The sense of wonder at the other, and the concern that literature grapple with ultimate questions about the limits of human consciousness (again, Lawrence on the sex act, and Eliot's ascent to meaning in *Four Quartets*), have established the very modern theme of writing for a new understanding of writing's own limits, rather than a predetermined concept of God or the holy.

So, "words, after speech," as Eliot says in the *Quartets*, "reach into the silence." No matter how tangible the felt experience is in the text—the plan of the garden in "Burnt Norton," the geography of *The Waste Land*, or Lawrence's urge to locate emotional recovery or despair in specific places around the world—Lawrence and Eliot never lose a preoccupation with the extent to which writing can be pushed to establish a silence over the facts of experience. What is the message of the bird in the garden in "Burnt Norton"? What is the significance of "our exile" in "Ash Wednesday"? Can the Waste Land really produce life and not only "the peace which passeth understanding"? What is the "tremulation on the ether" which Lawrence finds in the spirit of every place?

Thus the question of a writer's inarticulateness arises—less a question, than a given fact. It lies not only in the failure of words to capture the ineffable, but also in knowing what cannot be said but must still be attempted. Throughout *Four Quartets*, for example, Eliot reiterates that writing can never be complete, that a negative knowledge dominates. What it does is establish the individual consciousness—feelings and language—in tantalizing uncertainty:

> . . . a raid on the inarticulate
> With shappy equipment always deteriorating
> In the general mess of imprecision of feeling.[4]

This Eliot had earlier only smiled at as Prufrock's mock-heroic crisis, before the poet came to East Coker. And Lawrence's main characters are obsessed by such inarticulateness after passing through mysterious psychosomatic illnesses, dark periods of self-awareness which somehow refine their garrulousness. " 'You can't go away,' " says Birkin in frustration with himself and Ursula, stoning the reflection of the moon in *Women in Love*. " 'There *is* no away. You only withdraw upon yourself.' "[5] The withdrawal from speech had already reached a significantly oblique expression in Birkin's neo-Platonism, his stumbling explanation to Ursula earlier that emotions urge us to go beyond language and social references, to accept the unspeakable pleasures of love as an abstraction: "There is . . . a final me which is stark and impersonal and beyond responsibility. So there is a final you. And it is there I would want to meet you—not in the emotional, loving plane—but there beyond, where there is no speech and no terms of agreement."[6]

The effort to come into consciousness, then, which must alone define the numinous, for there is no other starting place, presupposes a radical introversion through writing which Lawrence and Eliot take pains to account for: Lawrence in the earnest, probing argument between his major characters, Eliot in the earnest ratiocination of his poetry. Despairingly, the introversion must reach abstraction, which the writer then tries to undercut. There is a constant strain for articulation in both these writers, out of the "void" which they acknowledge establishes consciousness. Their pressure to enforce a metaphysics of their own presence amidst the absence of certainty about what can be known is continual. It is always the circular path of speech, passing through silence and meeting continually the erasure of metaphysics in writing which defines their efforts. There is an understandable uncertainty over that whole process which is quite clearly announced. Birkin does learn that he cannot really go "beyond speech," and struggles to find Ursula "enough." Lou Witt is left in self-chosen exile away from people. Mellors finds everyday speech inadequate to express sexual feelings. And there is, of course, Eliot's "knowledge of words, and ignorance of the Word":

> . . . a limited value
> In the knowledge derived from experience.
> The knowledge imposes pattern, and falsifies
> For the pattern is new in every moment.[7]

Is there any question, then, that the effort by these two writers to come into understanding of fact, let alone numinous fact, reveals their insistence on some disjunction in the beginnings of individual consciousness, and the continuing failure to unify it? There is but a short step from the awareness of this as a problem inherent in language itself to diagrams for the split of consciousness in literature. Behind the text, forming each attempt at completing knowledge, yet condemning it to incompletion, lies the belief that no constant center can be found from which the writer may perform, nor any means of assuring himself of appropriate form for the meaning he intends to express. The chance of ever filling the void of consciousness is tragically kept from us, ironically by the very act of writing itself which can find a center only to lose it:

> There is only the fight to recover what has been lost
> And found and lost again and again: and now under
>   conditions
> That seem unpropitious. But perhaps neither gain nor
>   loss.
> For us, there is only the trying. The rest is not our
>   business.[8]

Lawrence's vitalist teleology attempts to locate understanding, even with a utopian intent, in unconscious motive, which is in its fullness absent from consciousness: "the bringing of life into human consciousness is not an aim in itself, it is only a necessary condition of the progress of life itself. Man is himself the vivid body of life, rolling glimmering against the void. In his fullest living he does not know what he does; his mind, his consciousness, unacquaint, hovers behind, full of extraneous gleams and glances, and altogether devoid of knowledge."⁹

To express the inexpressible, then, is to begin with a major paradox: the intent to be persistently articulate about essential things leads only to the loss of a center from which one begins. The conscious act of creating the text begins from negative knowledge, and always keeps in full view an inevitable incompletion: the circling of fact from silence to silence through a clamor of possible meaning. Discourse is always a no-man's land between the void of consciousness and the imaginary fullness of desire. Both Lawrence and Eliot are very much aware of having to write their way out of this uncertain position, and thereby begin to take on the mythical conditions of language. For each writer, the transition from the isolation of natural signs (the events prompting understanding in both the external world and feeling states) to symbolic representation is constantly watched and evaluated, tested especially for sentimentality and imprecision. Lawrence's frequent rewriting of his novels, and Eliot's close refinement of every word, may appear to have achieved quite separate results, but the intent of their refinements is much the same. Lawrence's honesty in documenting the rhythms of despair and euphoria at times seems simply repetitious, but he emphasizes that discovery only takes places through repeated acts of writing. Eliot, especially in *Four Quartets*, is equally vulnerable, pointing the way with doubt and humility as to the validity of his own questioning and his ability to make metaphor.

Yet the rhetorical persistence of these writers with the question of the sacred reveals their effort to be unequivocal about the kind of knowledge that demands equivocation. They are aware of the exhaustion of language (as in Lawrence's almost paranoid skepticism over the word "love" and Eliot's attempt to find the right vocabulary for the poetic statement about transcendence), yet they persist in exhausting it. Art-activity may be the business of giving form to the meaning of events, but in purely athletic terms, that requires a constant reengagement of writer with sign, such as Lawrence trying to find a vocabulary for the ineffable in sex in novel after novel, or to prove that he might yet locate the "New World." Or there is Eliot, trying to acquire just a touch of sainthood as poet explaining the Incarnation. The paradoxical status of all discourse is sharply obvious to Lawrence as he insists that, although the pleasures of the body are not to be cerebralized, there is no good sex until the "mind has caught up with the body." And Eliot constantly returns to the rational, argumentative effort in the *Quartets*, as a means of bypassing the vagueness of faith.

What is implied is that the sense of the numinous in experience may be the dramatic alternative to the void of consciousness for the writer, but any statement about that begins in paradox, and its achievement depends on not demanding the complete removal of the void, and on not allowing easily the euphoria of transcendence, but on arguing with a certain rational effort. Anna must pull Will down as he blissfully contemplates the spire in Lincoln Cathedral in *The Rainbow*; Ursula must deflate Birkin's self-serving pomposity in "Excurse" in *Women in Love*; Mellors resorts to the earthy vernacular with Connie in *Lady Chatterley* in their most intimate moments. Eliot makes constant reference throughout his poetry to historical and mythic paradigms, and to events from memory, which modify his own position and ironically deflate his overstatement. He shows even an academic familiarity with literature itself, to assure us of the reasonableness of his argument. With each author, specificity of place, impression, and close analysis are persistently part of the performance of writing in order to give their art a firm basis.

It is nothing new to say that both Lawrence and Eliot are highly conscious visionary writers: we surely need no introduction to Lawrence's Christian revisionism via Theosophy and Quetzalcoatl, or to Eliot's born-again Anglo-Catholicism. But they also know that language must fail to establish ideal presence. The recovery of the numinous, they sense, has something to do with a union of ordinary writing and extraordinary vision. Both must be rooted in the almost mundane void of the writer's starting-point. This is why I have reminded the reader of Lawrence's and Eliot's interest in the "dissociated sensibility." We may "shrink," as Wallace Stevens puts it in "The Motive for Metaphor," from "the weight of primary noon. . . . The vital, arrogant, fatal, dominant X." That shrinking, however, produces a split in consciousness to parallel the split in the sign. In short, we have to find words for that "X" in order to declare its facticity. It surely bears repeating again that, in terms of the artist's discovery of the intentional structure of writing, the void of desire, and the tortuous path of consciousness out of which the Romantics and Symbolists made the subject of their art, is no less central to modernism and no more modern with Eliot and Lawrence than it was with Wordsworth and Mallarmé. But that is a discovery of the peculiar fate of poetry (religious or otherwise) as language which must be reworked over and over again in a secular world. The "dissociated sensibility" then acquires an allegorical presence as a definition of consciousness. It is the shrinking of consciousness in writing, a negative knowledge of the self, that is the instigation for resisting the "primary noon." The poet has to be an inarticulate at heart, stripping away vision before vision can be discovered.

So allegorical forms of fiction-making in poetry or prose seem inevitable in order to create and then maintain the tension which the dissociated sensibility imposes. Lawrence, for example, constantly battled between "blood" and "mind" in the effort to "come through" into consciousness and an acceptance of sexuality as a cure for the split and distinctly Oedipal personality. Eliot insisted that art presupposes a gap between suffering and creation: the play between the two deflates Prufrock, creates the Waste Land, requires the penitence of "Ash Wednesday," and discovers the "barely pray-able" prayer of the bone "to Death its God" in "Dry Sal-vages." The agony can only give way to the resignation of the "condition of complete simplicity," if suffering and creation, the "fire" and the "rose," are seen as one, as Eliot argues they can be in "Little Gidding." In fact, where would modern lit-erary studies be without what Freud termed the "disease called man," consciousness forever reproducing itself into a crisis state to prove it is alive. No tautology survives quite so easily in modern literature and literary studies as the divided con-sciousness. That tautology preserves, ironically, the relation between religion, myth, and literature, even if only by making the recovery of the numinous an act of intending to unify consciousness. And that is inseparable from writing, which must court anxiety by its very performance. It is this kind of creative anxiety that provides the ground for the allegories of modern art, and no simple moralism can cope with that. It is, quite distinctly, an allegory of writing and reading, derived from the sharp awareness of the ontological limits of language, which is characteristic of the modern style. The dissociated sensibility is beginning and end. In order to create an unsen-timental and accurate art, it must lead us straight to the limits of sign-making through the kind of deliberately simplified drama we associate with allegory.

There are, of course, various models for "allegory," and I should explain my use of the term here as one closely tied to post-Structuralist theory. Readers of Angus Fletcher's brilliant study—*Allegory: The Theory of a Symbolic Mode*[10]—will note that he anticipates some of the more deconstructive uses of the term which are well enough known now, especially thanks to the work of allegorists of reading as different as Paul de Man and Harold Bloom. Fletcher emphasizes the his-torical development of allegory as "a figure of inversion," a term to include most forms of saying one thing and meaning another, from chivalric and picaresque romances to melo-drama and science fiction. But he notes too that allegory is always a function of the sophisticated reader, a matter, as he says, of "reading into" as well as "about." This idea that all literature is in some sense allegorical has long been a stable of literary theory, implied alike in Goethe's distinction between allegory and symbol, Coleridge's organic form, Frye's anatomy of allegorical criticism, and de Man's ideas that a text is the allegorical narrative of its own desconstruction. Of course, there are many subtle variations on the theory of allegory in the history of poetics—for which the reader is referred to Fletcher—but we do find that the term allegory is used both as a function of literary form and with reference to a psychological model of reading and writing.

There is no need for a dualistic split between the linguistic and the psychological, as I hope I have shown in my first chapter. In the same way that a union between Structuralism and interpretation theory is both desirable and necessary, so any contemporary theory of allegory cannot very easily emphasize only one of its sources in order to make its point. Either way, allegory is a metaphor of inversion. It is the subsuming trope of tropes, for it insists at once both on the self-sufficiency of its own rhetoric, and on a rhetoric dependent on interpretation. There can be no allegory without reading implied. The reader, therefore, will sense that I am returning him to the same repetitive point of the early chapters: allegory is an inescapable condition of language, namely, the figure resulting from an overdetermination of meaning in the face of language's broadly nihilistic ontology. There can be no idea expressed without metaphor, and no metaphor without allegory. So in saying that all literature is allegorical, and all reading too, we are constantly reminding ourselves of the "prison-house" which is language.

Allegory is the distinctive mode of argument of the modern, at once the expression of felt limitations to understanding and the means by which those limitations can be escaped. Nothing expresses existential despair or the ardent need to recover the mythic more clearly than the two-dimensional world of allegory. Allegory seems to offer defenses against expanding knowledge, and allows relief at our having found a world plain enough to inhabit. And all along, we know that the allegorist, at his best, is only showing us his preliminary hand, the condition in which he must invent a form of himself (because no coherence has seemed possible) where that unity will appear arbitrarily imposed. The value of allegorical argument, then, lies in both accepting and transcending literalness. In other words, allegory can stifle us and be opaque, or it can be a transparent symbol allowing transformations of its terms. But it can never escape the fact that it is the trope of doubt. It develops from the babble of suggesting too much and ends by demanding silence. No matter how transparent it becomes, the origin of writing in allegorical modes of consciousness always implies the futility of expecting to understand existence as it really is, be it Lawrence's desire for apocalypse, or Eliot's careful blending of self-control and ardent prayer.

To put it another way, the motive for allegory is the motive for myth. However richly symbolic the sign may become, it is consciously limited not so much by the incompleteness of human knowledge as by the incompleteness of the sign itself which, in turn, makes more urgent the search for numinous fact. In allegory—and I am using the term in the sense that all literature is allegorical—that daunting amalgamation of rhetoric and metaphysics which has been described throughout this study is evident. On the one hand, allegory *is* a trope, a deliberately "achieved dearth of meaning," as Harold Bloom has discussed the ideal of strong poetry.[11] But it is also, again to quote Bloom, the "oxymoron where achieved outweighs dearth." One can think of allegory, in Bloom's sense, as a legitimate "map of misreading," a "properly drastic model for creative reading and critical writing." In short, allegory insists on reading as the "troping of the trope," as Bloom has shown. So one technique of revealing the allegorical nature of literary discourse is to indulge those figures of the power of reading until trope becomes *topos*, as Bloom puts it, until the work is not merely a highly intricate metaphorical system but a "place of invention," a location of intention.

There is a certain optimism to Bloom's treatment of the

allegory of literature—albeit rather too gnomic and willful, at times—that is not shared by other readers aware of this function of the text. De Man's interpretation, for example, faithfully adheres to the Derridaean point that allegory is always allegory of metaphor, and the interpretation of a sign is not a meaning but another sign.[12] The allegory of reading is always, as he puts it, an allegory of "the impossibility of reading." The reader—true to de Man's view of man—is a metaphor "detached from the empirical in the reflective self-experience." But de Man's habit of seeking the unreadable in a text, of pointing out mutually exclusive assertions determining meaning, still bears a necessary (even if uneasy) relationship to the "promise" of reference which a text both subverts and asserts at once. It is really only Derrida himself, in a third kind of allegorical reading, who indulges, with almost sadistic pleasure, the disfiguring figuration, the seemingly limitless play of tropes without reference, which requires the circumlocutory variety of running commentary he has become so adept at in his texts and subtexts. There is, too, a fourth possibility of allegorical reading, one more faithful to impressionistic habit but nonetheless closely linked to linguistic theory—namely, the Lacanian deconstruction of the "I" of the reader / writer which I have discussed earlier. (D. H. Lawrence's texts for example, are very susceptible to the psychological maneuvers of the phallogenetic language of the self.)

But having asserted that the foundation of modern myth criticism must be tied to theories of language, psychology, and interpretation, I want to rescue some version of the allegory of intent from a theoretical nihilism. If the mythicity of language and the allegory of reading or writing have close links, then myth is surely an allegory in which reading *does* appear possible, no matter how fantastic, surreal, misread, or unreadable it obviously also is. Myth, no less than allegory, is a science of the signifier over the signified, but it is also a science countering the nihilism of the split in consciousness— even as it depends on it—by opening up value systems. The allegorical nature of the text is an aspect of the mythicity of literature, but what is needed now is a definition of allegory which gives full credit to the *topological* as well as the *tropological* contortions of narrative and poetic invention. Again, the union of structure and interpretation will take us in that direction. The allegory of reading and writing is available to us not just as a map of misreading, or initially exclusive assertions, or phallogenetic determinism, or of limitless play— though it is *all* these things. It is an allegory which, like all allegory, can disfigure for logical and inventive purposes; in a very conscious way it can reveal progressions of thought, and even an approach to the ineffable, as it appears bound by the disfiguration which every figure implies. It perhaps should not be forgotten in the modern that allegory has, in Fletcher's very subtle psychology of the term, paradoxically offered "a maximum of wish-fulfillment with a maximum of restraint." That is, it has always suggested, by its very self-conscious espousal of the limitations of reference in language, that there is a peculiar power to stories which allegorize human experience of the sacred. As Fletcher puts it, the "oldest idea about allegory" is that "it is a human reconstitution of divinely inspired messages, a revealed transcendental language which tries to preserve the remoteness of a properly veiled godhead."[13] "Veiled godheads" and "a revealed transcendence of language" are rather less appropriate now perhaps, but our more cautious efforts at examining a "revealed transcendence" in language remain relevant. So let us turn, in necessarily short and simplified terms here, and certainly without indulging all the phenomenological possibilities of allegory which I have hinted at above, to two versions of this interest in Lawrence and Eliot.

LAWRENCE'S HOLY WAR

Allegory is the mode of expressing meanings available on the borderlines of consciousness, and the allegories of reading and writing are parables for coming *into* consciousness. They have a way of suddenly making a point clear, even if by deliberately simplifying it, by somehow stylizing contradictions. The allegory of coming-into-consciousness can be both confused or tranquil, oppositional or unified. Evidence for this is readily available in the work of Lawrence and Eliot. Lawrence's allegorical roots are certainly more extensive than Eliot's, are more clearly polemical, and therefore perhaps easier to sum up. They appear to have a cosmopolitan and peripatetic history, in contrast to Eliot's restraint and Anglophilia. If the effort of all thought which sees itself as aiming to reach the essential relies on a careful interlocking of paradigmatic "life" values and logical argument, then Lawrence certainly displayed a stubbornness in trying to rationalize the sacred, to develop lived-in paradigms. In Lawrence we find both confusion and calm. The primary allegory of his writing is that the text is the body erotic, which is a source of neurotic conflict depending very much on a resolution of tension, in his terms, in erotic play. The text is the self writ large with a talent for substituting one erotic paradigm after another. His art is deliberately sensationalist in his attempt to establish his own metaphysics of presence. The body, its feelings and desires, is the metonymy underlying the metaphors for the theological and political systems which abound in his works. The movement in his thought is away from the unreadability of the world to the "precise" allegorical reference of the body in the world.

Hence the fundamentalist yet erotic nature of Lawrence's interest in the opposition between "love" and "death" never really fades from his work, from the early fabular writings on the triumph of death over love (*The White Peacock* and *The Trespasser*) to his equally fabular treatment of the triumph of love over death in *Lady Chatterley's Lover*. He never lost a fascination with the fundamentalist demands his Christian upbringing made on him, with its parallelisms and rhythmic, ritual expression. It is the music of the English Hymnal and the King James Version of the Bible that is evident in his prose, particularly in *The Rainbow*. Within that form, the faith remained stubborn too: the mystery of Trinitarian thought he also maintained in the transition from essays like "The Crown" and "The Reality of Peach" to *Apocalypse*, as he tried to secularize the Holy Ghost as the tension between "opposites," the mediator between the lion and the lamb. In other words, his is primarily a synchronic art, the offering of a hierarchy of paradigms for experience, and his sense of history is always subservient to this condition. Lawrence made this clear in *Movements in European History* and the *Studies in Classic American Literature*, where history is only made intelligible through repetitive cycles of power and the exemplary behavior of Great Men. Then, in novels like *The Plumed Serpent*, *Kangaroo*, and *Aaron's Rod*, together with the essay "Reflections on the Death of a Porcupine," he develops fictions and theory in which politically heroic uses of energy seem necessary to give social significance to the colorless flux of experience. Even his sexual aristocrats, such as they are in their uncertainty (like Birkin and Mellors), must demand something of an heroic dimension to sexual performance. Birkin for one "sat still like an Egyptian Pharoah . . . as if he were seated in immemorial potency, like the great carven statues of real Egypt." The sense of the heroic—and the mythic— is born not from an emphasis on evolution or history, but from a single-minded synchrony.

But there is more to Lawrence than an anecdotal and self-serving use of dualistic beginnings. We must look more closely at this, for it is the persistence of dualistic thinking that defines the recovery of the numinous for him. It is well known that all his expository prose reveals his attempt to reanimate thinking as an eternal struggle between polarities of meaning (light / dark, male / female, active / passive, and so on), polarization being the attempt to reassert the presence of the self. His main effort is to restore Christianity to its pagan and animistic roots, especially through the revival of totemistic knowledge, which Lawrence quite atavistically thought of as a direct communication of nature to the primitive mind (as in *The Plumed Serpent*'s Quetzalcoatlizing, *Apocalypse*'s dragons, his fascination with snake and horse totems—in *St. Mawr* and *The*

Rainbow, especially—and the constant presence in all his fiction of sexual taboos). In other words, what Lawrence wants most of all is the allegory of Christian thought in its double meaning: the Platonism of spirit and flesh. He constantly wants to get all attempts at revelation in writing back to redramatization of dualistic thought and thence to a "metaphysics" for sexual presence.

As he explains it in the metaphysical essays from "Thomas Hardy" on, he has to return to the "two halves" of the psyche, the warring spirit and flesh, the *bellum intestinum* in which, as he says in "The Reality of Peace," the lion never lies down with the lamb. The "union" in the "Holy Ghost" is at best a coming together of opposites in tension. His aim, that is, is not simply to emphasize the binaries of human thought, nor to play out the opposition of nature and culture, but to get thinking back to a real crisis point, to set the stage for apocalypse by getting us literally into a warlike state when mind conflicts with the body. Eliot may be prepared to suffer this in embarrassment—"Ridiculous the waste, sad time / Stretching before and after"—when he is not announcing his faith, offering up a prayer, tolerating a Prufrock, or entering the "interminable night" of discussion with his "familiar compound ghost." But Lawrence insists that there must be war the moment that discomfort, compromise, or contradiction occurs, a fact which is most clearly available to us in the battling between Ursula and Skrebensky, Birkin and Ursula, Gerald and Gudrun, and Harriet and Somers. Myth is atavism and violence; as if drawn only from *The Golden Bough* and *Totem and Taboo*, it returns consistently to the battle of the Sons against the Fathers, the predatory goddess against the sacrificed male.

This ancient need for a melodramatic *psychomachia* is updated for us in one of the most detailed modern expositions of the Freudian allegorical awareness (what can be more allegorical than Freud's id, superego, ego, and libido?). The Oedipal crisis, which lies behind all of Lawrence's early work up to and including *Sons and Lovers* (and some have argued for its continuance far beyond),[14] has long been taken to be the psychological key to Lawrence's allegorizing—but not with Freud's ontological pessimism. It is not seen by Lawrence as his peculiar fate but, as he said of Paul Morel, the fate of most "nice" young men in England. But he then proceeds to treat it as a myth for asserting logic as bodily and the holy as erotic, with so theosophical an interest that readers are still arguing over just how much of Freud he might have known when he wrote *Sons and Lovers*. His own Oedipal crisis is taken as the model for general experience, and as a sanction for paradigmatic thinking: that is, for neurosis as normalcy bearing out the dualistic battle we are all heir to between body and mind-centered motives. The "battle" between men and women must repeat that original crisis as an unavoidable human fact. Birkin's lengthy explanation of "star equilibrium" in *Women in Love* ("Mino"), is precisely the result of trying to retain a persistently dualistic view of male and female role-playing centered on body-mind attributes; meeting and a mingling are possible, but not a merging. It is devised by Birkin as much as a defense against Ursula's insistent "battle-cry" for "love," as it is a myth of sexual origins, proclaiming that he (Birkin and Lawrence) had found a solution to sexual anxiety.

Lawrence's insistence on restoring us to allegorical origins in the body-mind split, and his avoidance of an unearned optimism about the fate of sex, lies most clearly in what can be called his Freudian revisionism. In *Psychoanalysis* and *Fantasia*, for example, he argues against Freud's determinism of consciousness, revealing yet again the persistence of his own allegorical vocabulary of neo-Freudian terms blinded with metapsychology and Blavatskian theosophical diagrams which relate centers of energy in the body (nerve and muscle centers, that is) to "cosmic" effluences. And so on, to his espousal of apocalypticism in the last works, as we see in the Waste Land imagery of Lady Chatterley's England. To pin down exactly the sheer variety of sources and implications by which Lawrence compounds his allegorical interests (with reference to the Bible, Theosophy, Nietzsche, Schopenhauer, Herbert Spencer, Edward Carpenter, and so on) is a massive task yet to be adequately completed.[15] But surely it is readily apparent in fiction and essay that Lawrence's turn of mind was fascinated by oppositional paradigms of all kinds for the body. How else to assert the need to "fill" the "void of desire"? So he is obsessed by heroes and the heroic use of power (even though he claims to have given up "leadership theories" after *The Plumed Serpent*), and especially by *sexual* salvation myths in which various men, vulnerable and messianic (Birkin, Gerald, Kangaroo, Ramon, Mellors, Jesus himself in *The Man Who Died*), develop Lawrence's pre-Reichean belief that revelation is only given to the body free to act sexually. It is logical for Lawrence to conclude, as he does, that the numinous is recoverable primarily in the sex act, which is treated as the very model of the oppositional nature of reality, and thence of the allegory of love.

Lawrence's interest in the mythic, then, does not take shape in any persistent theories of Romantic organicism. It lies in the eternal battle between the natural and the civilized which is located very tangibly in the life of the body, that central exchange system of ideas and feelings. He argued consistently against idealist merging, or a monism of the spirit, but turned in a characteristically post-Freudian manner to the body as the source of the numinous: distinctive in opposition to other bodies. Even in his earliest essay, "Art and the Individual,"[16] he implied that writing itself is erotic, that art can unify imagination and body, can remove neurotic compromise and dramatize a freedom of thought in the sheer sensuality of its performance. And that is only part of a larger theory. In all his essays, the sexual opposition between men and women becomes the clearest statement of the contradiction which must create the numinous experience. But is there anything further to say once contradiction has been established? To answer this, we must make a transition at this point from an awareness of the strictly allegorical origins of his thought to the possibility of an epiphany making its way out of the duality of experience, an epiphany which is quite literally believed to be sexual orgasm.

Nowhere is Lawrence's need for recovering the numinous out of the pessimistic nature of reality more apparent than in his mythologizing about sex. At times, he is intensely controlled, cerebral, and moralistic about sensuality (he hated promiscuity and prostitution), and at other times he is plainly the sexual anarchist of his age (in his treatment, say, of the Oedipal crisis in Paul Morel or anal intercourse in *Lady Chatterley* and *Women in Love*, Birkin / Gerald's homoeroticism, Birkin's bisexuality, Anna Brangwen's sexual destruction of Will, Ursula's of Skrebensky, Gudrun's of Gerald). But in both his anarchistic and democratic moments, he shows a highly sensitive accounting of a growth into consciousness in the major figures of *Sons and Lovers*, *The Rainbow*, and *Women in Love* which may very well be among the most heuristic writing about sexual desire and its drama we have. In short, Lawrence may not be consistent in inspiration, but he is the first to argue in modern writing (as he does with Tom and Lydia in *The Rainbow*, and Birkin and Ursula in *Women in Love*) that revelation is indeed largely erotic. He argues this way even with his apparent failures to convince us that consciousness can grow (as with Cipriano, Kate, and "the woman who rode away"), failures determined by an allegory of solipsistic love. He is prepared to acknowledge, as Birkin must to Ursula, that all the "pollyanalytics" about love, and all the tea-party metaphysics, will not achieve sexual happiness. It remains that being saved for Lawrence means acting as if one is free to do what one wants with one's own body. That is the ideology of his writing. In a personal sense, it meant writing freely of the restoration of contradiction: that is, the allegory of the "dissociated sensibility."

But there is a problem here. We can empathize with the psychological drama of his characters' search for orgasm and ideal, yet their arguments (and his) are so relentlessly repetitive—always returning to the same metaphor, that of the erotically constrained body—that his writing seems doomed to a circularity which cannot metamorphose. For the moment we return to allegory to justify an act, as Lawrence does, we can feel—as we do, say, in *Lady Chatterley's Lover*—that human experience has been dramatically oversimplified, and the play of feelings neutralized. For example, we find that Lawrence often needs to revert to isolation and separation in the opposition between men and women, as a fatalistic reaction to the problem and a deliberate mystifying of the numinous. This is even a part of Birkin's famous "star-equilibrium" theory. Thinks Birkin:

> There is now to come the new day, when we are beings each of us, fulfilled in difference. The man is pure man, the woman pure woman, they are perfectly polarised. . . . There is only the pure duality of polarisation, each one free from any contamination of the other. In each, the individual is primal, sex is subordinate, but perfectly polarised. Each has a single separate being, with its own laws. The man has his pure freedom, the woman hers. Each acknowledges the perfection of the polarised sex-circuit. Each admits the different nature of the other.[17]

There is a good deal of irony about this statement, which is perhaps the most ethereal version of the heterosexual ideal in the modern novel. It is true that Lawrence does, at least, make a refusal to go along with the sentimental androgyne, as far as that fashionable theory indicates a utopian need to do away with differences altogether. Nor does he suggest some biological or mythic basis for the theory of love as the search for an ultimate "merging." He does rightly emphasize that men and women must have confidence to admit the different nature of the other. But the contradiction is that Birkin's definition of "star-equilibrium" is a definition of a neutral state, a perfected dualism—parodied bitterly, perhaps, in the relationship of Gudrun and Loerke—which indicates inertia rather than nirvana.

We also find an expression of this inertia in those frequent references Lawrence makes to the "spirit of place." He often allows his characters only a retreat back to what appears to be a narcissistic womb of nature. Although he had a strong sense of the eroticism of place, often evoked in his novels and travel books in richly impressionistic descriptions of landscape, there is something disturbingly sterile about this womb of the land. Lou senses it in the desert and even the Rockies, Somers in the "fourth dimension" of the Australian bush, Birkin in the long grass after Hermione strikes him with the lapis, Kate in Mexico, Mellors on the farm, and so on. Part of Lawrence's search for the "New World" seems to be for a place where no-one will interfere. Nature may be an abrasive other, but it finally numbs. By its clear otherness, it intimidates Lawrence and his characters back into a belief in the sharp dualisms between self and society.

But the real problem with Lawrence's allegorical frame of mind in both essay and fiction is even more obvious in its relation to his treatment of sexuality. He often takes an aspect of love and tries to show that it is normative, as in the sexual meetings in *Lady Chatterley's Lover*. That men and women are different is not the truism at stake. What is the issue, of course, is his insistence that what men and women do sexually is determined by the essential roles which he claims to have justified for them in his "pollyanalytics" in *Psychoanalysis, Fantasia*, and the other metaphysical essays. These are thinly disguised patterns of behavior based on his own sexual anxieties, as has often been said. Lawrence's imagination is constantly restrained by his need to attribute various physical and psychological roles to women (passivity, idealism, the symbolic use of light and cerebrality) and then by the remarkably arrogant male need to find woman waiting to be opened up to consciousness by the "dark potency" of the phallus. Obviously there can be little defense for a love ethic which is so atavistic, which depends on asserting the pompous imperialism of "the sons of God" coming to the "daughters of Men," as Ursula is supposed to feel it all in "Excurse":

This was release at last. She had had lovers, she had

known passion. But this was neither love nor passion. It was the daughters of men coming back to the sons of God, the strange inhuman sons of God who are in the beginning.

Her face was now one dazzle of released, golden light, as she looked up at him and laid her hands full on his thighs, behind, as he stood before her. He looked down at her with a rich brown brow like a diadem above his eyes.[18]

So one of the major problems of Lawrence's insistence on rooting love in such dualistic role-playing is that he constantly insists on a norm for its behavior. He wants structure and form above all else. But such atavism can demythologize precisely what it needs to restore. The art is relentlessly metonymical in its repetitions. The interrogation of sex will never be contained in a book, so he has to *state* the mystery over and over again. Ironically, he must search for some metaphysical meaning for the sex act, which is an important enough enterprise except when it is layered upon the neurosis of warring opposites and interferes with what is otherwise a rich phenomenology—mysterious enough—of erotic desire in his writing. We see here, particularly, the enormous problem of recovering the mythicity of sex out of allegorical beginnings when metaphor (and myth) is not trusted. There is nothing wrong with allegory if the dualism is not pervasive. But the heroic aspects of Lawrence's male sexuality and the gesturing toward the holiness of sex can keep strictly to the oppositional nature of experience and not allow transformations of fact. This is part of our traditional Freudian anguish over reconciling nature and culture, but with Lawrence the reconciliation in the body has a certain authoritarian ring to it. The allegory stretches at times even to what men and women are supposed to feel in sex. That Lawrence presumes to know what a woman feels is one thing that women writers since Simone de Beauvoir have rightly attacked him for; and to that must also be added the charge that his illusions of solipsistic grandeur do not adequately represent what a man need feel either. The descriptions of sex in *Lady Chatterley's Lover* and *The Plumed Serpent*, as well as the particular incident I have quoted from *Women in Love*, are open to the obvious criticism that they, at least, are over-allegorized. For sex, unlike love, has a habit of resisting preconceptions. The overweening male authority, the persistence of women as Circe, do not do Lawrence or experience justice, and resist the recovery of the numinous.

In *The Plumed Serpent*, to quote an extreme example, what might be called heterosexist role-playing is legislated as part of Kate's experience of entering the mystic commune of the ranting "sons of the Mexican Gods." Even Lawrence, by the end of the novel, knows how strident have been the demands Cipriano and Ramon make on Kate, so that he allows her the complaint: " 'But you won't let me free.' " But that comes to us, surely, as the author's last-line gesture toward what should have been explored three hundred pages earlier. And in *Lady Chatterley's Lover*, too, the mystique of the sensitive phallus demands its own terms. Lawrence attempts to show in this book—tired as even he clearly was by then of dramatizing his dualisms of men and women (though he saw no way out of it)—that the oppositional theory of love can remythologize sex once and for all. But his is an extraordinarily theoretical book; it is excessively rational. We sense that it decrees the moment of illumination, the numinous experience of men leading women to the mutual orgasm. The novel then is opaque allegory, however much it rightly and passionately intends to speak for "tenderness." The references beyond the text, which presumably control its meaning, are those tight, constrained terms of Lawrence's metaphysics and Birkin's "star-equilibrium," to which is added the mechanistic therapy of sexual orgasm.

But let me leave berating the static allegories of intent in Lawrence when they harden into authoritarian gestures and nonprogressive contradictions, and repeat that however scathing one can easily be about particulars in his fiction, Lawrence also achieves wonderfully successful allegories of love which have rarely been equalled in the novel. Much of *Sons and Lovers* and *The Rainbow* and large sections of *Women in Love* and *Kangaroo* work this way as his characters move with a self-critical growth of consciousness and a wealth of unconscious motive becoming articulate which can only serve to make contraries open up to progression. At all times, anyhow, we must be somewhat in awe of Lawrence's nakedness, his unswerving honesty and high-toned refusal to back down from his utopian intent to explain the nature of essential experience, and to come through from the *bellum intestinum* and declare sex holy. Lawrence may not exactly be an idealist, but he has ideals nonetheless, and they center on the need for freedom for the body from the compromise of ideas and society. The rhythms of all his fictions, especially the experimental meetings between men and women described with such a close eye to detail (for example, Anna and Will stacking sheaves in *The Rainbow*) can at best direct us back to the body as sign and text. We are asked to enter a world in which no feelings are neutral—even if they can be neutralized—and everything to do with the body is important. Above all, we are asked to suspend judgment on all but a very few characters (plainly not on the side of life, as F. R. Leavis would say), and consider whether human relationships can be made simpler without oversimplifying the nature of experience. (Whatever their limitations, for example, we do not dismiss the simplemindedness of Tom or Will Brangwen, even if Skrebensky is but a straw man.) Plainly Lawrence is constantly adopting strategies by which to reach a solution to his allegorical bounds. He wants to extend the reader's consciousness toward an awareness of the very uncompromising nature not only of sexual experience, but of writing about it. The modern novel has never had a more ambitious, even if peculiarly earnest, mandate to recover a sense of the sacred for love and sex.

Yet it is only the open-endedness of fiction dependent on metaphoric shifts that can offer confirmation of the realism to which Lawrence's utopian intentions aspire. If utopia were possible, then there would be no need for the novel, whose transformational, experimental logic must contradict the relentlessly two-dimensional structures which are the characteristic of utopias as well as of allegories. The central paradox of all utopian thought is that it is a desire to abolish desire itself, to recover the holy as a pure fact which has no contradiction. So although the theory of star-equilibrium is about the necessity of contradiction, it is stated blandly, and we have no real counterargument offered to it even when Ursula berates Birkin. Ironically, the oppositional nature of thought cannot exist for Lawrence without the allegory of the split in consciousness. But Lawrence at times allows his yearning for a world free from anxiety to push the novel close to an assertion of the numinous consciousness, in such a way that the novel itself ceases to exist (as it turns into the "preach" for much of Birkin's talk). Again, the irony is: what else can the allegorical consciousness do but confirm its yearning for no contradiction at all?

It is a fascinating experiment with the novel which can receive only the shortest treatment here. No other major modern novelist is at once so uncompromisingly fundamentalist and yet so honestly erotic, and at all times so vulnerable about it. True, the allegorical beginnings of his thought, the relentless desire for paradigmatic meaning, push him toward an end to desire and ambiguity—to utopia, that is. And there are moments in his fiction when he fails to give us a subtle accounting of the *dialectical* nature of consciousness, reducing everything to an interminable holy war between men and women, solved only in star-equilibrium. But he can also pull back from the feeling that the numinous must be impossibly utopian and atavistically pre-apocalyptic. It attends the everyday with certainty—Anna with Tom in the stable, Ursula and Paul growing up, Somers in the Australian bush—and allows a contradictoriness of spirit to invade the novel, which establishes for some of his fictions the same structural open-endedness we have found in myth.

It can also be said that even if much of the writing pushes his characters to Hell or the Promised Land, Lawrence still has the insight to pull back from any conclusive endings. In fact, it is the endings of his fictions that offer us his clearest perception of the numinous as dependent on accepting contradiction but allowing the oppositions to work themselves out. If the inherited Christian dualisms, together with the Oedipal crisis, have from the earliest work created the need to initiate writing, they also ironically create the refusal to complete any of the novels. A study of Lawrence's endings would reveal that they are not deliberately left wide open as if in mere deference to relativity, or to make an obviously Existentialist point, but because Lawrence knows there is no solution to the allegory of love other than what the reader can complete for him or herself.

The allegory of the mythic as the binary domination of thought, that is, is persistent in Lawrence's best writing and in his worst. It restrains the imagination in *The Plumed Serpent* but allows for an earned recovery of illumination by Ursula in *The Rainbow*. Throughout, it sustains Lawrence's creative energy and identifies his mythical intentions to seek out the essential about human nature. Paul Morel turns to the lights of the town. Will he live, or "drift towards death"? Ursula looks through the rainbow to an uncertain future. Birkin wants "two kinds of love." What will he and Ursula do next? Kate wants and does not want the Quetzalcoatl submission. Mellors and Connie write to each other from limbo, rather than from a tranquil separation, talking about the future, communes, and socialism. And so on. Each novel is an open-ended, incomplete structure which the reader must try to resolve. We are always thrust back to those culprit arguments for the "split" in consciousness, to which we must find an alternative other than a sentimental and false unity, according to Lawrence. There is no perfected time in past or future at the end of the novels (though *Lady Chatterley's Lover* turns halfheartedly to the latter). The endings of his books are set in a present which allows no consistently transcendent vision other than a yearning for sexual completeness kept alive by the abrasiveness of human contact. The dualisms have not finally been suppressed by the close of any of his novels, but a curious thing has happened. However stylized and at times infuriatingly narrow-minded Lawrence's allegory of love and sex has appeared, he always demands that it is the reader who must accept the responsibility for recovering a sense of unity by erasing the terms of that allegory—ironically, by bypassing the text. In the steps of Augustine, who likewise insisted that revelation can only follow an acceptance of the manichean nature of reality, Lawrence begins and ends his novels with radical alternatives.

Eliot's Embarrassment

If Lawrence turned to the abrasiveness of myth as a power struggle between opposites, Eliot, we can say, willingly risked at first the embarrassment of having no myth at all. He had a self-trust which seemed not to require constant feeding and defense in order to prove he was still alive such as we find in Lawrence. We may lose something of Lawrence's range of experience, the sensuality of his myth-making, and his energetic experimentalism, but there is with Eliot an equally modern mythopoeia. His is the strain from disbelief to orthodoxy, and then finally to conventionally Christian allegorical boundaries. This does not make his experiment any less important than Lawrence's—it may even make it more accessible (as Leavis has suggested) in spite of his supposed phlegmaticism—for no less than with Lawrence, a key version of the modernist phenomenology of belief is apparent. Lawrence's life was undoubtedly the exception rather than the rule in its intensity—"I take my living damnable hard," he said—even if his exile must be considered along with the therapeutic peripeteia of Forster, Durrell, Joyce, Pound, and Hemingway. But if a stereotype of the tactful English scholar-poet has emerged in the last thirty years or so, it is Eliot, who carefully indulged with a certain conscious expatriate irony the playing of the restrained role, be it Old Possum, Prufrock, the Hollow Man, the Fisher King, the Composite Ghost, or the Literary Critic.

Subtly, he is in his poetry the conscience of the academic. He is, even for us today, an exemplary sensitivity, slow to anger, carefully balancing the fate of opposites, less impetuous certainly than Lawrence, and the first major modern poet in English to take deliberately to poetry as a hermeneutic exercise.

The geography of Eliot's search to recover the numinous in poetry is less vast than Lawrence's. His sense of space is abstracted rather than geographical, even if he retained spiritual homes in various parts of the United States, the East, and "the green fields of Russell Square." But just like Lawrence, he shows great wariness when it comes to establishing vision simply as a credible or an incredible account of an event. Instead, he takes on the whole question of making the creative act analogous to religious aspiration. While Lawrence is obsessed with writing as a struggle through the prolix to the proverb, using language profusely to eradicate the need for language and to direct us back to the instincts, Eliot is more occupied with extending beyond the void of consciousness to a restrained, formal awareness of conflicting coordinates for the word: the word as pun, as paradoxical meaning. In fact, we might say that his semiological awareness is more acute than Lawrence's. He does not obviously have a vocabulary of paradigms to draw on, but tests the word for validity in the act of every interpretative event. Lawrence tested writing in place, extroverting the drama in extended settings for the body. Eliot, in the tradition of Hopkins, inscapes the world, develops a mythical allegory of instressed reference. The numinous in Lawrence is discoverable in the energetic act of living among and retreating from people, however confining his allegories can be. In Eliot, it is achieved (as it was for Hopkins) in the privacy of poetic insight, the fascination with ontological issues of how the moment might be "in and out of time":

> The moments of happiness—not the sense of well-being,
> Fruition, fulfillment, security or affection,

Or even a very good dinner, but the sudden
    illumination—
We had the experience but missed the meaning,
And approach to the meaning restores the experience
In a different form, beyond any meaning
We can assign to happiness.[19]

We must look for Eliot's version of the numinous, "beyond
any meaning / We can assign to happiness." Whereas Lawrence has rooted it quite concretely in the vagaries of human
sensuality, the impressionism of the bodily text, Eliot develops
quite logically and theoretically an ontological paradox. The
numinous, recoverable or not, by definition is the "timeless"
moment. But it cannot avoid being in time as well, reasons
Eliot in *Four Quartets*, in order to be defined at all. Here,
then, is Eliot's key contradiction, even a conventional one we
might say now, but only because we have rather taken his
experiment for granted: the numinous is determined by the
legacy of history and precedent (the Incarnation of Christ) but
is discoverable in the metaphorical language of poetry, as he
explained it in the *Quartets*, written in the full face of history.

But it was not always this way. To talk of Eliot's uses of
the past is misleading, for the past for much of his career more
clearly uses him. History, he knows in "Burnt Norton," is
lived in and appropriates us long before we even consider
reacting, and then when we do, it makes our response seem
heavily ironic. This is not simply a tidy academic aphorism,
but Eliot's consistent belief, as he expressed it in "Gerontion":

    Think now
History has many cunning passages, contrived corridors
And issues, deceives with whispering ambitions,
Guides us by vanities. Think now
She gives when our attention is distracted
And what she gives, gives with such supple confusions
That the giving famishes the craving.[20]

Furthermore, history takes over writing as well. If we survey

Eliot's poetry from "Prufrock" (1917) to the "Choruses from *The Rock*" (which appeared in 1934), we find that he had an extraordinary respect for the diachronic, for the patterns moments make in time. Coinciding with his theory of the dissociated sensibility, history is an anxiety-ridden continuum. Vision in the early poetry is strictly controlled by the systematic use of allegorical language: allegorical because the poem always refers back to the unavoidable and tragic split between past and present. From Prufrock's "formulated phrases" and "overwhelming questions" we have no freedom in time, which must lead us to the "last twist of the knife" ("Rhapsody on a Windy Night"), and the "heap of broken images" in *The Waste Land*.

Certainly, Eliot made many now familiar attempts, as he puts it in "The Hollow Men," to "wear deliberate disguises," but the disguises do not help: it is always the same voice, the measured tone, the dry wit, relentless time's intonation. Even when he reaches the decision at the end of *The Waste Land* to put his "own lands in order," time is not fooled. For what can be done when, as the Hollow Men say,

> In this last of meeting places
> We grope together
> And avoid speech
> Gathered on this beach of the tumid river.[21]

Or as the poet puts it wearily in "Portrait of a Lady":

> And I must borrow every changing shape
> To find expression . . . dance, dance
> Like a dancing bear,
> Cry like a parrot, chatter like an ape.
> Let us take the air, in a tobacco trance—[22]

And, of course, Eliot will not avoid speech, yet when speech is attempted, it must play continually between the names of things and states of consciousness, irreconcilable opposites on earth at least:

Between the idea
And the reality
Between the motion
And the act
Falls the Shadow[23]

Whatever substance we give to the Shadow, the controlling fact of the early poetry is the obvious present, rooted in the allegory of past domination and in the control of reinforced opposites: categories like "idea" and "reality," "desire" and "spasm," "essence" and "descent." The litany of allegorical alternatives carries with it the poet's insistence that he "sit still" and be calmly fatalistic, as in the restraint and pathos of lines like these:

I am moved by fancies that are curled
Around these images, and cling:
The notion of some infinitely gentle
Infinitely suffering thing.
Wipe your hand across your mouth, and laugh;
The worlds revolve like ancient women
Gathering fuel in vacant lots.[24]

In *The Waste Land*, Tiresias, timeless, blind, and bisexual, attends the seduction scene between "the young man carbuncular" and the "lovely" typist who has "stooped to folly." He is Eliot's "most important" person, at Eliot's own admission, not simply because he represents in myth the ideal unity of the sexes, of which this unsatisfactory version of intercourse going on before his eyes is a real travesty, nor because he can be blasé about seduction, but because knowing even past, present, and future, he cannot be satisfied. He embodies conflict in time, and for that he is more human than superhuman. Tiresias is important to Eliot not because he knows the future or knows too much—although he knows too much to make sex anything more than habit—but because of his uncertainty over what to do with his knowledge (his problem in Sophocles' *Oedipus Rex*, too). And then Eliot also knows too much about

232

the tragic nature of history to allow the numinous to appear with any confidence. Time is always linear and repetitive for him before the *Quartets*; it is predictably tragic. The blessing at the end of *The Waste Land* only reconciles us to our disinheritance in time. In the early poetry, that is, the idea of myth as naturalized history dominates: poetry and consciousness are controlled by a perspective which allows no real dialectic, only the tragic allegory of past time. Poetry is mediated by this fact, visionless till "Ash Wednesday" perhaps, except for a fleeting, enigmatic moment of "Looking into the heart of light, the silence" (*The Waste Land*, I). Consciousness is directed toward controlling rhythms, which are incantatory and restrained. Ratiocination follows the mood and does not create a way out of it.

Now this is not to say that the early Eliot is merely pessimistic, but that the poetry is controlled by the literal, unrelenting efforts of diachronic time. And how does this affect the function of poetry, specifically? History, for Eliot, only serves to make things more literal than they might appear. There is very little room for metaphor, for unrestrained pathos, the lines from the "Preludes" being one of the few exceptions. Poetry tries to establish itself as the bare fact of an historical moment, an allegorical image willed to recovery amid the heaps of broken images. The onrush of time only encourages impressionism. Each poem is at best, then, a reasonably reconstituted image—"These fragments I have shored against my ruins"—each fragment a metonym clung to desperately. Even the lyric recall—the "bats with baby faces in the violet light"—does not disturb the metonymical emphasis. Such short moments of expressionist license only heighten the horror which confronts the poet in committing himself to contradictory fact:

> My friend, blood shaking my heart
> The awful daring of a moment's surrender
> Which an age of prudence can never retract
> By this, and this only, we have existed . . .[25]

The rhetorical stance here is created by myth as history dominating consciousness, and not just consciousness of the historical fact of language. Anxious time can live only in the present / past. This means that it allows no present or future to cover the negative consciousness creating the poem, which can now only speak in measured terms of allegorical conflict and restraint, even of the defeat of knowledge.

What I am saying is that Eliot's respect for history affects the metaphorical expansiveness of his poetry. Before the *Quartets*, it forces him to make the poem an object, an obelisk in time. We know well his emphasis on the objective correlative, but we can make the mistake of playing up "correlative" to the detriment of "objective," as though Eliot is referring specifically to metaphor-making. There is very little metaphor-making in the early Eliot, for correlative means "alongside," and "objectivity" makes the language of poetry one of metonymy rather than metaphor: that is, the conscious attempt to make the poem realistic. But the problem for Eliot is that anxious time only allows objects to relate by their proximity or juxtaposition: equivalence is not possible, the gap can never be filled with signs. Remember:

> Between the desire
> And the spasm
> Between the potency
> And the existence
> Between the essence
> And the descent
> Falls the Shadow[26]

Metaphor is the exception rather than the rule, and then, perceptibly, an enormous effort, as in the last line of this quotation from "What Thunder Said," which aims to compound opposites into a "synthesis":

> Here is not water but only rock
> Rock and no water and the sandy road
> The road winding above among the mountains

234

Which are mountains of rock without water
If there were water we should stop and drink
Amongst the rock one cannot stop or think
Sweat is dry and feet are in the sand
If there were only water amongst the rock
Dead mountain mouth of carious teeth that cannot spit[27]

The opposing facts are too pessimistically aligned to produce
anything but a deeply moving strain over creation, felt by a
poet who insists that even metaphor is in the control of myth.
The poem is dominated by events in frightening proximity to
each other and to Eliot, and there is little open questioning
in *The Waste Land*. So even this residual metaphor of "Dead
mountain mouth of carious teeth" is a relief. This is a fine
instance of poetry shoring up its own ruins in the face of
history. We have to say that ironically it is the metonymy that
saves Eliot no less than Lawrence. He continually finds a
narrow but definite space to sit among the rocks. This is his
location of the real: the small, defined, and defensive space
the author occupies in the poem. He lives among the allegory
of analogues: a mark of his extraordinary control, lack of
sentimentality, and stubbornness.

From the Waste Land to the Promised Land is less of a
transition than we might expect, scarcely a matter of transformed speech. As "Ash Wednesday" makes clear, it is "Because I know I shall not know" that the poet must "renounce
the voice." The poet can only turn away from his thought to
"the wind, to the wind only for only / The wind will listen."
This often seems a routine literary gesture, a demand on nature
which borders on pathetic fallacy, but which nonetheless indicates the enormous burden of intent and the weight of ontological gloom. But the second section, the song of the bones
and the litany to the "Lady of Silences," for the first time
proposes a union of opposites in contemplation, "speech without word":

Lady of silences
Calm and distressed

Torn and most whole
Rose of memory
Rose of forgetfulness
Exhausted and life-giving
Worried reposeful
The single rose
Is now the Garden
Where all loves end[28]

This is an epiphany which is not exactly undeserved. After *The Waste Land*, who would criticize a moment of respite? But it seems unearned argumentatively and is even deliberately mystifying. Again, history has not changed: the litany is Christian, Dantesque, celebrative, exterior, even in the poet's drama of temptation and control in the poem—literally a moment in which to recontemplate poetry, to remember specifically "one who moves in the time between sleep and waking." But if memory is the protagonist of "Ash Wednesday," it is still memory of "an ancient rhyme." The Eliot who has been previously disposed to be determined by some structure of ordered time, to need some comfort in the emotional repetitiveness of history, turns to Christian time, which offers little variation on this. It is true that we must now choose our fate, but time still has a relentless certainty, enforcing life or culminating in death. That is what makes Eliot's context for poetry alternately annoying and highly interesting. There is so little space to move in the Waste Land or the Garden that we can only admire Eliot's ability to stay alive. The Christian belief in the Incarnation in "Ash Wednesday," unlike its function in *Four Quartets*, finally seems to make history hopelessly parallel to present time, with no earned intersections.

Intuitions are, again, of an exterior source of hope: gaudy intuitions, even when not sharply restrained, as in the recall of Dante's Procession in the *Purgatorio* (XXIX):

The unread vision in the higher dream
While jewelled unicorns draw by the gilded hearse.[29]

But the real energy actually lies in the constraint of Eliot's insistence on a myth of history, his refusal to trust metaphor. In the litany to the "Lady of Silences," compounding metonymical figures are put under the stress of liturgical rhythms rather than the metaphorical imagination. This is the poetry sustained by the rhythms of a stylized desire. "The single Rose" is "the Garden," a union of "memory," "forgetfulness," "worry" and "life." Yet there is no guarantee from the extensive analogues that such a correspondence should emerge. There is no problem when Eliot has God say "Shall these bones live? Shall these / Bones live?", or even his own "Pray for us sinners now and at the hour of our death," because that is direct, literal speech, a lyric poetry of simple effusiveness. But when he says that the rose *is* the garden, we wonder why, because the metaphor has not justified itself; it has been decided on arbitrarily in the face of history's message, and we must ask ourselves if this metaphor is, indeed, any resistance to history. The answer must be that it is not, for the impact of the rose has been as a product of historical meaning: Dante's rose at the end of the *Paradiso* (XXX, 100-112), the image of perfected reality. This is not really the poetry of apodictic experience, because the word will not be heard or even spoken till "after this our exile." But it is certainly the poetry controlled by mythology if not myth. The numinous is not recovered, but spoken about mysteriously: the experience of an uncertain release from fact.

So it is not surprising that Doris says in "Sweeney Agonistes," "I'd like to know about that coffin." For Eliot is now accepting the implications of exile and imagination's death: eternal wandering in the effort to make consciousness whole, as he describes it in the "Choruses from *The Rock*" (I):

> The endless cycle of idea and action,
> Endless invention, endless experiment,
> Brings knowledge of motion, but not of stillness;
> Knowledge of speech, but not of silence;
> Knowledge of words, and ignorance of the Word.

All our knowledge brings us nearer to our ignorance,
All our ignorance brings us nearer to death
But nearness to death no nearer to GOD.[30]

The allegorical implications of the split in consciousness are
now fully stated (if not worked out, for that has to wait for
Four Quartets). "The Rock" itself speaks like Ibsen's Brand,
manichean no less in the despair of this knowledge:

In all my years, one thing does not change.
However you disguise it, this thing does not change:
The perpetual struggle of Good and Evil.[31]

After "Ash Wednesday," and before *Four Quartets*, Eliot becomes declamatory, polemical, and rarely at ease with anything less than the full impact of his own version of the Holy
War between virtues and the vices. But he is not yet really
vulnerable to the *paradox* of such an aphoristic view of morality, but continues to trade axiom for axiom fatalistically:

. . . if the Temple is to be cast down
We must first build the Temple.[32]

For some eighteen years of poetry, between "Prufrock" and
"Burnt Norton," Eliot was fully appropriated by the myth of
history, first pessimistically, then by offering salvation on dog-
matic Christian terms. This had an enormous effect on his
poetic language, as he says sadly in the fifth section of "East
Coker":

So here I am, in the middle way, having had twenty
years—
Twenty years largely wasted, the years of *l'entre deux
guerres*—
Trying to learn to use words, and every attempt
Is a wholly new start, and a different kind of failure
Because one has only learned to get the better of words
For the thing one no longer has to say, or the way in
which
One is no longer disposed to say it.[33]

It is this kind of discourse—more analytic, more probing and rational, even if it retains Eliot's characteristic discursiveness—that marked the turning point in Eliot's relationship to time. What is new in the *Four Quartets*—which allows Eliot to pause for a moment in "East Coker" and talk like this for the first time—is that he finds a new power in writing as a resistance to time, and the possible creation of the "timeless moment." In effect, he discovers the hermeneutical intensity of myth in the first section of "Burnt Norton."

These are still perhaps the most difficult lines in the *Quartets*, outside the opening lines of "Little Gidding" with their equally oblique "unimaginable zero summer." But this section is the center of the poem in two ways. First, in terms of the way the poem creates its spatial metaphors: the garden in "Burnt Norton" is the focal setting; consciousness is discovered there and expands out to a wider world, creating paradox as before, but returning hopefully in the last lines of "Little Gidding." Second, in terms of the way a poem creates its sense of time, these lines are as close as Eliot ever came to an extended recovery of the numinous consciousness as a matter of locating the wholeness of experience:

> . . . Into our first world.
> There they were, dignified, invisible,
> Moving without pressure over the dead leaves,
> In the autumn heat through the vibrant air,
> And the bird called, in response to
> The unheard music hidden in the shrubbery,
> And the unseen eyebeam crossed, for the roses
> Had the look of flowers that are looked at.
> There they were as our guests, accepted and accepting.
> So we moved, and they, in a formal pattern,
> Along the empty alley, into the box circle,
> To look down into the drained pool.
> Dry the pool, dry concrete, brown edged,
> And the pool was filled with water out of sunlight,
> And the lotus rose, quietly, quietly,

The surface glittered out of heart of light,
And they were behind us, reflected in the pool.
Then a bird passed, and the pool was empty.
Go, said the bird, for the leaves were full of children,
Hidden excitedly, containing laughter.
Go, go, go, said the bird: human kind
Cannot bear very much reality.
Time past and time future
What might have been and what has been
Point to one end, which is always present.[34]

So careful is Eliot's discussion of time in spatial terms in this section that these two aspects of the poem's phenomenology, its sense of history and moment, clearly intersect. Time can now be lived in consciously, even in the diagram of the garden, and poetry is dependent on our conscious efforts to inhabit an imaginary as well as a bodily space in a way which resists history even as it occurs in time. It establishes for a lyrical moment, at least—as Mallarmé had hoped—the possibility that writing might appropriate time.

Now, instead of telling us about the academic "single rose" of the "garden where all love ends," Eliot actually enters the garden. We might assume, when we read the riddle about time past and present, that we are back in the show of ambivalence to be found in "Ash Wednesday," where resolution depends on either a double meaning or a translinguistic fact. But we are not. There is a genuine openness to history now, which leaves Eliot free to act, to be dispersed through the text, to show the uniqueness of the events in the garden. What are these events, then, and why is diachronic time now so much less of a threat? In the opening lines, Eliot is telling us that historical time is relentlessly linear, and there is no escape from that; but in its movement, it allows moments of acute insight. Radical intuition is now disinterred from history. Depending on how we look at it, either history is "a pattern of timeless moments," or the timeless moments only make sense because they exist in history. But we cannot have one

without the other, and especially we cannot have one perspective on time without the other. So mythicity of time, once
we have succumbed to its determinism, leaves us an opening.
There will be occasions when the moment controls time as
well as the very reverse, but all interpretation depends on their
possible intersection.

> Time present and time past
> Are both perhaps present in time future,
> And time future contained in time past.
> If all time is eternally present
> All time is unredeemable.
> What might have been is an abstraction
> Remaining a perpetual possibility
> Only in a world of speculation.[35]

This is not simply a riddle, but designed to lead us to understand why there is paradox in the function of time, and how
it is inevitable. Time is necessarily linear, but its psychological
demand is to make us accept the necessity of history and
future projection, or else "All time is unredeemable"; there
would be no present to inhabit. But there is also hypothetical
time, "What might have been"—the desire for hindsight,
hopes, dreams, and even imaginary needs—which moves us
back and forth from the dominance of the moment over time
to another sense of being compromised by history. Hypotheses
too must exist in time. But either way, Eliot says, in fact or
in fiction,

> What might have been and what has been
> Point to one end which is always present.[36]

This is where Eliot establishes his independent *cogito* most
clearly with a concern to indulge the phenomenology of writing. For the first time in his poetry, he is genuinely "putting
his own lands in order," putting himself both in and out of
time in an imaginative dialectic with the myth of history.
Whether we think of history as a literal or as a hypothetical
truth, we can only do so because we argue from a present

point of view: *all time must flow into the present because it flows from and into consciousness.* The exemplary, religious significance is not merely reportable now, but open to be created afresh. Not only does time require a point of view to establish the metaphysics of presence, but the pressure is now on the poet not to be appropriated by history, but to resist it by establishing his own *cogito* as reliable within the flux of writing: an attempt which Lawrence also saw as the only hope for modern writing. Now the coordinates of history are not a matter of relentless linearity, with heaven and hell waiting for us at the end, with either our sitting it out or merely being brave. Now the coordinates of the diagram of intersecting time, which Eliot gives us in the opening lines, allow the moment to have a lively relationship to other events, even if it is still a problematic one: we are not so sure of tragic history any more, because we have our own timeless moments to discover and recover in poetry. This is, I·think, one of the clearest moments of intuiting the mythicity of poetry writing.

It is now the synchronic aspect of time which, in effect, creates space to live in, makes consciousness evident, and obstructs history, even as it depends on it. And this opens the door to the garden for Eliot, "into our first world." Eliot goes down the passage he has not taken before into a garden which is not obsessed by significance (past significance, that is). The rose does still have literary antecedents: it is Dante's rose, the image of perfected reality, the emblematic rose, the sexual rose of courtly love, and it is also in an empirically realized rose-garden. Its geography is available to us in the tangible details of pool and shrubbery together. The rose is not necessary to a discovery of extratextual meaning (as in, say, "Ash Wednesday"), nor is it an objective correlative for anything. Now it is all there is, arbitrarily the signifier making its own transformations, complete with dust on "a bowl of leaves."

The poet wants to keep the incident as direct and literal as possible, but it is a different kind of literalness from that of *The Waste Land*. There we sense that the poet speaks directly out of emotional restraint, expressing the literal as a parody of emotion, even when lyrical. But now the metonymy is a poetic beginning rather than an end: not a lyric recall, but lyricism itself, a refinement of language not down to bare correlatives, but to signifiers so compressed that they beg to become metaphor—expressing desire, but hiding it, carefully refining it, suggesting absent meaning. Why the garden? What is the bird doing? Why the thrust? Why the pool? The answers do not matter, for we are in a Mallarméan vacuum in which time is suspended, yet encroaches at the edges of meaning. This is no less metonymical than the earlier poetry, but it is less anxious, more likely to expand into metaphor. "Our first world" is recoverable as a kind of familiar but vaguely felt reconstruction of a moment in which history has mattered (it is still Dante's rose) but has not mattered as much as it once did. There is no transcendence, but a genuine truce between past and present, desire and fact, in which consciousness is now no longer obsessed by anxious time but can consider its own status.

Eliot offers us a secular world of bare geographical facts, such as the cleverly innocent "corner" and "gate," which are precise because consciousness has now no mandate but to be empirically accurate. And it is only then that the act of interpretation can establish the numinous better than any inherited historical meaning. The experience is made so interior, and yet it is so precise and diagrammatic, that though we might call it allegorical, we know we are pushed to a state where language is distinctly transparent. Whatever the events really are, it does not matter much, because consciousness has made some progress in defining its own coordinates, assuring us of its own future. The filling of the pool and the rising of the lotus become subtle analogues for the growth of consciousness, and the emptying of the pool for its confident recession. This contrapuntalism of mind is again nothing less than mythic thought. To contrast with this movement, the facts remain in the garden, in themselves neutral but real, "looking out and looking in," accepted and accepting, established as signifiers. Events in space, too, are poised and alive, and await the movement of consciousness in time which pays close attention to detail: "moving without pressure over the dead leaves."

The world is now strangely alive and reverberating for Eliot in a way it has not been before. The events in the garden, whatever the expectations of desire, have been discovered for their own reality, and become the content of the numinous consciousness. They are in a dialectical relationship to the poet who also accepts and is accepted, moving on quite realistically as the pool empties. The rhythm of understanding is no more or less than the rhythm of consciousness, testing its every move, moving unpredictably as a function of desire (Eliot's need here is to see the world clearly, as if for the first time), and removing itself when it has seen enough: "human kind / Cannot bear very much reality." There is a genuine humility on the poet's part as he discovers that modern writing can resist history, so he will not now indulge impressionism, but predictably return himself to present time.

In effect, historical time has never been clearer in Eliot, nor more vulnerable. The Christian paradigm has always been too easily accepted, too much a determination of the present by history and forced into immanence. Now Eliot makes a secular beginning to recover the numinous, and the Incarnation (central as it is to the *Quartets*) must justify itself in human time. This is now the poetry of earned introversion. We do not begrudge the lotus, redeemed from time, even transforming itself into a paradigm (Eastern now, ecumenically in league with the Western rose)—perhaps the first real epiphany in Eliot's poetry—because consciousness has established itself and the world with clarity.

But unfortunately this does not last long for Eliot. He is more a discursive poet and less a thoroughgoing Symbolist. Quite realistically, we must return in the *Quartets* to historical time, the power of transformation available to us because "history is a pattern / Of timeless moments." The remainder of the poems offer an attempt to recover the diachronic axis, the conditions creating the moment. This is why "Little Gidding" can so confidently announce that

> . . . the end of all our exploring
> Will be to arrive where we started
> And know the place for the first time.[37]

It is really the rest of the *Quartets* which concern themselves with the recovery of the numinous, even while they must ironically question the possibility of ever doing so.

The sharp limiting of the senses in the opening section of "Burnt Norton" is Eliot's cue: he will confine his argument now to recovering patterns of consciousness which have yielded understanding. He will argue that vitality depends on structure, which in this first *Quartet* is a pattern of circles and ritual dances about the "still point." If the lotus had been the earliest still point, now the circulation of the blood and the movement of the stars emphasize that at the center is not simply stillness, but reconciliation of opposing forces ("garlic and sapphire," "boarhound and boar," "the inner / And outer compulsion," "a new world / And the old," and so on). Gradually, consciousness and ratiocination—their dialectical pattern and fascination with binaries—are reestablished, encroaching on events both real and imaginary. There is a release from the opposition of interior and exterior compulsion in writing itself, and an understanding that timelessness is not only given in revelation (as with the lotus), but in the attempt to interpret the present, insofar as we can only be fully conscious of a present. Yet it is understood that the numinous depends on the intersection of memory and perception:

> Time past and time future
> Allow but a little consciousness.
> To be conscious is not to be in time
> But only in time can the moment in the rose-garden
> The moment in the arbour where the rain beat,
> The moment in the draughty church at smokefall
> Be remembered; involved with past and future.

Only through time time is conquered.[38]

The allegory of the split in consciousness has become the allegory of the split in the word: consciousness caught up in the interplay of history and timeless moment—literally, language and word. No escape is possible from this, and Eliot makes it clearly his new restraining structure for the imagination: the opposition out of which dialectic and epiphany are made. Through the rest of "Burnt Norton," Eliot tries to recapture "the moment," to restore the "flicker / Over the strained time-ridden faces," by trying to purify language. He re-creates the times when contradiction is most acutely felt—moments ranging from "tumid apathy" in the underground station to the stillness of the Chinese jar—when the give and take of events in consciousness begin to refine themselves out in "perpetual movement" to heightened consciousness. This is finally orchestrated to the cries of the children in the foliage, heard at last, which break the spell of the first section. That, with appropriate modesty, leaves "only" the "ridiculous . . . waste sad time / Stretching before and after" to be redeemed, which he proceeds to try and do in the remaining poetry of the *Quartets.*

So "East Coker," in its turn, explores repetition in the hope of an answer, primarily the inevitable circularity of words and fact: all events have happened before, "I am here / or there, or elsewhere." Poetry can only wrestle with its "worn-out poetical fashion," hoping at best for a "limited knowledge" and endless "humility," since it is confronted with the absence of meaning, the descent into darkness, "the growing terror of nothing to think about." An exterior vision is resisted as the poet insists on remaining with his own perspective, though he begins to despair of ever finding a new way of saying. But there is no easy alignment of the poet's despair over the word, and religious mortification over recovering the Word. Finally, the only hope is to keep going along the tenuous middle way, the journeyman way of making poetry, expecting no more than momentary illumination, and the chance to start over and over again.

Eliot labors this because consciousness does not easily metamorphose for him here. It is defined by repetition and not change, and it becomes plain to him that there is something sisyphean about linking poetry and belief, when consciousness is all the time in the thrall of negative knowledge. He is acutely aware of "what you do not know" as "the only thing you know." So "to be restored, our sickness must grow worse." Presumably, things must appear this way—especially our sickness with history—in the endless "raid on the inarticulate," unless we are prepared to think of our actions not fatalistically, but as a continual "new beginning," and "exploration" into "further union, a deeper communion." The recovery of the numinous now can only take place, since it has been tasted before, through even more intense poetic activity.

It is because we anticipate this situation that "Dry Salvages" appears something of a failure of creative energy. There is comfort for the poet, but it is in the stated dominance of linear history: as a collective experience, "not the experience of one life only / But of many generations," and as "the assurance of recorded history." History, it is true, is not easily a legacy of collective achievement, for the poet admits that it brings with it "the backward half-look . . . towards the primitive terror": the horror of going back to the starting point in the unconscious, which is always the logical end of memory. There is overconscious linearity once more. But Eliot is willing to be dispossessed in humility. The mind is capable of progress, he tells himself, by transforming experience: "approach to the meaning restores the experience / In a different form." The approach seems hollowly optimistic, however, relying on images of journeying, on memory and continual effort which do not detail the discoveries but stress the unrequited nature of desire once more: the sea-journey, for example, aims to suspend time, "the murmuring shell," yet expects to re-create the still point only by the effort of prayer—and not poetry—and

247

by following "hints" with "ardour and selflessness and self-surrender."

We know at this point that Eliot is talking with some exterior aid to poetry very much in mind, namely, the example of Christ's "ardour and selflessness":

> . . . the gift half understood, is
> Incarnation.
> Here the impossible union
> Of spheres of existence is actual[39]

Yet this sense of exemplary meaning is an *a priori* to the poem. The "right action" and the "significant soil" seem a rather moralistic encroachment on the careful structure of interpretation set up in "Burnt Norton" and "East Coker" in their effort to capture the numinous consciousness. The poet seems momentarily afraid of remaining open, and must state salvation in the "proof" that earthly time has been conquered by Christ. This makes neither the poem nor Incarnation easier to understand. A lesson from history intrudes to appropriate writing once more through an exterior myth. The allegory of warring opposites finds unity outside the poem, even though the poet tries to keep the reader with him by asserting that, as far as we are concerned, these are only "hints and guesses," and that "right action" is "Never here to be realised." All that remains is the need to "keep trying"; we "are only undefeated / Because we have gone on trying."

So where is Eliot's poetic confidence in the Incarnation? Sadly, there seems none now beyond faith, and then only the circumstantial evidence of "recorded history." But he does know that he must say more about how we can be delivered from the eternal dialectic of event and meaning in time, so the enigmatic opening lines of "Little Gidding" return us to the Garden by way of the "unimaginable / Zero summer." The first section tries to re-create the moment in and out of time through the metaphor of time "suspended . . . between pole and tropic": literally a time in no particular time or place, a radical introversion in which the numinous consciousness states its claim to take over some event, even though we never know what or why. But the lines following "if you came this way . . . " are less idle than we may think, for they locate the poet as euphemistic Everyman, making his way to the shrine of Little Gidding, where he must reckon his fate. That fate, we discover, is that he cannot "verify" "sense and notion." Even metonymy must fail, for the "intersection of the timeless moment / Is England and nowhere"; it is in place, ironically (where Eliot comes close to Lawrence's physiocratic ideal), but no place. So we look to see if it can be in the poem, but instead, Eliot seems anxious to accept history once more, to have done with the battle of finding the moment again in the lyric cry of desire and confession caught in time, and in the death of the body through ritual purification by air, earth, water, and fire. Writing has again somehow flattened into direct speech. We might expect the poetry of "Burnt Norton," with its earned insight, at the end of such an enquiry as well as at the beginning. But there seems no possibility of this now for Eliot.

He turns to commune with his compound ghost, or rather the compounded unsolved questions in his own mind created by the poem. This is both an amazing hubris (as he aligns himself with Christ on the road to Eumaeus, Dante meeting his former pupil in hell, Shakespeare, Yeats, and Mallarmé), and a tragic sense of self-effacement in that symbol of modern hell, London after an air-raid. But the inflation of his own effort to "purify the dialect of the tribe" in the second section is countered by the dubious "gifts reserved for age." Dubious, because sense is not simply dessicated; now it is expiring, and with age seems to come the loss of balance and the recovery of a voice known only for the moment of speech. If this is a tragic and moving reassessment of his vocation as a writer, it seems to stress again for Eliot that the poet can only rely on the "refining fire" of the Holy Ghost (as the Provençal poet was saved in canto XXVI of the *Purgatorio*). We cannot physically fight on indefinitely, and can only try and resist growing indifference with a more persistent urgency of memory.

What is left? A very direct offer of the advice that only our "motive" (poetic, religious) can purify us "In the ground of our beseeching." If we fare forward, it is inevitable that memory slowly dies, and "we die with the dying." But from Christ we at least have "A symbol perfected in death," and a guarantee of the "refining fire." But that is not, unfortunately, felt to be the assurance of writing. However strikingly honest and totally accepting Eliot may be of his fate as a poet, there is an imaginative leap in the final section that takes us out of the poem, as the poet tries to assure us that he has really been talking about returning to the Garden all along even as he speaks of Christ.

Then what has death to do with the rose-garden? "The end is where we start from . . . / We are born with the dead." But are we? Has it all simply been circular? Is it really adequate to say that we are reborn with the "complete consort" of words "dancing together"—that is, in the poem—when the poem itself (after the opening section of "Burnt Norton") has encouraged only several hundred lines of confining reference to the tragedy of history? Eliot the humanist makes his position plainer at the end than Eliot the myth-maker: poetry *cannot* sustain its resistance to time; poetry cannot be written in a vacuum without reference to time. Poetry, finally, meets insuperable odds in recovering the numinous. There has been only one timeless moment in the poem, even though the Incarnation has become for Eliot an intersection proven by history. The last lines of the poem, calling for the return to the start, are brave indeed—"A condition of complete simplicity / (Costing not less than everything)"—but they do not assure us that the poet who can write in resistance to time in "Burnt Norton" and "East Coker" will want to return to that task. As brilliant as those two *Quartets* are in asserting that it is consciousness which creates the timeless moment, that mythicity can be recovered in the modern, we are left in the last line of "Little Gidding" with the dominance of linear time, and the simple wish-fulfillment of "the fire and the rose" as one.

But why can the poet say this? It is true that history forces him to value every moment; that once he enters the Garden, he must leave it again for further refinement in time, must enter the unreal world. It is also true that we can only admire the honesty of the personal struggle Eliot makes to recover the numinous "in and out of time." He has brought us in the *Quartets* to a moment of considerable importance in modern poetry by forcing us to see the text caught in the history of language, its evasiveness as sign, and the timelessness of the word. Yet outside "Burnt Norton" he still weighs his work down with the word in time, even if in "Little Gidding" he pretends he is outside time. He is still too much of a realist to let writing create its own terms with sharper refinement of its objects. He will not give himself up to either fact or history willingly, but remains positive that the numinous exists by exterior example, above all by the example of Christ. In effect, Eliot shows us that poetry cannot finally be religion, nor religion poetry, for religious belief is too powerful a myth to leave the moment unattended, and the mythic nature of poetry too open-ended to allow a single significance. He exemplifies, therefore, the evasiveness of myth-making in the modern even as it searches to replace religion by a sense of the numinous. Insofar as Eliot allows language to become transparent in the first two *Quartets*, he comes as close as any modern poet to showing how the numinous consciousness is caught in the split in the word. But this is a highly compromising position for him, and not one he chooses to remain in for long. Perhaps what Eliot has really wanted has been that condition of "complete simplicity," and ironically, it is religion and not poetry which finally seems to offer it to him.

COMPARATIVE REMYTHOLOGIZING

How then can we summarize the play of religion in the service of literature offered by Lawrence and Eliot? For Lawrence, the allegory of the sacred and profane is rather more conventional than for Eliot. Lawrence wanted to show, specifically, that experience needs remythologizing back to its dualistic religious origins, and that writing itself can be allegorical in dramatizing those origins. In his fiction and essays he wanted literally to remythologize sexuality, to make it sacred even while it is repaganized, to show that there is an eternal dialectic between body and spirit. The numinous, it is quite apparent in Lawrence's fictions, is erotic, evoked by the sensual word returning to the body. Writing is about the thematics of the split in consciousness. Eliot, on the other hand, wanted to show that the split is homologous to the split between word and meaning. So even the Christian Incarnation is a living event, and its mystique of intersecting time—sacred and secular—can be recovered in the making of poetry. For poetry is a probe into the ontology of the word, not simply its physicality. Clearly, for both Lawrence and Eliot, the Gods, savage and otherwise, make different demands, but they do have in common the attempt to make writing part of religious aspiration. I have been considering the different ways these writers have "raided" the "inarticulate" and shown us two major aspects of the allegory of the dissociated sensibility. What Lawrence calls the "living quick" and what Eliot says is "the still point" are both not simply the end of desire and the condition of faith, but the numinous moment to be recovered, with varying degrees of self-consciousness, in writing.

So, ironically enough, the numinous has structure for these writers, certainly a pattern of desire and fulfillment in the body for Lawrence, and an intersection of individual consciousness with historical meaning for Eliot. But art only authenticates the numinous insofar as it reveals that illumination is lived through—even as writing—as well as being a visionary event: a moment for the reader and writer to progress toward. It is, therefore, all a question of interpretation, which takes careful account of how we are caught in the contradiction between form and meaning. Art can only offer us the phenomenology of belief, the play of consciousness in language. Lawrence is right to insist that this is truly erotic (Roland Barthes has elaborated this point in *The Pleasure of the Text* more recently), and Eliot is right to insist that the diagram of intersecting time can show us the way "there and back." While Lawrence was greatly concerned with happiness for the body, Eliot seemed more concerned with interpretation theory. Each, in what are surely complementary (and exemplary) ways, tried to raise writing to the status of the numinous event, desired, intuited, and lived in. This motive of mythical thought is consistently the intentional factor, and for both men even becomes a matter of allowing vision to appropriate the text. "Vision" is irrevocably tied to allegorical forms.

Surely the modern has learned something from the experiment of both these writers. Between them, they offer us a range of possibilities for interpreting the way the mythical intention is tied to language. Their successes, I have tried to make clear, result from their consciousness of having to push art to the point of "saying it all," of deconstructing the sacred and not merely using myth. But, on the one hand, it seems inevitable that to return the word to the body will bring the novel to sensationalist limits, and either eradicate the play of the senses by overconscious effort, or demote consciousness to sense evidence alone. That is Lawrence's problem. On the other hand, it would seem inevitable that Eliot's union of the "fire" and the "rose" is a matter of spiritual interest only if it reduces the numinous to a theory of intersecting time, to be recovered only in moments of rare contemplative zeal. Both the body and history, that is, have a habit of creating fatalistic limits, and whatever we mean by the numinous is somehow dependent on breaking free from these allegories of consciousness and the closed systems of meaning that we can derive from them.

What can we conclude then about the place of myth in modern writing in the light of Lawrence's and Eliot's efforts? From a purely Structuralist viewpoint, Joyce has made us concerned with plot transformation, but Lawrence and Eliot are more ambitious about the fate of the word, Eliot most of all. What we find in the work of all three is that the text, as a mediation between the writer and the world, both uses the writer and is used by him. The author can literally only occupy the split in the sign, the borderline place. The more religious the intent in writing, the more pressure for the text to be all things to all men, to suggest a fusion between event and meaning. But the more intelligent the writer, the more vulnerable he becomes to the mythicity of his genre, and the more he realizes the impossibility of closing the gap. The text both controls discourse and yet demands that the author never stop talking. Myth is, then, creating and created, belying the numinous and demanding it, a function of the writer's vision which must in some way be unmediated—that is, able to move among and possibly unify even discrete events—*and* a mediation. The ideal is to establish the mythicity of both fact and vision, which means, first of all, as the Symbolists made clear, establishing the intensity of the physical evidence. Both Lawrence and Eliot insist on beginning with art as a metonymical statement. But then they are plainly troubled by the next step confronting reader and writer concerned about the religious motive in writing. We are never quite sure whether the recovery of the numinous means the recovery of the object itself, the facticity of events, particular and unique—or whether it means the primacy of some absent event and the freedom to make everything unique with constant metaphorical play. Furthermore, if we pursue one side or the other of this argument, we must create straw men of both, and make the numinous potential of consciousness simply commonplace or ethereal.

Lawrence and Eliot have shown us that we have no escape from this manichean presence of reality, though it follows that we must resist it with some dialectical and not dualistic theory of writing and its mythical intent. A sense of fact will always lend itself to allegorical meaning, if for no other reason than that we know we can never be in possession of complete knowledge. In that sense, all literature is allegorical in its treatment of the real. It is too reliant on language itself, on finding simply the "right word" (as Eliot discovers) which, when words fail, leaves us without metaphor at all. On the other hand, those visions which deny their own allegory demote reality into the endless movement of consciousness. What we might see then from the experiment of Lawrence and Eliot is that the truly numinous text is neither exclusively "unmediated vision" nor "mediated fact."[40] Writing attempts to be interpretative by reinforcing fact with the imaginative transformation into metaphor, but it also has to push the extremes of vision to the extremes of problematic fact. I am saying that what modern criticism may declare—in the light of language theory—to be the inevitability of deconstruction in serious texts is in fact what one of our more conventionally established modernists, T. S. Eliot, discovered in the act of writing. Ironically, here text supports theory rather than the other way round.

More perhaps than any other kind of writer, the author with religious and mythical intentions must embrace the dichotomous function of the word as vision and as fact. It is there, surely, that the pleasure, the uncertainty, and the anticipation of discovery for the reader and the writer begin. And one uncertainty is impossible to avoid. We are constantly in doubt as to whether literature is appropriating myth and other pursuits of the essential, or the other way round. If it is the former (as I have indicated it might be with Joyce) then religious beliefs in fictions are not truths to be discovered, however much they are presumed to be true, but signposts to a truth which can now reside in a new form, namely, in literature itself. I have been arguing largely from that standpoint as a counter to the predominant view that myth lies beyond the text. On the other hand, Lawrence and Eliot do at times assume that it is religion, visionary activity, that really takes over writing—which, again, it might very well do since it is itself a mythical system—and so words are pushed to a presemiological state, bare numinous events themselves which resist appropriation in any other way. Hence Eliot's early predilection for metonymy.

As Lawrence and Eliot come to realize—most acutely in Birkin's speeches in *Women in Love*, the cyclical patterning of *The Rainbow*, and in the early poems of the *Four Quar-*

tets—writing is not in an equation with consciousness, but a highly problematic function of it, whose complex nature must be part of any meaning the writer intends to offer. But sometimes this complexity, not surprisingly, is ignored, and there are moments in their writing when meaning becomes appropriated to such an extent that it overwhelms form, and the circle of attraction between fact and desire turns to pure mythopoeia. In other words, desire comes to dominate literature, and writing seems no longer exploratory. Then we find ourselves, as readers, on the side of literature as the underdog, wishing that Lawrence would forget Quetzalcoatl and get back to Kate, or wanting to leave the prayer to Mary (in "Dry Salvages") and return to "the bone's prayer to Death its God." We can only say that the mark of Lawrence's and Eliot's talents as writers, then, is their ability to resist ideology even as they are plainly seeking an elevated status for their own art. Similarly Joyce must resist the literal nature of the Ulysses story in order to keep the myth and his own art alive. Such, again, is the highly suggestive paradox of myth: it is discourse resisting mere ideology.

The text truly mediates, that is, when its vision and its own metaphysics of absence are one, when the extreme subjectivism of belief draws out toward the extreme uncertainty of the word as unstable meaning. In the best writing, neither pole ever really holds sway, and the text approaches aphorism and tautology, yet draws back realistically into more discursive modes. The aphorism deconstructs, showing its self-reflexive but productive nature. We find the writer deliberately moving in a tension between opposites, originally created, of course, by the drama of the gap between form and content. He is tied to the reference of the senses, the area of feeling-states, and all the welcome ambiguity of consciousness, even while he finds there the motive for metaphor in the gap between word and thing.

What Lawrence and Eliot have done for modern literature, in their different ways, with a uniquely energetic performance (unique, that is, to the effort to recover the numinous) is to

burden literature with the continual rediscovery of fresh consciousness and new relations among word, vision, and fact.
In short, they are concerned with the problem of belief in
writing, with the text carrying the full responsibility of jus-
tifying a vision. This latter need points up the very issues I
have been referring to concerning the mythicity of literature.
Indeed, Lawrence and Eliot converge on a central problem of
modern writing, which is the question of whether writing can
carry belief at all.

So self-conscious are the modern and the postmodern about
establishing the ontological status of literature, that whatever
is asserted thematically often appears appropriated by highly
self-conscious form (as in Hawkes's and Barth's use of mythological motif; the heady associative logic of Pynchon's or
Barthelme's surrealism; or Golding's clever concern with the
closely linked growth of consciousness and language expressed in allegorical plots). This modern reinvention of Structuralist interest has been called many things, and in its extreme
cases (especially with Pynchon) fits what Roland Barthes has
usefully referred to as the "subversion of writing," the creation
of a literature aiming not for expansion of meaning out into
the world, but "infra-signification." Or, as Lévi-Strauss would
say, modern fiction has become obsessed by the weakening
in myth of its own repetitiveness. Not only can the circle
break, as I have just said, when myth and religious aspirations
appropriate the novel's structure—it also does so when form
is appropriated with greater emphasis than meaning. If the
dialectic between the symbol as numinous and the symbol
as fixed model is not maintained, writing either way is sub-
verted. Lawrence and Eliot may have the same intention of
recovering the numinous in writing, but they take part in this
experiment of subversion by appropriating form—by encouraging the inevitable infra-signifying of language—in quite different ways. Lawrence wants the body to subvert writing;
Eliot wants the word to stand still with increasing refinement.
(Joyce wanted writing to subvert through the imperialism of
the pun.) Which brings us again to the question of the par-

adoxical status of the sign, forced to mediate these aims, as the source of the mythic.

We can say, in sum, that we have no way of discussing the problem of mythical or religious writing except as writing, which forces us to start with the ontological status of the word itself, as we saw Eliot doing in *Four Quartets*. It is only language that essentializes meaning, that assigns meaning to forms, thereby not merely allowing the writer and speaker to appropriate meaning, but insisting that they do so. Language is the object the writer must find new forms for. Meaning may be emptied, adjusted, or tampered with in many ways, but it can never be entirely impoverished, must be always somehow essential, and yet never really sufficient. To look for essence, then, is to look for undeniable fact which, as Eliot kept on saying, is also the "right word." But, as we have noted, it can never be the word alone. For all we have in the sign systems we call reality are signs about signs, waiting to be further interpreted, before we even get to thematics and immanence. The numinous fact to be recovered, first of all, is a matter of expository tact. For the word must always appear appropriated in some way and never be entirely pristine; it can only lead us on to other words, as Eliot asserted—that is, to language not only differentiating essences, but creating new facts. The word as sign is always a potential emblem in the play between metonymy and metaphor.

This is not a nominalist enterprise, for again, every intentional act in writing is made unintentional by the paradoxical function of writing. Words have the potential to be transparent, to suggest meanings which merge and obliterate themselves in the play of the consciousness they encourage. Yet, quite simply, we are not involved in the interpretative act of either reading or writing if we do not return to the word as opaque, stopping consciousness, and causing us to become involved in its cut or split. Although he need not be fully conscious of this, the writer or reader can never escape this semiological role-playing, and it is this situation, in particular, which is of great significance for defining the mythic. If we believe, as I have tried to show Lawrence and Eliot believed, that the word itself tries to be all, even with some translinguistic fact driving our attempt to recover the numinous (from orgastic pleasures and theosophical "powers" to the conventionally Christian myths of salvation), then regardless of what that fact is, we are assuming that language has some transparency to carry even the "hints and guesses" of the ineffable. In fact, as it would seem Eliot realizes in the *Quartets*, it is only that transparency which is the hint. And the more we intend to use words as signposts to that which cannot be expressed in words, as Lawrence also aims to do in his descriptions of place and in his treatment of human sexuality, then the more words develop an opacity and appear (misleadingly) to equate themselves with things. Similarly, if we choose, in the manner of a Robbe-Grillet, for example, to emphasize the opacity of words, to locate events as words, we are still pushing our intentional meaning to extremes, and inevitably causing the reader to want to break out of the bondage of empirical fact, to go back to a sense of immanent meaning. We have no escape from this dialectic of semiotic meaning, this peculiar ability language has to appropriate the function opposite to the one we intend for it. And it is Joyce, Lawrence, and especially Eliot, I want to suggest, who capture its significance for the modern tradition in English. Their search for the word in its interpretive function is always a fully conscious movement in and out of the transparency of language, as well as in and out of the more easily identifiable oppositional models (visionary and factual) for full and empty living. The paradox is that Lawrence's obsession with the numinous in love must codify it, and Eliot's attempt to recover the moment in the garden elsewhere than in the garden must end in superstition. As highly energetic beliefs, Lawrence's vitalism and Eliot's Christianity (not to mention, of course, Lawrence's Christianity and Eliot's vitalism) do at times take over the writing, but the saving grace for each writer is that he knows that it is writing which must win in the end.

For both writers, writing is ontology and it is fact. There

is no doubt that they felt that literature factualized their religious motives, but more important, it suggested to both of them that there must be a point at which the sense of the numinous is not only literal but can be said to be open to progression. That is, the recovery of the numinous is possible only insofar as writing tries to develop its intent to literalize experience, to remain married to both the body and its metaphysics of absence.

It goes without saying that this tautology does not relieve us of a central paradox in the act of reading and writing. The sense of the numinous and the sacred—any apostrophic term to convey the idea of the holy on which religion depends—is both inside and outside the text at once. The experience of the holy outside the text, which may infiltrate writing, can only be mediated in discourse. It resists writing and speech, yet it is only in writing and speech that the definition of the boundaries of the holy and the uniqueness of the experience can take place. We can say that the religious motive in literature is not *a priori* a mystery-in-itself, but only as evasive or factual as the function of language. How literal can we then expect the numinous to be? To answer that question, we are left with the impossible task of defining both "literal" and "numinous," without presupposing either. From the point of view of defining the numinous, we can say that it is nothing if not the paradox of exteriority demanding interiority. For the numinous to remain a useful term, it must remain problematic. To define it, then, from the perspective that Rudolf Otto has taken, is to use repetitively analogous terms for the "full" and "empty": "mighty" and "fearful" *mysterium tremendum*, and the "empty distances" of "silence," "darkness," and "void." But that is evasive, turning merely to function to account for the numinous. We are reminded also that what Otto describes as the elusiveness of *numena* is no stranger, of course, to the nonreligious poet. The familiar existentialist poetics of the void and the silence, while skeptical of the sublime and declaratively secular, has acquired certain religious connotations in its own right, not to mention its profound influence on modern Christian and Jewish thought.

We are not, it is clear, any nearer to knowing what the numinous is, even when we can offer interminable analogues for the "full" and "empty," or show that its expression is fraught with ambiguity and doomed to inaccuracy. Instead, perhaps all we can say about the numinous consciousness is that it leads to certain persistent sets of opposites, to a dismantling of its own terms to show its hermeneutic structure, a fondness for a dualistic and allegorical explanation of experience, a necessary mediation between the transparent and the opaque, the interior and the exterior, as reasonable extremes which force us to seek a hypothetical synthesis. In a sense, it does exactly what we have found in the linguisticality of myth in the preceding chapter. The text itself is nothing less than the attempt to show that the numinous depends on the linguistic allegory of intent.

There is no easy conclusion to be reached from the intentions revealed in the work of Lawrence and Eliot and the allegorical origins of their split in consciousness. Clearly the paradox of the numinous is as much a paradox of language itself, and as readers we have nowhere else to start but there. But the catalogue of emotions and reasons we associate with a contemplation of the holy in no way establishes an increasingly complex set of objective attributes for the subjectivity of "God language." Such language does not, of course, prove the objective or essential presence of God or the mythic in a limited, definable way, separate from the metaphysics of discourse. The catalogue could be said to presuppose a sense of the numinous, but that begs the question. Or it could be said to demand the numinous, or a God concept vast enough to unify its attributes, but that leaves the door open to the relativity of its demands on consciousness, and even questions of sensibility and taste. Even so, it is not surprising to find our writers arguing from the consciousness of the numinous to consciousness of God, and from God back to the numinous, thereby literally having the best of both worlds.

Eliot, in "Religion and Literature" (1935), for example, makes his position as a believer in the supernatural quite plain, and from there he can safely argue in his essays for an "unconscious" Christian literature, because a conscious or objective one is unnecessarily obvious, too clearly devotional or propagandistic, and easily prone to the attempt to sound literary. Such statements are possible, because Eliot can take it for granted in his essays—not in the poetry, I hope I have shown—that "the common ground between religion and fiction is behaviour. Our religion imposes our ethics, our judgement and criticism of ourselves, and our behaviour toward our fellow men." So, "it is our business, as readers of literature, to know what we like. It is our business, as Christians, *as well as* readers of literature, to know what we ought to be like."[41] Do we trust this to work for his poetry? No, for the split between Christian and poet, even the man who suffers and the man who writes, constantly undergoes close scrutiny in the poetry. Eliot does not forget that his subject, if he is to be concerned with illumination, must be consciousness itself. A reliance on the devious paths interpretation must take and a compounding set of questions about the validity of the poet's own experience are then central to his task.

Lawrence, too, pretends to have a clear argument in his expository prose, a relatively certain starting point which is not reflected in his fiction: "the real problem for humanity isn't whether God exists or not. God always is, and we all know it. But the problem is, how to get to him." Lawrence's irony should not escape us, for as neat as his arguments seem to be in the essays of the *Phoenix* collections, the continual reworking of doubt about the recovery of the numinous, let alone how to get there, is clear in the long metaphysical discussions his characters have in the major novels after *The Rainbow*, as well as in his euphemistic preoccupation with sex as holy. Clearly, if we refer to their literary works, Lawrence and Eliot are both aware that a God concept, present and justified, can work against the expository tact of fiction and poetry; but that awareness, for them, does not negate the need to recover a sense of the mythic and the numinous in the nature of writing itself.

NOTES

Chapter 1

1. Carl Jung, "Instinct and the Unconscious," in *The Collected Works of Carl Jung*, ed. G. Adler, M. Fordham, and H. Read, trans. R.F.C. Hull, Bollingen Series XXX, vol. 15 (Princeton: Princeton University Press, 1966), p. 81.

2. Jacques Lacan, *The Four Fundamental Concepts of Psychoanalysis*, ed. Jacques-Alain Miller, trans. A. Sheridan (London: Hogarth Press, 1977), p. 153.

3. Jung, *Collected Works*, 15, p. 82.

4. Jung, *Collected Works*, 15, p. 81.

5. Jung, *Collected Works*, 15, p. 98.

6. Jung, *Collected Works*, 15, pp. 104-105.

7. G. S. Kirk makes this point in his book, *Myth: Its Meaning and Functions in Ancient and Other Cultures* (London: Cambridge University Press; Berkeley: University of California Press, 1970), pp. 275-276. His reference is to Jean Piaget's *Play, Dreams and Imitation in Childhood*.

8. Jung, *Collected Works*, 15, p. 80.

9. Jung, *Collected Works*, 15, p. 80.

10. Jung, *Collected Works*, 15, pp. 80-81.

11. Jung, *Collected Works*, vol. 9i (Princeton: Princeton University Press, 1969), pp. 40-41.

12. Jung, *Collected Works*, 9i, pp. 22-23.

13. Northrop Frye, "The Archetypes of Literature," in *Fables of Identity* (New York: Harcourt, 1963), pp. 8, 10, 12.

14. Frye himself writes in "Literature and Myth," in *Relations of Literary Study*, ed. James Thorpe (New York: Modern Language Association, 1967), p. 38 that the "tradition of allegorical interpretation played an important role" in the transition from myth to literature.

15. Frye, "Literature and Myth," p. 38.

16. Frye, "Archetypes of Literature," p. 15.

17. Frye, "Archetypes of Literature," p. 15.

18. There are now a number of introductions to semiotics and I have found the following useful: Umberto Eco, *A Theory of Semiotics* (Bloomington: Indiana University Press, 1976); Roland Barthes, *Elements of Semiology*, trans. A. Lavers and C. Smith (New York: Hill and Wang, 1968); Pierre Guiraud, *Semiology*, trans. G. Gross (London: Routledge and Kegan Paul, 1975); Terence Hawkes, *Structuralism and Semiotics* (London: Methuen, 1977). Perhaps the most useful general introductions to interpretation theory in its literary application are David Hoy, *The Critical Circle* (Berkeley: University of California Press, 1978) and Paul Ricoeur, *Interpretation Theory* (Fort Worth: Texas Christian University Press, 1976).

19. Paul de Man, *Allegories of Reading* (New Haven: Yale University Press, 1979), p. 5.

20. See René Girard's *Violence and the Sacred* (Baltimore: Johns Hopkins University Press, 1977) for a theory of how violence makes the sacred possible and understandable.

21. Jacques Derrida, "Structure, Sign and Play in the Discourse of the Human Sciences," *Writing and Difference*, trans., introd., and additional notes A. Bass (Chicago: Chicago University Press, 1978), p. 286.

22. Girard, *Violence*, pp. 299–300.

23. In addition to the references in note 18 (especially Hoy) the following is useful on Schleiermacher: *History and Hermeneutic*, ed., R. Funk (New York: Harper and Row, 1967), especially Heinze Kimmerle's essay "Hermeneutical Theory or Ontological Hermeneutics."

24. Wilhelm Dilthey, *Gessamelte Schriften* (Leipzig and Berlin, 1927) is yet to be translated into English. Kimmerle's essay cited in note 23 is useful.

25. See especially Rudolf Bultmann, *Essays Philosophical and Theological*, trans. J. C. Greig (London, 1952).

26. See Martin Heidegger, *Being and Time*, trans. J. Macquarrie and E. Robinson (New York: Harper and Row, 1962) and Hans-Georg Gadamer, *Truth and Method*, ed. and trans. G. Barden and J. Cumming (New York: Seabury, 1975). See also Hoy (note 18) and Wolfhart Pannenberg, "Hermeneutics and Universal History," trans. P. J. Achtemeier, in *History and Hermeneutic*, ed. Funk (note 23) for a useful outline of Gadamer's view of history.

27. Hoy, *Critical Circle*, pp. 419, 426. Emphasis added by Hoy.

28. See especially Jacques Derrida, *Of Grammatology*, trans. G. C. Spivak (Baltimore: Johns Hopkins University Press, 1976).

29. See Norman Holland, *Poems in Persons* (New York: Norton, 1973) and especially Jean Starobinski's article "The Inside and the Outside," in *Hudson Review*, vol. 28, no. 3, Autumn 1975, pp. 333-351.

30. Paul Ricoeur, *The Rule of Metaphor*, trans. R. Czerny (Toronto: University of Toronto Press, 1977).

31. Emil Benveniste, *Problems in General Linguistics*, trans. M. E. Meek (Florida: University of Miami Press, 1971).

32. See Paul Ricoeur, "The Metaphorical Process," in *Critical Inquiry* (special issue on Metaphor), vol. 5, no. 1, Autumn 1978.

33. Ricoeur, *Rule of Metaphor*, p. 131.

34. Ricoeur, *Rule of Metaphor*, p. 198.

35. Jean Cohen, *Structure du langage poétique* (Paris: Flammarion, 1966).

36. See fifth section of this chapter, "The Unconscious as Lack." The relevant works in English by Jacques Lacan are *The Language of the Self*, trans. and notes A. Wilden (Baltimore: Johns Hopkins University Press, 1968); *Écrits: A Selection*, trans. A. Sheridan (London: Tavistock Publications, 1977); and *The Four Fundamental Concepts of Psychoanalysis* (see note 2). Since writing this study, I have read Maria Ruegg's useful article "Metaphor and Metonymy: The Logic of Structuralist Rhetoric," *Glyph 6* (Baltimore: Johns Hopkins University Press, 1979). This is an excellent summary of the way in which Lacan attempts to restore a fundamental monism to Structuralist theory.

37. Ricoeur, "Metaphorical Process," p. 159.

38. Ricoeur, "Metaphorical Process," p. 146.

39. Ricoeur, "Metaphorical Process," p. 156.

40. Ricoeur, "Metaphorical Process," p. 148.

41. Ricoeur, "Metaphorical Process," p. 151.

42. Ricoeur, "Metaphorical Process," pp. 153, 155.

43. Ricoeur, *Rule of Metaphor*, pp. 84-85.

44. Ricoeur, *Rule of Metaphor*, p. 98.

45. Lacan, *The Four Fundamental Concepts*, p. 212.

46. Lacan, *The Four Fundamental Concepts*, pp. 247-252.

47. Holland, *Poems in Persons*, p. 83.

48. Holland, *Poems in Persons*, p. 83.

49. Holland, *Poems in Persons*, p. 151.

50. Holland, *Poems in Persons*, pp. 152-153.

51. Starobinski, "The Inside and the Outside," p. 335.

52. Starobinski, "The Inside and the Outside," p. 342.

53. Starobinski, "The Inside and the Outside," p. 348.

54. Derrida, *Of Grammatology*, pp. 271, 275.

55. Lacan, *Écrits*, p. 65.

56. Lacan, *Écrits*, p. 66.

57. Lacan, *Écrits*, p. 49.

58. Lacan, *Écrits*, p. 52.

59. Lacan, *Four Fundamental Concepts*, p. 22.

60. Lacan, *Four Fundamental Concepts*, p. 31.

61. Lacan, *Four Fundamental Concepts*, p. 25.

62. Lacan, *Écrits*, p. 138.

63. Lacan, *Four Fundamental Concepts*, p. 44.

64. Lacan, *Four Fundamental Concepts*, p. 218.

65. Lacan, *Four Fundamental Concepts*, p. 204.

66. Lacan, *Écrits*, p. 274.

67. Lacan, *Écrits*, pp. 166-167.

68. Lacan, *Four Fundamental Concepts*, p. 176.

69. Two very useful commentaries on Lacan in English are A. Wilden's edition and commentary on Lacan's "Function of Language in Psychoanalysis" (from *Écrits*) in *The Language of the Self* (see note 36) which began Lacan studies in this country; and Fredric Jameson's brilliant essay in *Literature and Psychoanalysis* (*Yale French Studies*, 55/56, 1977), which substantially revises his view of Lacan in *The Prison-House of Language* (Princeton: Princeton University Press, 1972). See also Maria Ruegg's "Metaphor and Metonymy" cited in note 36.

70. Lacan, *Écrits*, pp. 5-6.

71. Lacan, *Four Fundamental Concepts*, pp. 277-282.

72. Lacan, *Four Fundamental Concepts*, p. 280.

73. Lacan, *Écrits*, p. 54.

74. Lacan, *Écrits*, p. 187.

75. Lacan, *Four Fundamental Concepts*, p. 206.

Chapter 2

1. Claude Lévi-Strauss, *The Origin of Table Manners*, trans. J. and D. Weightman (New York: Harper and Row, 1968), p. 131.

2. Roland Barthes, *Sade / Fourier / Loyola*, trans. R. Miller (New York: Hill and Wang, 1976), p. 7.

3. See Claude Lévi-Strauss, "Jean-Jacques Rousseau, Founder of the Sciences of Man" in *Structural Anthropology*, vol. II, trans. M. Layton (New York: Basic Books, 1976).

4. Claude Lévi-Strauss, *Tristes Tropiques*, trans J. and D. Weightman (New York: Atheneum, 1974), p. 62.

5. Lévi-Strauss, *Tristes Tropiques*, p. 412.

6. Lévi-Strauss, *Tristes Tropiques*, pp. 413-414.

7. Lévi-Strauss, *Table Manners*, p. 131.

8. Lévi-Strauss, *Tristes Tropiques*, pp. 414-415.

9. Claude Lévi-Strauss, "The Story of Asdiwal," *Structural Anthropology*, vol. II, p. 184.

10. Claude Lévi-Strauss, *The Raw and the Cooked*, trans. J. and D. Weightman (New York: Harper and Row, 1969), p. 12.

11. Claude Lévi-Strauss, *The Savage Mind* (Chicago: University of Chicago Press, 1966), p. 252.

12. Claude Lévi-Strauss, *Structural Anthropology*, trans. C. Jacobson and B. G. Schoepf (New York: Harper and Row, 1963), p. 203.

13. Lévi-Strauss, *Tristes Tropiques*, p. 209.

14. Jean Piaget, *Main Trends in Interdisciplinary Research* (London: Allen and Unwin, 1973), p. 22.

15. Lévi-Strauss, *Savage Mind*, p. 254.

16. This is the theme of René Girard's *Deceit, Desire and the Novel* (Baltimore: Johns Hopkins University Press, 1965) and is taken up again in *Violence and the Sacred*.

17. Lévi-Strauss, *Savage Mind*, pp. 257-260.

18. Claude Lévi-Strauss and Roman Jakobson, "Charles Baudelaire's 'Les Chats,' " trans. R. and F. de George in *The Structuralists from Marx to Lévi-Strauss* (New York: Anchor, 1972).

19. Lévi-Strauss, *Savage Mind*, p. 263.

20. Lévi Strauss, " 'Les Chats,' " p. 124.

21. Lévi-Strauss, "The Structural Study of Myth, " *Structural Anthropology*, pp. 206-231.

22. Lévi-Strauss, " 'Les Chats,' " p. 124.

23. Claude Lévi-Strauss, *The Raw and the Cooked*, trans. J. and D. Weightman (New York: Harper and Row, 1963), p. 18.

24. Lévi-Strauss, *The Raw and the Cooked*, pp. 14-15.

25. Roland Barthes, *Image-Music-Text*, trans. S. Heath (New York: Hill and Wang, 1977), pp. 165-166.

26. Barthes, *Image-Music-Text*, pp. 166-167.

27. Roland Barthes, *Mythologies*, trans. A. Lavers (New York: Hill and Wang, 1972), p. 144.

28. Barthes, *Mythologies*, p. 120.

29. Barthes, *Mythologies*, p. 129.

30. Barthes, *Mythologies*, p. 123.

31. Barthes, *Mythologies*, pp. 123-127.

32. Barthes, *Mythologies*, p. 135.

33. Barthes, *Mythologies*, p. 135.

34. Barthes, *Mythologies*, p. 133.

35. Barthes, *Mythologies*, p. 136.

36. Lévi-Strauss, *Tristes Tropiques*, p. 44.

37. Paul de Man, *Blindness and Insight: Essays in the Rhetoric of Contemporary Criticism* (New York: Oxford University Press, 1971), p. 75.

38. de Man, *Blindness*, p. 76.

Chapter 3

1. James Joyce, *Ulysses* (New York: Vintage, 1961), p. 50.

2. Claude Lévi-Strauss, *From Honey to Ashes*, trans. J. and D. Weightman (New York: Harper and Row, 1973), p. 473.

3. Claude Lévi-Strauss, "Four Winnebago Myths," *Structural Anthopology*, vol. II, trans. M. Layton (New York: Basic Books, 1976), p. 204.

4. Lévi-Strauss, *From Honey to Ashes*, p. 473.

5. James Joyce, *Stephen Hero* (New York: New Directions, 1963), p. 211.

6. Joyce, *Stephen Hero*, p. 213.

7. Extracts from the *Paris* and *Pola Notebooks* in *James Joyce: The Critical Writings*, ed. E. Mason and R. Ellmann (New York: Viking, 1964), pp. 141-148.

8. James Joyce, *Portrait of the Artist as a Young Man* (New York: Viking, 1964), p. 206.

9. S. L. Goldberg, *The Classical Temper* (New York: Barnes and Noble, 1961), p. 223.

10. Roland Barthes, *Mythologies*, trans. A. Lavers (New York: Hill and Wang, 1972), p. 123.

11. Barthes, *Mythologies*, p. 155.
12. Clive Hart, *Structure and Motif in "Finnegans Wake"* (London: Faber, 1962).
13. Hart, *Structure and Motif*, p. 63.
14. Hart, *Structure and Motif*, p. 87.
15. Margot Norris, *The Decentered Universe of "Finnegans Wake"* (Baltimore: Johns Hopkins University Press, 1974).
16. Norris, *Decentered Universe*, p. 85.
17. Norris, *Decentered Universe*, p. 139.
18. Norris, *Decentered Universe*, pp. 56-57.

Chapter 4

1. Roland Barthes, *Mythologies*, trans. A. Lavers (New York: Hill and Wang, 1972), p. 159.
2. Mircea Eliade, *Myth and Reality*, trans. W. R. Trask (New York: Harper and Row, 1963), p. 191.
3. Eliade, *Myth and Reality*, p. 192.
4. Eliade, *Myth and Reality*, p. 192.
5. Rudolf Otto, *The Idea of the Holy*, trans. J. W. Harvey (London: Penguin, 1959). See especially Chapter V, "Analogies and Associated Feelings."
6. B. Malinowski, *Myth in Primitive Psychology* (1926), quoted in Eliade, *Myth and Reality*, p. 20.
7. Barthes, *Mythologies*, p. 123.
8. See Geoffrey Hartman, "Structuralism: The Anglo-American Adventure," in *Structuralism*, ed. J. Ehrmann (New York: Anchor, 1970), pp. 154-155.
9. John White, *Mythology in the Modern Novel* (Princeton: Princeton University Press, 1971).
10. C. Lévi-Strauss, *Structural Anthropology*, trans. C. Jacobson and B. G. Schoepf (New York: Harper and Row, 1963), p. 216.
11. Lévi-Strauss, *Structural Anthropology*, p. 246.
12. James Joyce, *Ulysses* (New York: Vintage, 1961), p. 270.
13. Paul Ricoeur, *Interpretation Theory* (Fort Worth: Texas Christian University Press, 1976), pp. 86-87.
14. See Jacques Derrida, *Of Grammatology*, trans. G. C. Spivak (Baltimore: Johns Hopkins University Press, 1976).
15. Derrida, *Of Grammatology*, pp. 36-37.
16. Derrida, *Of Grammatology*, p. 50.

17. Derrida, *Of Grammatology*, pp. 62-63.
18. Derrida, *Of Grammatology*, p. 65.

Chapter 5

1. D. H. Lawrence, "The Novel," *Phoenix II*, ed. and intro. W. Roberts and H. T. Moore (London: Heinemann, 1968), p. 416.

2. T. S. Eliot, "Virgil and the Christian World," *On Poetry and Poets* (New York: Noonday, 1961), p. 137.

3. John Harrison, *The Reactionaries* (London: Gollancz, 1966) is a useful summary of the reactionary elements of both Lawrence's and Eliot's work. For an interesting critique of Lawrence's "Heroic Vitalism," which has certainly drawn more criticism than Eliot's politics, see Eric Bentley, *The Cult of the Superman* (Gloucester, Mass.: Peter Smith, 1969; reprint of the British edition of 1947).

4. T. S. Eliot, "East Coker" V, *Four Quartets, Collected Poems 1909-1962* (New York: Harcourt, Brace and World, 1970)—hereafter referred to as *CP*—p. 189.

5. D. H. Lawrence, *Women in Love* (New York: Viking, 1960), p. 238.

6. Lawrence, *Women in Love*, p. 137.

7. Eliot, "East Coker" II, *CP*, p. 185.

8. Eliot, "East Coker" V, *CP*, p. 189.

9. D. H. Lawrence, "Study of Thomas Hardy," *Phoenix*, ed. and intro. E. D. McDonald (London: Heinemann, 1936), p. 431.

10. Angus Fletcher, *Allegory: The Theory of a Symbolic Mode* (Ithaca: Cornell University Press, 1964).

11. See Harold Bloom, "The Breaking of Form," *Deconstruction and Criticism* (New York: Seabury, 1979), pp. 1-37.

12. See Paul de Man, *Allegory of Reading* (New Haven: Yale University Press, 1979), especially "Semiology and Rhetoric," pp. 3-19.

13. Fletcher, *Allegory*, p. 21.

14. See Daniel Weiss, *Oedipus in Nottingham* (Seattle: University of Washington Press, 1962) and David Cavitch, *D. H. Lawrence and the New World* (New York: Oxford, 1969) for the most consistent applications of the "Freudian" reading of his fiction.

15. At this point, perhaps Mary Freeman's *D. H. Lawrence: A Basic Study of His Ideas* (New York: Grossett, n.d.; original edition,

University of Florida Press, 1955) is still the best summary of a wide range of intellectual influences on Lawrence.

16. "Art and the Individual," probably written between May and July 1908 when Lawrence was 23; in *Phoenix II*, pp. 221-226.

17. Lawrence, *Women in Love*, p. 193.

18. Lawrence, *Women in Love*, p. 305.

19. Eliot, "Dry Salvages" II, *Four Quartets*, CP, p. 194.

20. Eliot, "Gerontion," *CP*, p. 30.

21. Eliot, "The Hollow Men," *CP*, p. 81.

22. Eliot, "Portrait of a Lady, " *CP*, p. 12.

23. Eliot, "The Hollow Men," *CP*, pp. 81-82.

24. Eliot, "Preludes," *CP*, pp. 14-15.

25. Eliot, *The Waste Land* V, CP, p. 68.

26. Eliot, "The Hollow Men," *CP*, p. 82.

27. Eliot, *The Waste Land* V, CP, p. 66.

28. Eliot, "Ash Wednesday" II, *CP*, pp. 87-88.

29. Eliot, "Ash Wednesday" IV, *CP*, p. 90.

30. Eliot, "Choruses from *The Rock*" I, CP, p. 147.

31. Eliot, "Choruses" I, *CP*, p. 149.

32. Eliot, "Choruses" VI, *CP*, p. 161.

33. Eliot, "East Coker" V, *CP*, pp. 188-189.

34. Eliot, "Burnt Norton" I, *CP*, p. 176.

35. Eliot, "Burnt Norton" I, *CP*, p. 175.

36. Eliot, "Burnt Norton" I, *CP*, p. 175.

37. Eliot, "Little Gidding" V, *CP*, p. 208.

38. Eliot, "Burnt Norton" II, *CP*, p. 178.

39. Eliot, "Dry Salvages" V, *CP*, p. 199.

40. For a useful discussion of these alternative interpretations of the poem as object, see Murray Krieger, "Mediation, Language, and Vision in the Reading of Literature" in *Interpretation: Theory and Practice*, ed. Charles Singleton (Baltimore: Johns Hopkins University Press, 1969), pp. 211-242. Also see G. Hartman, *The Unmediated Vision* (New York: Harcourt, 1954, 1966).

41. T. S. Eliot, "Religion and Literature," *Selected Essays* (London: Faber, 1951), p. 399.

SELECT BIBLIOGRAPHY

Bachelard, Gaston. *The Poetics of Reverie*, trans. D. Russell (New York: Orion, 1969).

Barthes, Roland. *Elements of Semiology*, trans. A. Lavers and C. Smith (New York: Hill and Wang, 1968).

———. *Image-Music-Text*, trans. Stephen Heath (New York: Hill and Wang, 1977).

———. *Mythologies*, trans. A. Lavers (New York: Hill and Wang, 1972).

———. *Sade / Fourier / Loyola*, trans. R. Miller (New York: Hill and Wang, 1976).

Benveniste, Emil. *Problems in General Linguistics*, trans. M. E. Meek (Coral Gables: University of Miami Press, 1971).

Bloom, Harold, et al. *Deconstruction and Criticism* (New York: Seabury, 1979).

Burke, Kenneth. *Language as Symbolic Action* (Berkeley: University of California Press, 1968).

———. *The Rhetoric of Religion* (Berkeley: University of California Press, 1970).

De Man, Paul. *Allegories of Reading* (New Haven: Yale University Press, 1979).

———. *Blindness and Insight: Essays in the Rhetoric of Contemporary Criticism* (New York: Oxford University Press, 1971).

Derrida, Jacques. *Of Grammatology*, trans. G. C. Spivak (Baltimore: Johns Hopkins University Press, 1976).

———. *Writing and Difference*, trans. A. Bass (Chicago: University of Chicago Press, 1978).

Eliade, Mircea. *Myth and Reality*, trans. W. R. Trask (New York: Harper and Row, 1963).

Eliot, T. S. *Collected Poems 1909-1962* (New York: Harcourt, 1970).

———. *On Poetry and Poets* (New York: Noonday, 1961).

———. *Selected Essays* (London: Faber, 1951).

Feldman, Burton and Richardson, Robert. *The Rise of Modern My-*

thology 1680-1860 (Bloomington: Indiana University Press, 1972).

Fletcher, Angus. *Allegory: The Theory of a Symbolic Mode* (Ithaca: Cornell University Press, 1964).

Frye, Northrop. *Anatomy of Criticism* (Princeton: Princeton University Press, 1957).

————. *Fables of Identity* (New York: Harcourt, 1961).

————. "Literature and Myth," in *Relations of Literary Study*, ed. J. Thorpe (New York: Modern Language Association, 1967).

Funk, Robert, ed. *History and Hermeneutic* (New York: Harper and Row, 1967).

Gadamer, Hans-Georg. *Truth and Method*, ed. and trans. G. Barden and J. Cumming (New York: Seabury, 1975).

Girard, René. *Deceit, Desire, and the Novel*, trans. Y. Freccero (Baltimore: Johns Hopkins University Press, 1965).

————. *Violence and the Sacred*, trans. P. Gregory (Baltimore: Johns Hopkins University Press, 1977).

Goldberg, S. L. *The Classical Temper* (New York: Barnes and Noble, 1961).

Hart, Clive. *Structure and Motif in "Finnegans Wake"* (London: Faber, 1962).

Hartman, Geoffrey. *Beyond Formalism* (New Haven: Yale University Press, 1970).

————. *The Unmediated Vision* (New York: Harcourt, 1966).

Heidegger, Martin. *Being and Time*, trans. J. Macquarrie and E. Robinson (New York: Harper and Row, 1962).

Holland, Norman. *Poems in Persons* (New York: Norton, 1973).

Hoy, David. *The Critical Circle* (Berkeley: University of California Press, 1978).

Jameson, Fredric. "Imaginary and Symbolic in Lacan," in *Literature and Psychoanalysis*, ed. S. Felman, *Yale French Studies*, nos. 55/56, 1977.

————. *The Prison-House of Language* (Princeton: Princeton University Press, 1972).

Joyce, James. *Finnegans Wake* (New York: Viking, 1959).

————. *James Joyce: The Critical Writings*, ed. E. Mason and R. Ellmann (New York: Viking, 1964).

————. *Portrait of the Artist as a Young Man* (New York: Viking, 1964).

————. *Stephen Hero* (New York: New Directions, 1963).

Select Bibliography

——. *Ulysses* (New York: Vintage, 1961).

Jung, Carl. *The Collected Works of Carl Jung*, ed. G. Adler, M. Fordham, and H. Read, trans. R.F.C. Hull (Princeton: Princeton University Press; Bollingen Series XXX; 1959, 1969).

Kirk, G. S. *Myth: Its Meaning and Function in Ancient and Other Cultures* (London: Cambridge University Press; Berkeley: University of California Press, 1970).

Krieger, Murray. "Mediation, Language, and Vision in the Reading of Literature," in *Interpretation Theory and Practice*, ed. C. S. Singleton (Baltimore: Johns Hopkins University Press, 1969).

——. *Theory of Criticism* (Baltimore: Johns Hopkins University Press, 1976).

Lawrence, D. H. *Phoenix*, ed. E. D. McDonald (London: Heinemann, 1936).

——. *Phoenix II*, ed. W. Roberts and H. T. Moore (London: Heinemann, 1968).

——. *Women in Love* (New York: Viking, 1960).

Lévi-Strauss, Claude. *From Honey to Ashes*, trans. J. and D. Weightman (New York: Harper and Row, 1973).

——. *The Origin of Table Manners*, trans. J. and D. Weightman (New York: Harper and Row, 1968).

——. *The Raw and the Cooked*, trans. J. and D. Weightman (New York: Harper and Row, 1969).

——. *The Savage Mind* (Chicago: University of Chicago Press, 1966).

——. *Structural Anthropology*, trans. C. Jacobson and B. G. Schoepf (New York: Harper and Row, 1963).

——. *Structural Anthropology II*, trans. M. Layton (New York: Basic Books, 1976).

——. *Totemism*, trans. R. Needham (Boston: Beacon, 1963).

——. *Tristes Tropiques*, trans. J. and D. Weightman (New York: Atheneum, 1974).

Norris, Margot. *The Decentered Universe of "Finnegans Wake"* (Baltimore: Johns Hopkins University Press, 1974).

Otto, Rudolf. *The Idea of the Holy*, trans. J. W. Harvey (London: Penguin, 1959).

Piaget, Jean. *Main Trends in Interdisciplinary Research* (London: Allen and Unwin, 1973).

——. *Structuralism*, trans. C. Maschler (New York: Harper and Row, 1970).

Richardson, Robert. See Feldman, Burton.
Ricoeur, Paul. *Interpretation Theory* (Fort Worth: Texas Christian University Press, 1976).
————. "The Metaphorical Process," in *Critical Inquiry*, vol. 5, no. 1, 1978.
————. *The Rule of Metaphor*, trans. R. Czerny (Toronto: University of Toronto Press, 1977).
Righter, William. *Myth and Literature* (London: Routledge, 1975).
Ruthven, K. K. *Myth* (London: Methuen, 1976).
Starobinski, Jean. "The Inside and the Outside," in *Hudson Review*, vol. 28, no. 3, 1975.
White, John. *Mythology in the Modern Novel* (Princeton: Princeton University Press, 1971).

INDEX

Index

Library of Congress Cataloging in Publication Data

Gould, Eric, 1943-
Mythical intentions in modern literature.

Bibliography: p.
Includes index.
1. Myth in literature.   2. English literature—20th
century—History and criticism.   I. Title.
PN56.M94G6   820'.9'15   81-47132
ISBN 0-691-06482-2   AACR2

Eric Gould is Associate Professor of English, University of Denver.